University Education Through Ages

University Education Through Ages

R. R. Santhi Devi

Ess Ess Publications

4837/24, Ansari Road,
Daryaganj
New Delhi - 110002.
Phone : 3260807

First published 1995

ISBN 81-7000-181-1

Rs. 375/-

Published by
Ess Ess Publications
4837/24, Ansari Road,
Daryaganj
New Delhi - 110002.
Phone : 3260807

Composed by :
Academy of Computer Studies
BG-1/42, Paschim Vihar
New Delhi - 110063
Phone : 5580312

Printed at : Cambridge Printing Work's, B-85, Naraina Indl. Area, Phase-II, New Delhi-110 028. Phone: 570 60 39

List of Contents

1

INTRODUCTION

1.1 SCOPE

The present study focuses on a coneptual analysis of University as reflected in Buddhist monasteries of ancient India. It is not a mere empirical enquiry. The study has included the factual details of the development of higher learning in ancient civilizations emergence of the centres of higher learning in medieval Europe and also focussed attention on the development and organisation of higher learning in ancient and medieval India.

This present study - a conceptual analysis of a university focuses on the evolution of the university in the Western Countries. It also attempts to trace the development of universities during Buddhist India. Ancient Buddhist universities like Nalanda, Taxila, Vallabi can be included for the Conceptual analysis in the context of the prevailing situation of the then India. This heritage is of great interest because these universities existed in one of the best periods in Indian history where philosophy, art and science and technology all flourished.

As a prelude to the Buddhist system of education, the Brahmanical system of education cherished the Vedic education in Indian soil. Vedic education nurtured the lofty ideals of Indian Ontology and Epistemology for the posterity. They survived the on-slaughts during Muslim invasions and side by side with Madrasas and Maktabs: Vedic schools received patronage from secular- minded kings and emperors.

The present Indian universities are basically formed on the pattern of the Western ideas. These ideas bear certain similarities in the basic infrastructure of the Buddhist monasteries. When medieval Europe boasts of Christian monast-eries which blossomed into universities later on, India is in no way dearth of such kind of centres of higher learning. Hence this study is an attempt to analyse the concept of university as reflected in the Buddhist monasteries of India.

1.2 PHILOSOPHICAL APPROACH TO EDUCATION

Man is declared as rational animal by the Greek philosopher Aristotle (384-322 B.C) and education is the privilege of the rational man. A basic character of education is that it informs a person and it enlightens him about things he does not know and thus initiates him into asking all sorts of questions about nature, about life, about society and its organizations. One is made capable of thinking for himself and finding answers to the questions which one considers important or significant for one's life. The term 'education' is used in a variety of contexts and with different shades of meaning. In its broadest sense, any act or experience that has a formative effect on the mind, character or physical ability of an individual can be called as educational. It is in this sense that travelling, reading, conversation or even living with someone can be an education. However, education may also connote a system of institutions organised by society to deliberately transmit its cultural heritage - its accumulated knowledge, values and skills- from one generation to another. The educational system of a society would, accordingly, comprise institutions such as schools, colleges, universities including teachers, administrators, curricula and courses, examination and certification procedure and so on.

In fact, education is a social institution responsible for modifying and moulding the individuals into amenable and amiable fellow beings of the society. Through education, the society transmit the rich lore of knowledge to its posterity, thus maintaining a sort of continuity and subserving the legacy of the past. Impartation of knowledge takes place different levels and impartation itself is done by different agencies of education. On the one hand, we have home or family and society in myriad forms to act as informal agencies of education. On the other hand, we have organised agencies like school and state to impart knowledge in a systematic way. They are formal agencies of education. Education is education of pupil: the individual. This is a truism so evident that its implication in the process of education remains unnoticed. In the system of education importance is given to curriculum, to content of the courses in various subjects, to the teacher, to the school and its management, to textbooks, to examinations and the rest. These are all important factors in the organisation of education: but it is essential not to forget that the individual pupil is the centre of all learning: it is his individual education with which we are primarily concerned. Viewed from this angle, what is essential in education is to stimulate and keep alive the sense of wonder, the thrill of mystery without which both life and learning are dull, and at the same time, to subject the self-within to rigorous discipline in the pursuit of truth. Education fails if it does not help the individual to cultivate the hardest of all hard arts- the art of life, viz, the art of self-determination inspired and guided by elevated thoughts, humane values and refined tastes. What level of education would enable the individual to acquire these lofty perspectives in one's life? What are the means for establishing accessibility to these higher perspec-tives? What type of agencies of education will draw the individual closer to their achievement ?

Rejoinder to the aforesaid questions makes the scholar look up at the higher level of education: and consider the traditional formal agency of education at higher level as the appropriate apex body. An inquiry into the nature, meaning and functions of this apex body makes the scholar land in the study of the concept of a university. The inquisitive pursuit of the scholar results in an attempt to analyse the meaning and functions of the university relevant to the life of individual and useful to the society. In the search for the meaning and functions of this educational institution viz. The university, the scholar, being a student of philosophy resorts to the philosophical analysis of the basic constituent elements of the concept of a university.

In short an attempt at analysing the meaning and function of the concept of a university is a budding study in the field of philosophy of education. A study into the interrelationships between the meanings and the corresponding functions of the university is a kind of innovative study in the field of higher education with a basis of philosophical analysis.

Why does the scholar resort to the philosophical method for deciphering the educational concept ?

The answer lies in the interdependency between education and philosophy Being a student of both the disciplines, the scholar is well aware that philosophy provides a comprehensive view of education. Philosophy and education are regarded as the two sides of a coin. thus representing contemplative side and dynamic side respectively. "Education is involved with both the world of ideas and the world of practical activity: good ideas can lead to good and the world of practical activity: good ideas can lead to good practices, and good practices can lead to good ideas. In order to behave intelligently in the educational process the educator needs the things philosophy can provide: that is, an understanding of thinking processes and the nature of ideas, the language we use to describe education, and how these may interact with practical affairs. For the educator, philosophy is not simply a professional tool but a way of improving the quality of life because it helps us gain a wider and deeper perspective on human existence and the world around us". [1.1] This peculiarity of philosophy is proved by the observation of Alfred N. Whitehead (Process and Reality, New York: Macmillan Co. 1919. page.4) that speculative philosophy is the endeavour to frame a coherent, logical, necessary system of general ideas in terms of which every element of our experience can be interpreted.

The scholar has understood that even before the advent of the British. India had a rich heritage of her hoary past. We have existing records of centres of learning and enquiry at Taxila (now in Pakistan), Kanchipura (in South India) Nalanda, Oantapuri (or Uddandapma), Sri Dharryakataka, Kashmira and Vikramashila. We get a valuable picture of the working of some these institutions from Chinese travellers. Fi-hien, Hiuen- Tsang and I- Tsang who visited India in the fifth and seventh centuries A.D. Fi-hien, for example, was in India between 399-414 A.D. and visited Nalanda but was disappointed and dismayed to see the ruins of the Buddhist monasteries. However, when Hiuen- Tsang came (629 A.D. to 645 A.D) he found a flourishing Nalanda University as a Buddhist Centre of learning which, by then, had a world -wide reputation. Its site has been found near Rajgir in Bihar, and excavations have revealed that existence of large buildings, a library and other academic and residential buildings. Though the European nations are acclaimed for their unique contribution towards the development of the university system of education, India can also be proud of her Buddhist monasteries functioning as Centres of higher learning prior to the emergence of the universities in Europe. This very semblance inspires the scholar to analyse the concept of university imbibed in the Buddhist monasteries.

In due course, the investigator tries to analyse philoso-phically the reflection of the concept of a university in Buddhist Monasteries in India. India is not educationally poor. Yet the advent of the British instilled the

1.1. Ozmon, Howard A, Samuel M. Craver. (Introduction: Page xiii) philosophical Foundations of Education (Fourth Edition) 1990 Merrill publishing Company, Columbus, Ohio, USA.

spirit of higher academic pursuit into us and modelled the centres of higher education on the European model, during their sovereign reign in India.

1.3 ISSUES INVOLVED

We have a large system of higher education. But the developments in the field has been extremely uneven. After India become free (1947) and set about the task of reorientating its educational system to suit the needs and aspirations of an independent nation committed to democracy, secularism and socialism, intensive and widerspread discussions have taken place on the aims and purpose of its higher education. These discussions have involved all concerned with higher education, teachers, students, parents, educationists and leaders in the community. Their views and thoughtful expressions have found place in important national documents like reports of commissions and committee and statement of National policies. The various aims proposed in the commission and committees revolve around the abiding concerns of education viz. individual, society and knowledge.

In its history university education represented a combination of three functions namely, development and perfection of the individual, dissemination of knowledge and its creation, preserva-tion and progress of society. The nature of these functions was different in different historical periods. In most modern societies, however, educational institutions are considered instruments of social purpose. Government formulate explicit educational policies and finance educational institutions on the assumption that education is necessary for both order and progress. On the one hand, education is expected to maintain fallowed traditions: respect for authority, obedience to the law, patriotism and the like. On the other hand, it is expected to promote political, economic and social development.

Falling in line with the aforesaid aspirations, the independent India has been trying to emulate the British legacy of Higher Education: We have regular universities on the European models. Most Indian Universities are basically formed on the pattern of western idea. Free India is bound to stretch her tendrils to extend the facilities of higher learning at distance. This has resulted in the open university system augmenting opportunities for higher education and thus promoting a flexible and innovative system of education. The Indira Gandhi National

Open University has been established with these objectives and come into existence in September, 1985. This university has been assigned the responsibility to coordinate the distance learning system in the country and determine its standard. We have had rural universities and Institutes which have been the fruits of Gandhian Basic Education Movement. Rural higher education received fillip with intensification of the freedom movement. In addition to several other thinkers, Rabindranath Tagore and Mahatma Gandhi gave special attention to establishment of comprehensive institutions for the rural people starting at the early childhood level, going upto the highest. Inspite of the difficulties faced by it, Gandhian Basic Education has survived in the country and comprises a vital feature of our system. A large number of Rural Institutes were set up under the auspices of voluntary agencies during the Second Five Year Plan. Over the Years, however, Gandhian Basic Education, rural institutes and other institutions primarily meant for rural areas did not receive sufficient support and encouragement. The national policy on education (1986) envisages the development of a pattern of education related to the needs of rural communities and strengthening the support of the programme of Gandhian Basic education. For this purpose, a Central Council of Rural Institutes has been set up by the Central Government to formulate and implement a well coordinated programmes, connected with the rural uplift.

Recently, we developed institutions which have earned a reputation for maintaining high standards and are bestowed with the status of what are now called deemed to be universities. In recent years some of our high level institutions such as the Indian Agricultural Research Institute at Delhi, the Indian Institute of Science at Bangalore have been brought into the university system by deeming them as universities under Section 3 of the U.G.C. Act. There is in our educational system a need for institutions having the academic status and privileges which ordinarily belong to a university but with more specific and limited functions and scope, while such institutions in their limited field should maintain the highest standard of teaching and research: their organizational set-up need not be the replica of a university. We would like to stress that in deeming institutions as universities under the UGC Act, the most careful attention should be paid to the question of educational standard. This provision under the Act gives scope for experim[illegible]tation and innovation but it should not become a cheap side or back d[illegible] university status.[1.2]

1.2. (Report of the Education Commission 1964-66 (p[illegible] [illegible]du[illegible]ation and Natio-nal Development, Ministry of Edn. Govt. of India, 1966

1.4 CRISIS OF HIGHER EDUCATION IN INDIA

In course of my study taking organization and development of Higher Education with special reference to India I have come across criticism about and crisis in Higher Education in India. There is a rat race for getting degrees which are believed to be useful for securing employment. In the event of the usefulness of degrees as a passport to employment getting diminished higher degrees are sought in order to gain a competitive edge over those with lower degrees. In the absence of alternative the demand for degrees continues to grow.

What makes it even worse in the case of higher education is that the social and political pressure has led to a system of subsidization that cannot be justified on grounds of either equity or efficiency: first comes the pressure of numbers. The mere increase of the relevant age groups, regardless of social policy, brings about a situation in which, if standards of admission are not to be continually raised, mere places must be provided. In addition to this and in a sense perhaps rival to it comes a second group of influences springing from an enhanced valuation of what Universities and such like instituions have to give. At once we are faced with the question to what extent can these needs be met simultaneously. To meet these responsibilities, the universities must function as institutions for training the young and fostering the advancement of learning.

To overcome the criticism that higher education in India remains largely unrelated to the needs of the society, more and more is the involvement of universities being witnessed in the socio-economic progress of the country. In recent past, we have witnessed emergence of Agricultural Universities. At present we are witnessing the blossoming of many Medical Univer-sities. These are the healthy sings of involving universities in the socio-economic progress of the Nation.

We have come across deemed universities being encouraged by the University Grants Commission. At the postgraduate level the University Grants Commission has already made a start along these lines by giving recognition as Centres of Advanced Study to promising departments in various universities. The concept of these centres can be expanded and made to promote the requirements of higher education in a more integrated fashion if the organisation of postgraduate education within universities is itself modified.

Conceptually, universities are usually divided into three types: the affiliating. the unitary and the federal. Each has its own characteristics and India has experimented with all of them in varying degrees. The development of most Indian higher education as we know it today derives from a particular style of British higher education even it is influenced by all the others. Even while accepting the basically Western origins of today's higher education in India, we must notice important and significant elements of India's own past which have also been influential in varying degrees. In the long distant past as also in the not so distant past. India had its institutions of higher education, some like the universities and others quite different.

We have existing records of centres of learning and enquiry at Taxila. Kanchipura, Nalanda, Odantapuri, Sri Dharryakataka, Kashmira, and Vikramashila. We get a valuable picture of the working of some of these institutions from Chinese travellers, Fi-hine, Hiuen-Tsang, and I- Tsing who visited India in the fifth and seventh Centuries A.D. When Hiuen- Tsang came (629 A.D. to 645 A.D.), he found a flourishing Nalanda University as a Buddhist centre of learning which, by then, had a world-wide reputation. Its site has been found, near Rajgir in Bihar, and excavations have revealed the existence of large buildings, a library, and other academics and residential buildings

After seeing these developments in the field of higher education in the Indian soil, I would rather feel the necessity of analysing the underlying concept of a university as the basic for higher learning. To concretize the analysis, the sample of ancient Buddhist universities are taken for the purpose of reflecting the concept of a university.

Chapter-I forms the introductory chapter. Here, the problem is introduced expounding the importance of knowledge and acquisi-tion of the same by humans. The precise nature of problem is also specified. This is a kind of identifying the crux for the study with its scope, need and limitations.

Chapter-II deals with the descriptive account of the method-lology, and the philosophical analysis of education and description is to identify the specific methodology for the study, justifying its selection for treating the problem. Further illustrations are also offered to elucidate the procedural treatment for the study. The function of the illustration helps the scholar to purse the ways wherein the present study is analysed and interpreted.

Chapter-III deals with review of the concept of university in ancient and medieval civilization.

Chapter-VI gives a descriptiive account of dissertation. The views and opinions regarding the idea of a university has been discussed

Chapter-V presents a detailed analytical It is reflected in the study of Buddhist monasteries as indigeneous university of ancient India.

Chapter-VI is designed to be conclusion and also incorporates findings and suggestion.

2

PHILOSOPHICAL ANALYSIS OF EDUCATION

2.1 RATIONALE FOR THE PHILOSOPHICAL ANALYSIS

Human knowledge works at two levels. At the primary level it acts as the basis of a useful human activity, as when a medical man uses his knowledge to heal patients or as when a teacher expounds his subject for the benefit of his students. At the secondary level knowledge is employed to produce increments in the existing knowledge. At this level knowledge is not merely utilitarian: it is not merely utilized or spread but its quantum is increased by howsoever small an amount. The activity which produces such quantum of knowledge is known as research. Research is an intellectual activity which brings to light new knowledge or correct previous errors and misconceptions and adds in an orderly way to the existing corpus of knowledge.

Knowledge differs from experience in being orderly, systematic and insightful. In experience we are merely exposed to certain events or observations. They occur in their own haphazard manner. In research such observations are ordered and analysed to answer certain crucial questions, and these answer, carefully stated, are the increments of knowledge we are after, Such knowledge implies as much deeper and fuller understanding of the true nature of phenomenal knowledge gained by research is thus knowledge of the highest order. All research is an advance on existing frontiers of knowledge. Research does not arise in a desert of ignorance: it represents, instead, the expansion of the periphery of existing knowledge. It must necessarily take us beyond the frontiers of present knowledge. This advance need not always be horizontal. A vertical type of progress would improve our existing knowledge by the simple action of subsuming many earlier laws and generalizations under a principle. This discovery of a higher, more comprehensive principle is as much research as the discovery of a new principle.

The present problem of the dissertation A Study of the Concept of a university as reflected in the Buddhist universities of India is a humble attempt aiming at the deduction of generalized principles in terms of meaning and functions which, together constitute the fabric of the Concept in general. The study is confined to the philosophical analysis of the ideas about university expressed by John Henry New man in his book 'The Idea of a University and by KARL JASPERS in The ideas of the University. The analysis has been attempted from the philosophical perspective and not from socio-political analysis. Being a staunch Catholic recluse with academic fervour, Newman portrays the picture of the ideas of the English (Oxford) University. On the other hand, Karl Jaspers, the existentialist, offers a philosopher's research for the deepest roots and the inner most core of those strange human enterprises that we call universities in the tradition of the western world. In so doing, he shows in a brief sample the continuing vitality and greatness of the German philosophic tradition.

Why has the investigator resorted to the philosophical inquiry? Being a speculative discipline, philosophy could contribute to a "faith for living" viz. (a) (it could contribute) a reflective, discursive, rationally examinable inquiry into the warrant of beliefs which lay claim to ultimate or final validity" (b)" (it could) be the intellectual conscience of the community - to measure all special interests, half truths, and half-hearted ideas which claim final authority or ultimate validity, by the most penetrating and comprehensive standards of truth and adequacy that can rationally be maintained. Philosophy is not merely an inquiry tool but a critique of thought also.

Educators expect from philosophers of education a clarification and elucidation of concepts and arguments used in educational literature, especially in the literature of educational controversy. Voucher systems, minimum competency testing, equality of educational opportunity, integration are examples of such concepts and issues. The educator expects from the philosopher of education (a) reasoned proposals to use terms in one way rather than another so that ambiguity, equivocation, and vagueness can be eliminated, (b) reasoned proposals that a controversy be adjudicated in one way rather than another. What school people cannot expect consensus on usage or judgement from the philosophers, because of the fact that philosophers are not likely to agree on philoso phical issues; issues cease to be philosophical when such agreement is reached at least they cease to be of philosophical interest once they are settled.

Further, educators also expect from philosophy of education a strong and steady advocacy of rational discussion, freedom of inquiry, and instead of a fixed faith "an interest and standard from which reliable beliefs can spring."

Basing the study on the philosophy of education the scholar relies on method of philosophy for analysing the basic principles underlining the university. An educator may develop a broad understanding of education, but this may lack a sense of focus and organization. Philosophy as a disciplined study is concerned with developing a coherent, logical, and comprehensive out look. Philosophy has traditionally involved itself with a wide range of issues and problems, and education has long been of importance to most philosophers. Thus, there is an extensive body of literature available to the educator to help develop understanding of education as a broadly based enterprise. When the educator becomes aware that philosophy contains comprehensive perspectives and tools for developing organized and structured views, the basic groundwork for a philosophical perspective on education has been laid.

The scholar has gone one step further to substantiate the concept of higher learning institute viz. University with philoso-phical background. The scholar is of the opinion that certain ideas and recommendations about education have a great deal of influence today, particularly in shaping public attitudes about "back to the basics" and "moral values" education. Nation is also swayed by the utterances of "Operation black board" and "Each one, teach one". Society gives scant attention to women's Liberation and Care and Girl Child (1990): people who advocate such things may lack any philosophical sophistication or knowledge of the origin of these notions, but philosophers have often recommendations. Philosophical systems and recommendations are part of many of the "working ideas" and traditions of our society today. Many of us assume these things to be true and obvious without any clear idea of why. Thus, we may blindly accept a large number of educational recommendations without knowing whether they are justified or not. The student who seeks to become an educator needs to be informed about these ideas and traditions in order to sift through rhetoric and argument and to reach a more intelligent understanding of the current scene.

2.2 NATURE OF PHILOSOPHICAL ANALYSIS

It should be admitted that philosophical research does not require any very elaborate techniques. It is largely a matter of erudition and analytical insight and synthesizing ability. It is a bookish business, even more so than history, having to dc largely with the close perusal of authoritative books and venerable tomes. It needs naturally a good knowledge of philosophical thought in general and familiarity with the major schools and trends. What it needs more than anything else is the gift of acumen, of penetrating insight and an analytical faculty which enables the researchers to smell the rich vein of pertinent thought concealed in the scattered source material and - separate it from the dross of irrelevancy. Also in - the overview of a period the general trends, movements - and governing principles are observed and traced by - the exercise of this faculty of insight which enables - us to "see the woods inspite of the trees" [2.1]

2.2.1 DEFINITION OF ANALYSIS IN PHILOSOPHY

According to the Dictionary of Philosophy, Analysis and Synthesis are in the most general meaning, the processes of mental or factual breaking down of a whole into its component parts and the reconstitution of the whole from the parts. Analysis and Synthesis play an important role in the process of cognition and take place at every stage. In mental processes Analysis and Synthesis occur as logical methods of thought that use abstract concepts and are closely connected with other mental operations - abstraction, generalization (qq.v) etc. Logically, Analysis consists in mentally dividing the object being studied into its component parts and is a method of obtaining new knowledge. Analysis takes on different forms according to the nature of the object of study. A multiplicity of Analysis is a condition for the all-round cognition of an object. The breaking-down of the object into its component parts reveals its structure: the division of a complicated phenomenon into simpler elements enables the investigator to separate the essential from the nonessential and to reduce the complex to the simple: one form of A is the clarification of objects and phenomena. The Analysis of a developing process reveals its various stages, contradictory tendencies etc. In the course of analytical activity, the mind advances from the complex to the simple, from the fortuitous to the necessary, from multiformity to identity and unity. The purpose of Analysis is the cognition of the parts as

2.1 Soltis, Jonas F. (edited by) - Philosophy and Education, NSSE, part I Eighteenth Year Book, 1981, Chicago, illinois (page 95)

elements of a complex whole. On the other hand, synthesis is the process of uniting into a single whole parts, properties, and relations isolated by means of Analysis. Going from the identical to the essential, to the different and varied, synthesis combines the common and the individual unity and variety, into a concrete living whole. Synthesis complements Analysis and is in indissoluble unity with it.

2.2.2 HISTORY OF PHILOSOPHY

Socrates (470-399 B.C.), claiming himself a philosophical mid-wife, used to proceed from the statement that he was an ignorant person and the only merit he claimed was to be aware of his ignorance. He tried to achieve the goal of clarity by eliciting answers to his questions. This Socratic Method of philoso-phical investigation and teaching used by socrates was largely the method of question and answer. Yet this Socratic method contains the origin of analytic method in fact.

Analyses from Zeno of Elea (490-430 B.C) through the philoso-phers of Megara to the Stoics of Greece and Rome most frequently were distinctively logical in character and were intended to show that the opposing positions involved paradoxes or unaccept-able patterns of reasoning. The analytic thrusts until the time of Plato (427-347 B.C) tended to be isolated criticisms which, like fables, had morals the listener was expected to see and apply. In contrast, Plato employed analysis as an integral part of his total philosophy. Plato subjected the view of knowledge as perception to a critical analysis. The procedures of analysis themselves must be metaphysically neutral, in the sense that they involve the testing of philosophical proposals by universal standards of reason rather than on the basis of particular content.

Aristotle's (384-322 B.C) sensitivity to and concern for language led him to formulate his Organon, the first systematic treatment of logic. Speaking generally, we may say that Aristotle studies judgments in their relationships to one another. A judgment is for him the basic unit of knowledge in which the subject of the proposition expressed stands for a substance and the predicate of the proposition stands for a substance and the predicate of the proposition stands for a belonging to the substance. Aristotle holds that the propositions expressed by our judgments reflect the structure of reality and that therefore the various relations that obtain among the propositions provide us with the key for achieving a scientific body of knowledge. Thus, for example, the lingustic fact that we may apply a given predicate to an entire range of subjects as in the instance. "All fish have gills" is paralleled by the ontological fact that a given form can secure as a property of various individual substances. And the linguistic fact that not all predicates apply to an entire range of subjects as in the instance. "Some fish are not edible," is paralleled by the ontological fact that a given form need not recur as a property of various individual substances. From a classification of judgments, each of which capture some aspect of reality in the propositions expressed, Aristotle moves to the study of the relations among these judgments. Various propositions expressed by our judgments are linked together through common terms. It is precisely this fact of language and indeed, of nature, which makes it possible to account for, to explain, to make intelligible one judgment in terms of others. After Aristotle there was a significant but spasmodic formal logic and a growing concern about the role of language in thought.

An awareness that language can lead us into error and a concern to develop an adequate theory of the relation between language and reality were abundantly in evidence throughout the Greco - Roman and medieval periods. The nominalist - realist controversy concerning the status of universals provides many examples of analytic thought in medieval times. An opponent of the extreme realists such as the nominalist Roscellinus (1050 - 1122), criticized extreme realism because it is committed to the view that particulars or individuals are real only in the sense that they exemplify collections of universals. An extreme realist, such as William of Champeaux (1070 - 1121), criticized the theory of Roscellinus extreme nominalism because it holds that only particulars are real and that so called "universals" are no more than general terms used to designate particulars. The only thing that is "real" about the universal is the name: only particular entitles "exist"

Among the most perceptive and influential attempts to resolve the issue are the counts of Abelard 1079 -1142) and Ockham. A brief review of Abelard's thinking leads us towards the study of the modern movement of philosophical analysis. Abelard, a student of Rosecellinus, rejected his teacher's view but stopped short of accepting the realist view. Whereas Roscellinus maintained that a universal is no more than a general term to describe particulars, Abelard insisted that a general word also expresses a meaning or universal concept. Abelard's account of "a universal concept" varied: he held both that it is a confused mental image and that it is the result of a process of abstraction carried out by the mind. Thus, in the first instance he claimed that the universal concept "dog" is a blurred composite image of the various dogs seen, while in the second he claimed that it is the mentally abstracted characteristics that serve to distinguish dogs from "non dogs". In the either of the accounts, the mind is a necessary condition for concept formation but the concept, in and of itself, is about the common characteristics of a collection of individual entities. Thus, while Abelard held that the universal concept or meaning is the result of psychological processes, he was unwilling to equate it with the psychological processes themselves. Furthermore, while acknowledging that a universal concept or meaning is objective rather than subjective, he resisted the extreme realist thesis that it has an ontological status independent of the particulars out of which the mind has composed or abstracted it.

Solutions to the problem of universals extend from the extreme realism of William of Champeaux (the universal exists independent of particulars and is discovered by the human mind) through the moderate realism of Abelard (the universal exists only in particulars which exemplify it and comes to be known through mental abstraction) to the extreme nominalism of Roscellinus (the universal is merely a term devised by the human mind to denote collections of particulars, which alone exist). Locke's (1632-1704) solution, sometime called "conceptualism" falls between the views of Abelard and Roscellinus. A universal is an abstract, general idea existing solely in the mind: a universal functions by signifying a common property of a collection of particular ideas. Our awareness of Locke's departure from both Roscellinus and Abelard is sharpened when we note that he confined us strictly to particular ideas of the mind: we can refer neither to particular things as Roscellinus does nor to properties common to particular things as Abelard does. Not only does Locke insist that our immediate knowledge is restricted to that of ideas rather than of objects and properties of objects, but he also insists that our words are mere symbols for ideas. For example, the word "man" is simply the agreed - upon symbol for the general, abstract idea "man." The impact of Locke's position (in conjunction with that of Descartes) on much of subsequent philosophy was to make the study of epistemology prior to that of ontology, that is, to make our answers to questions about the relation of language to things (of "man" to man) depend on our answers to questions about the relation of language to thought (of "man" to our idea of man). since Locke held that the nature of thought is decisive, he focused attention on this problem. He proceeded by asking question "What is the origin of our ideas? that is, from where do "the materials of reason and knowledge" Locke began the exposition of his own position by insisting that all genuine ideas must have their origin in experience, either sensory or introspective.

Locke went on to provide us with an account of complex ideas and to advance a doctrine concerning the ways in which simple ideas are "compounded", Locke found that the mind engages in the processes of uniting, comparing, and abstracting ideas and that it is only through these processes that we pass beyond simple idea. Ideas of substance, such as the idea of a man or a dog, are produced by our uniting such simple ideas as those of a specific colour, shape and so on. Ideas of relations, such as the idea of a grey colour patch "A" being "darker than" the grey colour patch B, result from our comparing one idea with another. Ideas of abstraction, such as those of whiteness or humanity, have their origin in our sorting our common features in a multitude of ideas.

An important feature of the Lockean account of knowledge that his successors, Berkeley and Hume, found unsatisfactory was the notion of "abstract general ideas". Even Locke was indecisive regarding them. The theory tended to favour most is the view that we arrive at an abstract, general idea by elimination from our ideas of particulars those characteristics that distinguish one idea from another. Berkeley and, in his wake, Hume, were quick to point out that, as Locke himself had maintained elsewhere, the only ideas a mind can entertain are particular ideas. This means, first that our ideas have specific rather than generic characteristics. Thus, for example, to have a simple idea of a colour is, say, to have an idea of a specific shade of red. Second, and even more drastic, to have a particular idea is to have a numerically singular idea rather than a "group" idea of a quality common to a class of particular ideas. Thus to have an idea of a specific red shade is to have in mind this distinct red image, say of a three-inch tomato.

Berkeley and, again, Hume developed one of Locke's less developed lines of thought in their effort to remain consistent empiricists while giving the necessary account of general ideas. Their key insight was that we achieve generality by employing a particular idea as representative of a whole class of particulars. that is to say, a particular idea is singled out by the mind to be regarded, not for its own sake, but rather as the standard for classifying other particular ideas through their resemblance to it. Thus move is similar to that of a geometer when he says, "Let this triangle stand for any triangle". For the abstractive process is being presupposed to range over a "class" of particular ideas, a "class" being a collection which in itself must be accounted for. To put it another way, for Locke the basis for calling a term "abstract and general" is that it refers to an abstract, general idea. For Berkeley and Hume there is no parallel basis for calling a term "general": a general term does not name a general idea, since there are only particular ideas. Rather, a term becomes "general" because of its capacity to evoke a particular idea that may be said to function loosely as representative of a group of resembling particular ideas. Specially Hume held that a term is called "general" when it is associated with a custom of the mind, with a disposition to evolve any one of a set of resembling particular idea from fresh experience to that set. What Berkeley started and Hume completed is the rejection of the traditional theory of meaning in which the meaning of a word is the single idea or object denoted by the word. Many contemporary analysts accept the Humean analysis and hold that general words, unlike proper names, do not stand in a one-to-one relationship with ideas or objects: at most these philosophers are willing to say, with Hume, that a general word stands in some sort of relationship to a disposition of mind to bring forth ideas which are similar.

This discovery was, in a small sense, the result of their rejection of the existence of abstract, general ideas and in a large sense, the result of their concern to be consistent empiricists.

Hume began by insisting that Locke failed to distinguish precisely between sensing something and thinking about it, between having and impression and having an idea. Because of this failure, Locke could not give a clear criterion for indentifying genuine ideas. The test Hume provided is that every simple idea has as its necessary condition a simple impression to which the idea corresponds in every way except that (1) it is less vivid and forceful and (2) it must occur subsequent to the original impression. In addition to simple ideas there are complex ones the result from the play of the imagination as it is guided by the laws of association: resemblance, spatial and temporal contiguity, and cause and effect. Having laid an epistemological groundwork of the sort we have indicated, Hume proceeded to apply the empiricist meaning criterion systematically to philosophical concepts in order to clarify those that are vague and to eliminate those that are meaningless. Hume claimed, for example, to have clarified the idea of "time". After having searched through his perceptions (ideas and impressions, simple and complex) in a futile quest for the origin of the idea, he concluded that the idea of "time" derives not from any single perception but from the succession of our perceptions.

An essential feature of the Humean analysis is the rejection of the thesis that a proposition such as, "Billiard ball `A' causes billiard ball `B' to move" has the same status as the propostion, "2+2=4. That these propositions are not similar may be seen through an examination of their contradictories. To say that "2+2 =4" is self-contradictory: to say that "Billiard ball `A' does not cause billiard ball `B' to move" may be false, but it is not self-contradictory. Thus, to admit that a mathematical relation implies a necessary connection is not to admit that a causal relation does.

The essential distinction between logical relation and factual relation, on which Hume had insisted, was given its most influential formulation by Immanuel Kant (1724-1804) showing that Hume's two categories of propositions were not exhaustive: Kant drew the following distinction: In every judgment of the subject predicate form, the predicate term in either included in the subject term, explicitly or tacitly or excluded from it. In the former case, the judgment is called 'analytic' while in the latter, it is termed "synthetic". The judgment that" A bachelor is unmarried" is analytic while the judgment that "The sun is shining today" is synthetic. Hume's test for distinguishing between relations among ideas and matters of fact, which consists is showing that the contradictory of the former type of proposition is self-contradictory and the contradictory of latter is not, was also utilized by Kant in distinguishing between "analytic" and "synthetic" judgments. For example, it is self-contradictory to deny that a bachelor is unmarried, but it is not self-contradictory to deny that the sun is shining today. It is also the case the every judgment is either a prior or a posterior- that is, the verification of every judgment is either logically independent of or logically dependent on sense experience. Kant concluded that the distinction Hume made is that between analytic a priori and synthetic a posteriori judgments because they would be required logically to be both independent of and dependent on experience for their verification: he insisted that there are no such grounds for eliminating the possibility of synthetic a priori judgments. He argued first, that there is no contradiction in asserting that a true judgment may have a predicate term that is not included in the subject term and yet not depend on sense experience for its verification. He argued, second, that such important statements as "7+5, = 12" and "Every event has a cause" cannot be classified as either analytic a priori or synthetic a posteriori.

Kant argued somewhat as follows: (1) *both analytic a priori* and mathematical judgments are apodictic (absolutely certain truths) (2) synthetic a posteriori judgments fail to be apodictic (3) analytic a priori judgments are such that their negations are self-contradictory, but this is not true of all mathematical judgments. Therefore, mathematical judgments are neither synthetic *a posteriori* nor *analytic a priori.* To put it positively, Kant believed that he had shown that there are *synthetic a priori* mathematical judgments and, by extending the argument, that there are also important *synthetic a priori* truths in such fields as ethics and epistemology.

Kant has made an elaborate attempt to distinguish as different in kind, mathematical truths from logical truths: Bertrand Russel (1982-1910) has made an equally elaborate attempt to deny the distinction. Drawing together and enlarging on the Aristotelian and Storic logics, the men in this movement widened the domain of the analytic *a priori* to a degree which Kant could not possible have foreseen. Armed with symbolic or mathematical logic, Russell sought to demonstrate that a mathematical proposition such as "7+5 = 12" was as equal to the statement "All tall men are tall". Russell attempted to obviate such as "All tall men are tall". Russell attempted to obviate or resolve philosophical problems by applying a principle known as Ockham's razor which commands "wherever possible, substitute constructions out of known entities for inferences to unknown entities." This principle in conjunction with the tools of the new logic led him both to reduce mathematics to logic and to sound a general philosophical alarm. As language grows more abstract, a new set of entities come into philosophy, namely, those represented by abstract words- the universals. Although Russell does not adopt a strict nominalism, he nevertheless aligns himself with the nominalistic tradition in its long-standing efforts to curtail fanciful excesses of realism. To a greater or lesser degree, his nominalizing tendency has been continued by a whole host of philosophical analysis.

Having accepted from classical logic the realist doctrine that all terms refer to something. Russell was confronted with a puzzle: Suppose we, "The round square does not exist." It seems that this is a true proposition, Yet we cannot regard it as denying the existence of a *certain object called "the round square. "For if there were such an object, it would exist: we cannot first assume that there is a certain object, and then proceed to deny that there is such an object.*

Russell attached this problem by insisting that a distinction be drawn between two kinds of symbols which occur as grammatical subjects. In the first place, there are symbols which directly represent objects of our acquintance. The meaning of a symbol of this kind is simply the object it represent and it has this meaning whether or not it occurs in a linguistic context. In the second there are symbols meaningful to use but not meaningful in isolation viz. "incomplete" symbols. Direct representation is not the test of an incomplete symbol, the test is rather that a statement containing an incomplete symbol be analysable into a form wherein each symbol does in fact represent something with which we can be acquainted i.e. into a significant statement in which the incomplete symbol has completely disapproved.

Thus when we say "the round square does not exist" we may, as a first attempt at such an analysis, substitute "it is false that there is an object `x' which is both round and square".

Russell quickly recognized that the theory of description was merely a striking instance of a distinctive form of analysis, "analysis as the resolution of incomplete symbols",. In this, one proceeds by the replacement of symbols of dubious representation with apparently synonymous symbols which unquestionably do represent objects. He has always spoken about such analyses as straddling the border line between logic and epistemology and metaphysics. Flushed with the success of the philosophical application of logical techniques, Russell came to believe that the grammar of ordinary language with a happenstance vocabulary leading to muddle headed metaphysical positions ought to be replaced by the strict syntax of logic combined with the scientific terminology leading to a single but clear-head metaphysics. This Russellian doctrine that an ideal language - a logicoscientific language - could be constructed and that it would directly and unambiguously reflect the nature of reality is called *logical atomism.*

By far the most influential and fullest statement of logical atomism was worked out by Ludwing Wittgenstein (1889-1951), a student colleague of Russell. The impact of Russell on the thinking of Wittgenstein was considerable but immediate. In the long- run, Wittgenstein was more thoroughly impressed with the commonsensical endeavours of the philosopher whom he was to succeed at Cambridge University, G.E.Moore (1873-1958). G.E. Moore insisted that the key to solving philosophical problems lay in the quite different direction of paying close attention to common sense and its language that is, ordinary language. As early as 1903, Moore in his Principia Ethics, set the modern fashion of viewing ethics as analysis. The key to his orientation was that before one wastes his efforts in attempting to answer an ethical question, he must clarify precisely what the question is that he is asking: philosophers, for example, have asked the question "What is good?" and then proceeded to search for an answer without even being clear as to whether they were dealing with "What things are good ?" or How is good to be defined ?" Because of his spectacular success in applying this simple method of logical procedure, he influenced not only philosophers who are working in the field of ethics but also many working in other branches of philosophy.

G.E.Moore, in his essay entitled "A Defense of Common Sense" (1925) spoke about another methodological principle for basic simplicity. It may be stated as follows: We must distinguish between the statements which are known to be true with certainty and the analyses of such statements which endeavor to determine their full meaning. Generally commonsense provides us with a body of realible but largely unanalyzed truths which, in turn, challenge philosophy, to determine their meaning. From Moore's viewpoint, the philosopher's task is mainly *that of coming to understand the truth rather than trying to discover* it. But it becomes difficult for us to determine whether it is better classified as a type of commonsense philosophy or as a philosophy of ordinary language. Credit goes to Ludwing Wittgenstein rather then G.E.Moore as the Prime mover in the development of the *ordinary language school* which now dominates much of philosophy in the English speaking world. A man reminiscent of Socrates in his ability to attract disciples and in his provocative styles of expression, Wittgenstein was also effective in launching the new movement because of the authority he had gained in the earlier analytic movement of the logical positivists which he renounced later. It has been observed frequently that the Wittgenstern who wrote the Tractatas (1922) and the Wittgenstein whose span of work between 1929 and 1945 is captured in his philosophical Investigations are two different philosophers. The late Wittgenstein is claiming that to ask for an analysis of a given statement is merely to ask how the statement is being used in a given context rather than to ask what the statement *really* means. He is objecting, in the first place, to the earlier analysts article of faith that the meaning of a statement is the method of its verification: in the second place, to their practice of analyzing actual expressions of language by equiring them with expressions which are more fully understandable. Wittgen-stein insists that we appreciate: the multiple uses of ordinary language, and that when, a statement employed in such a way that it cannot possibly be verified we are merely to conclude that it is not being used rather than to be carried away by our discovery that it is non-referring and conclude dogmatically that it is meaningless. This sensitivity to the various ways in which statements are used leads the ordinary language philosopher to speak of each statement as having as its own "logic", its own function to perform. While there are, indeed, resemblances in the ways that various statements are used, we must not run the risk of arbitrarily imposing our own categories upon them by classifying them and by regarding them as units of an all-pervasive logical structure. Language is a subtle instrument in which many tasks are being performed at a variety of levels. This being so, we stand forewarned that unheeding analysis leads us not only to underestimate the power of language but also to deprive ourselves of much of the communication that it brings.

Many of the questions that the philosophers have asked from the earliest reflective period to the present have been unanswerable precisely because they make false presumptions about the language. Wittgenstein suggests that this is the case with perennial puzzles which arise in connection with statements involving "meaning", "understanding", "believing", "true", "fact", "time", "space", "beautiful", "good", and the like. He suggests us to trace historically an aspect of a actual language uses to which such words are and can put, if we hope to escape the "bewitchment of our intelligence." Let us look a bit more closely at what Wittgeinstein in advocating and what the trap is into which we have fallen. Consider the problem of meaning. In this context we are concerned to trace the conflict between nominalism and realism. We may say that many nominalists and realists have regarded themselves as irreconciliably opposed to each other. According to Wittgenstein, however, it remains that each has been presuming the words name-whether particular or universal in a way completely analogous to the way in which a proper name or general noun refers to an individual or kind of individual, respectively. They have taken such conspicuous naming circumstances to be paradigms of the relationship of language to the world. Once conceived, such a thesis seemingly unifies the whole meaning issue: once adopted, it require us to invent and dispute about a whole series of processes, entitles, and categories, for which there is no other justification and which ultimately fails even to sustain our unitary account. To say, for example, that "Five" denotes a number in the sense that "slab" denotes a building block is seen to be patently false when we remain alert to the various possible concrete language situations in which terms might occur. Let us suppose that a mason's assistant is told to fetch five slabs. Is it seriously open to him to complain that while he has found the slabs, he can't find the five ? The absurdity of this situation points but the danger of imposing a unitary theory of meaning upon these terms. The Wittgensteinian point to see in this example, is that "five" and "slab" have different roles to play in the effective language situation of a mason communicating with his apprentice. The language - sorting process that we have begun with this example must be extended by the philosopher, and once entered into, carries the case against any unitary theory of meaning. In brief, the moral of Wittgenstein' s writings bids us abandon our preoccupation with explaining the meaning of language and concentrate on describing the rich variety of ways in which language functions. Whether Wittgenstein is ultimately prepared to identify meaning and use is a moot question. However, he has stimulated legion of philosophers to undertake the task of describing the actual and possible uses of language as undebatable.

The investigator draws an example of John Austin, an extremely influential pioneer in the ordinary - language wing of analysis. His article "Other Minds" illustrates the distinctive ways in which ordinary language philosophers may be said to interpret age old problems and to seek their solution. As an ordinary language philosopher, Austin contributes to the philosophical task of distinguishing between the various ways in which we ordinary use such key terms, as "know" and "believe". He notes, for example, that when someone reports that he knows something, he is speaking in a different way than he reports that he believes it. In the first instance, it is fair to ask the person "How do you know ?" but not "why do you know ?" However, in the second instance, the appropriate question is "why do you believe ?" and not" How do you believe ?" Austin patiently pursues his inquiry into the uses of "know" by delineating several types of questions arising from knowledge claims. It may develop in conversation, for example, that in asking "How do you know?" one is really concerned to ask the more specific question "How are you in a position to know?" or again to ask the more specific question "How can you tell ?"

There is a singular difference between the two forms of challenge: "How do you know "? and "Why do you believe ?" We seem never to ask "Why do you know?" or "How do you believe ?" Either question, "How do you know?" or "Why do you believe ?" may well be asked only out of respectful curiosity, from a genuine desire to learn. But again, they may both be asked as pointed questions, and when they are so, a further difference comes out." How do you know?" suggests that perhaps you don't know it at all, whereas "Why do you believe?" suggests that perhaps you oughtn't to believe it. There is no suggestion that you ought not to know or that you don't believe it. If the answer to "How do you know?" or to "Why do you believe ?" is considered unsatisfactory by the challenger, he proceeds rather differently in the two cases. His next retort will be, on the one hand, something such as "Then you don't know any such thing," or "But that doesn't prove it, in that case you don't really know it at all, " and on the other hand, something such as "That's very poor evidence to go on; you oughtn't to believe it on the strength of that alone". The "existence" of your alleged knowledge is challenged. If we like to say that "I believe" and likewise "I am sure" and "I am certain" are descriptions of subjective mental or cognitive states or attitudes, or what not, then "I know" is not that, or at least not merely that: it functions differently in talking. It is stated that I know is obviously more than that, more than a description of my own state. If I know, I can't be wrong. You can always show I don't know by showing I am wrong or may be wrong or that I didn't know by showing that I might have been wrong. That's the way in which knowing differs even from being as certain as can be".

The normal procedure of language could be schematized as follows: first, it is arranged that on experiencing a complex of features C, then we are to say "This is C" or "This is a C". Then subsequently, the occurrence either of the whole of C or of a significant and characteristic part of it is, on one or many occassions, accompanied or followed in definite circumstances by another special and distinctive feature or complex of feature, which make it seem desirable to revise our ideas: so that we draw a distinction between "This looks like a C, but in fact is only a dummy, etc." and "This is a real C (live, genuine etc)" Hence forward we can only ascertain that it's real C by ascertaining that the special feature or complex of features is present in the appropriate circumstances. The old expression "This is C" will tend as heretofore to fail to draw any distinction between "real, live etc. "and "dummy, stuffed etc." "If the special distinctive feature is one which does not have to manifest their in any definite circumstances (on application of some specific test, after some limited lapse of time etc.) then it is not a suitable feature on which to base a distinction between "real" and "dummy, imaginary etc." All we can then do is to say "some Cs are and some are not, some do and some don't : and it may be very interesting or important whether they are or are not, whether they do or don't but they are all Cs, real Cs, just the same "Now if the special feature is one which must appear in (more or less) definite circumstances, then "Thus is a real C" is not necessarily predictive: We can, in favourable case, make some of it.

2.3 CONCEPTUAL ANALYSIS

2.3.1. DEFINITION OF A CONCEPT:

The word "Concept" means an idea underlying something general notion (as given in Oxford Advanced learners Dictionary of Current English A.S. Hornby, Fourth Edition, Oxford University Press 1989 P. 240) According to the Dictionary of philosophy (edited by I FROLOV, Progress Publishers-Moscow 1984), Concept is one of the forms of reflecti on of the world at the stage of cognition associated with the use of language (q.v) a form (method) of generalising objects and phenomena. Concept also denotes thought which generalises objects of a certain class according to their specific attributes. Moreover, the objects of one and the same class (atoms, animals, plants, socio-economic formations etc) can be generalised to form concepts according to different aggregates of attributes. The more essential are the attributes that comprise the content of the objects and according to which they are generalised, the higher the scientific value of the concept. The concept becomes a definite system of knowledge as other general attributes of objects, generalised in a concept are inferred from the attributes which comprise the basic content of concept. Progress of knowledge signifies above all the development of concept a passage from one concept (of a given object) to another, fixing the deeper essence of objects and, therefore representing their reflection more adequately. Concepts impart the sense to the words of a language. One of the logical functions of concept is to single out in thought by definite attributes the objects which interest us from the point of view of practice and of cognition. Every science operates with definite concepts in which knowledge accumulated by science is concentrated. The formation of concept, the transition to it from sensory forms of reflection, is a complicated process that sees the application of such methods of cognition as comparison, analysis and synthesis (qq.v) abstraction, idealisation, generalisation, and more or less complex forms of inference (q.v). At the same time, scientific concepts are often created intitally solely on the basis of hypothetical assumptions concerning the existence of objects and their nature (that is how, for example, the concept of atoms emerged). On the basis of knowing laws and trends of development, the concept of some objects may be formed before the emergence of objects or phenomena themselves (concept of communism). Thus, the formation of concepts is a manifestation of the active and creative character of thought, although the successful use of the concept created depends entirely on the precision with which objective reality is reflected with them. Every concept is an abstraction, which makes it appear to be a deviation from reality. As a matter of fact, with the help of a concept a more profound knowledge of reality is obtained by singling out and investigating its essential aspects. Moreover, the concrete which is incompletely reflected in particular concept may be reproduced to a certain degree of completeness by an aggregate of concept, reflect its various aspects. The Dictionary of philsophy further clarifies the extent and content of concept. They are the two inter connected sides of a concept (q.v). Extent is a class of objects generalised in a concept: content is the sum total of (usually essential) properties, according to which objects are generalized and singled out in the given concept. By formulating the content of a concept we single out the identical (general) in objects of the given class: a characteristic of volume i.e. differentiation of elements (objects which are —— of the properties comprising the content) and parts (species, subclasses of the given class) brings out the difference between objects of the given class. There is a connection between content and extent expressed in formal logic by the law of inverse relation.

2.3.2 RICKETS THEORY OF CONCEPT FORMATION:

According to Henrich Rickerts theory of concept formation, the establishment of objective knowledge of empirical reality is one of the goals pursued by humans. The efforts which are necessary to reach it occur in the form of specialized activities viz. scientific investigations. Rickert in accordance with the opinion prevalent at the time, conceived of knowledge as a mental state: when humans have knowledge of empirical reality they have something in their minds. But he rejects the idea that this may simply be described as a copy in the mind of a world existing outside it. For humans can only be aware of that which they have in their minds, and there is no way of finding out whether this faithfully reproduces a reality existing outside it and independently from it. Things as they are unmediated by the mind, independent from how humans perceive them and are aware of them, are not accessible to human reason.

Man can never know things as they are as such, but only as they appear to him as they appear in the mind as so-called phenomena. Thus, what humans have in their minds when they have knowledge of empirical reality, is not copies of things as such: it is phenomena. How may phenomena be described? What do they consist of? Rickert starts by saying that the analysis of the cognitive content of the human mind i.e disregarding subjective states like feelings, emotions, etc reveals the presence of a mass of most basic, least differentiated and unorganized elements given in the consciousness. These "sensations" or "impressions" constitute the lowest possible level of awareness. They may be called "immediate (or directly given) experiences", but this expression must not be misconstrued as faithful copies of a reality existing beyond or transcending the awareness of them. They are the basis of everything else, and it is not possible to go beyond them by reducing them to more original or immediate components. Sensations occur as an undifferentiated flow of diverse and unclear states of consciousness. Having such sensations, according to Rickert, does not constitute knowledge. Rather, he argues that they are the objects of knowledge. Knowledge must be knowledge of something: sensations are its raw material. For nothing more immediate is accessible to the human mind. Rickert says that knowledge can be adequately described as a copy or reproduction on another mental level, of the immediate sensations or directly given experiences, and that knowledge thus consists in having "notions" or "ideas" of these basic states of consciousness. But he thinks that this conception is unsatisfactory; for the analysis of what is usually called "knowledge" reveals that there is more to it than just having ideas of something. For example if some one asks : Is the sun shining?" he has the ideas "Sun" and "Shine" but he certainly has no knowledge. For the conception of knowledge implies that it can be either true or false, yet a question cannot be true or false although it can contain ideas. Only assertions can be true or false, and ideas alone do not assert anything. Rickert, therefore, concludes that knowledge consists in asserting something of an idea; having notions (i.e ideas) is not the same as having knowledge; the contents of consciousness (i.e. immediate experiences) become objects of knowledge only through thinking i.e judging (i.e asserting something of the ideas of these experiences). Thus, according to Rickert, when someone says "This is a Cat", he asserts something of the notion "cat" namely that it exists. The notion or idea of one or more immediate sensations - in this case "cat" - is called "content" of knowledge. "Existence" which is asserted of it is the form in which in this case knowledge is had. The combined form-content is what is usually called a "concrete fact". It is the idea of segment singled out from the undifferentiated mass of dimly experienced states of consciousness on the level of immediate sensations, which is given the form of "existence" i.e which is thought to be "real". Thus, when something is stated to exist, to be real, it is not asserted to exist outside the mind. It is only stated that, as a central content, it is thought of in a certain form, that of existence, rather than in another for instance, that of "possibility". A concrete fact, the combination of an idea and the form of existence is not something which simply occurs in the human mind on its own force. A form and content have to be combined and this is a volitional act. Its performance is intentional activity. Rickert argues that men constitute facts in their minds because they want to create something which can be said to be true. This is truth they want because they recognize truth as a value. Otherwise, there would be no reason for them to assert anything at all. They could be content in remaining on the level of just "experiencing" their immediate sensations, which they cannot help having. It is the recognition of a particular value as being valid which compels humans to combine a form with a content i.e to make a judgment. Thus, a judgment always involves a claim to truth, truth being a value. There are several forms in which contents are judged to occur, and their totality comprises any form in which man can have knowledge. The form-element is called the "category". Existence" is one of them.

For instance, in the statement "This is a man" the notion "man" is a content which is given the form of existence. Every concrete "fact" therefore is categorically formed. People refer to such facts when, in the empircal sciences, they speak of "objective reality' or "empirical reality" Concrete reality consists of contents of consciousness which are judged by everybody to be "real". Objective reality in its totality is the subject-matter of science: it is the concrete material which constitutes the object of scientific investigations. In science, the "real" existence of the content of consciousness is not seen as being problematic: it is taken for granted. Instead, the establishment of the substantive diversity of the content is focussed upon. It must be the task of science simply to state what the facts are that is, all facts everything which is thought as real. But Rickert has reason to think that it is not the task of science to state all facts; a selection is necessary. Thus, the principle of selection comes into question. Rickert argues that there are infinitely many facts and that therefore, it is impossible to state them all on the assumption that the human mind is limited. By this Rickert means, that on the level of ideas, humans are just not able to grasp all available contents; they cannot have them all in the mind. Now as far as its content only is concerned, disregarding the form in which it occurs, it is correct to describe knowledge as a number of ideas or occurs, it is correct to describe knowledge as a number of ideas or images or picture which humans have of their sensations. If, then, due to the limitations of the mind, humans can never have complete knowledge of empirical reality, it is obvious that their knowledge cannot be perfect in the sense that their minds can never contain an exact mirror-image of the sensation-contents of the consciousness in all their details. It cannot hold the totality of ideas which would exhaust the content of immediate experiences. The mind can embrace only a finite number of such ideas. This, of course, requires that a selection be made. The fact that human knowledge of concrete reality in its entirety is impossible, and therefore must be selective, must involve abstraction poses for Rickert the problem of the "objectivity" of scientific knowledge. For this situation creates the possibility that each scientist's knowledge is different from everybody else's, that everybody abstracts in a different way and thus arrives at a merely subjective, private picture of the world. However, all science is based on the idea that it is possible to achieve objective knowledge of empirical reality, viz to establish the same knowledge in every scientists mind. Since the establishment of knowledge is due to an effort of the will, it is reasonable to assume that scientists would apply the same methods of abstraction only if they were all interested in identical knowledge. In Rickerts opinion, this commonality of interest is indeed the case. With this the task of establishing Rickerts conception of "objective knowledge" is finished. For him, "objective knowledge" is knowledge of those selected facts which everybody wants to know. This knowledge is, therefore, intersubjective. "Science" is the systematic effort to establish this knowledge. Hence it can said that according to Rickert, every exposition of facts can legitimately claim scientific status, which is accepted by all those (scientists) whose aim is to establish knowledge. However such an exposition can be presented only after a previous selection from among all available facts. Thus, its legitimacy has to stem from the circumstances that a standard of selection from the circumstances that a standard of selection has been applied which is intersubjectively recognized as valid. A standard is recognized as valid when in involves a method of abstraction leading to the establishment of those facts which every scientist wants to know. Conversely when there is an agreed upon standard of selection, it is used because it leads to generally desired knowledge. Therefore, if the knowledge of laws of nature is the only knowledge which everybody wants to have, then the method leading to their formulation is the only legitimate scientific method.

Scientific knowledge, as far as its content is concerned, is a partial "image" on one level of the human mind of the sensations which occur on a different level. Such an image cannot be likened to a mirror reflection. It is a selective image which has to be constructed, or formed, with the intent of intersubjectivity. Its selectivity is asserted to be valid for everybody: it is assumed that what is said is true. Asserted now is the legitimacy of the selection of particular and true facts for an account of empirical reality i.e. the conformity to a valid standard of selection. The process of selection involved in the establishment of scientific knowledge, in Rickert's view, is a formative process. Its end product is a certain account of empirical reality, thus displaying a certain form in which the substantive content appears. This form is called concept by Rickert. In this terminology, then the formal aspect of scientific investigation is a process of concept formation. Its established outcome is a concept. Strictly speaking. "concept" refers only to the formal aspect of scientific knowledge. However, the term is also used loosely by Rickert to denote the form-content combination as a whole. The conceptual content consists of facts, the conceptual form is the kind of abstraction from concrete reality which they represent, and due to which they are judged to constitute a valid account of this reality. This kind of abstraction is a function of the standard of selection applied in the process of concept formation. The application of such a standard represents for Rickert a method of overcoming the "irrational" infinity of reality. It is a method of rationalizing it i.e. treating it such that it can be grasped by human reason. Therefore, Rickert calls concepts "methodological forms" as opposed to the categories, which are Constitutive forms" since through them objective reality is constituted. The analysis of the methodological forms is the object of "methodology". It is the existence of these forms which makes science possible at all. Without them, humans could not have scientific knowledge but could only try to grasp the infinite whole of the concrete world through intuituion or some other kind of all-embracing inner experience.

According to Rickert the fact constituting objective reality are categorically formed notions of sensations. The category or "constitutive forms" of existence was mentioned as the form which makes humans think of such notions as "real". Another such category is "possibility". Now still another is "Causality". This may be expressed by saying that the human conception of objective reality is governed by the principle of causality which means that every single form of objective reality which is given this form is conceived as causing and being caused, not more or less. This is not synonymous with any particular causal law. For in laws, general causal relationships are described which exist between all phenomena which are members of certain classes. Since objective reality confronts man as a totality of individual object, causes and effects, assertions about general relationships have to be the result of comparing and ordering many individual facts. Causal laws, then cannot be formed through which objective reality is constituted in the human mind. Instead they must be treated as forms in which humans have scientific knowledge of reality, that is, as forms of abstraction. As such they are methodological forms, concepts or ways of overcoming the infinite multiplicity of empirical reality. It is now necessary to turn to the description of these methodological forms.

If there is to be knowledge at all, the infinite multiplicity of things has to be somehow eliminated or overcome. This is accomplished by concepts. They reduce the mass of facts representing the empirical world to proporitions which the mind is equipped to handle. Thus, without concepts any knowledge of the world, any grasp of physical reality in our minds, would be impossible. Concept formation, therefore is necessarily connected with any judgment about reality which can be expressed in words. The scientific observer can overcome the infinity of reality only by limiting himself to the establishments of selected facts. The selection in order to be valid requires the application of a standard of selection which is recognised as valid by everybody who wants to have scientific knowledge. This standard states what parts of reality are to be considered as "essential" for its valid representation. Thus, being " essential" is not an inherent quality of certain facts, but a characteristic ascribed to facts by the scientist who is applying a particular selective criterion. Rickert refers to this situation when he says that it depends on the point of view adopted by a scientist i.e. the standard of selection applied by him, whether a fact is essential or not. Empirically one finds, according to Rickert, two different formal principles of selection. Their application makes it possible to arrive at two different kinds of representations of reality. Each principle is recongnized as valid by all those who are interested in the corresponding kind of knowledge. One of the standards prescribes the selection of those empirical elements which are common to many concrete phenomena. The elements are considered to be essential, whereas individual differences are neglected. The other standard requires the selection of those component elements of one individual phenomenon which is their combined occurrence constitute the unique features of this phenomenon and distinguish it from all others: everything else is neglected as irrelevant. The former method leads to "general" concepts. According to Rickert, it is characterstic of the natural science. The latter procedure results in "historical" or "individual" concepts. In their most elaborate form they describe complex historical development e.g. the decline of the Roman Empire. The use of the term "concept" for such descriptions is uncommon. However, in Rickert's terminology "concept" denotes any kind of thought construct, any methodologically formed mental content which is intended as a valid representation of empirical reality, no matter how complex its verbal formulation.

Rickert's considerations are based on a specific conception of empirical reality. The main idea involved is that every concrete phenomenon - be it a "thing", be it a process - is composed of smaller concrete parts: that every concrete component point, in turn, is a structure consisting of even small concrete elements, and so on. Further more, every concrete phenomenon is viewed as being caused and as having an effect:

the same is thought to hold true of all the concrete component parts of phenomena, of the parts of the parts. etc. On any given level of complexity on concrete phenomenon is exactly like any other. Every concrete phenomenon in its totality is a unique, individual structure of component parts, uniquely causing. However, the concrete composition of any phenomenon, as well as its cause and effect, may be partially the same as or like, that of other concrete phenomena. In this case, some of their component parts, and the ways in which they are related to each other, are alike. The same also holds of their causes and their effects. When a scientist decides to acquire knowledge of only these common features of phenomena, then causes and their effects, he decides to generalize. When he decides to ignore them and instead to focus on the particularities of just one concrete phenomenon those component parts and their interrelationships which make this phenomenon unlike any other, he decides to individualize. In either case, the method of ignoring some facts in favour of others involves the selective procedure usually called "abstraction." All concept formation involves abstraction. Therefore, as far as the content is concerned - scientific concepts are in Rickert's view abstracted accounts of reality.

The procedure which scientists use to approach this final goal, according to Rickert, consists in comparing many and even more, phenomena in order to identify the component parts which they all have in common the constellations which are common to all. Eventually a specific constellation of specific constellation of specific parts shared by many phenomena is established (e.g an organism with four legs, which is furry and barks): this is what scientists are aware of what they have in their minds, when they "have a concept" of something (of a dog in this case). They are conscious of a combination of parts which they designate by a term, and every concrete phenomenon displaying this combination is "subsumed" under the concept. Such concept may represent things or relations of cause and effect between things: they are "things - concepts" (e.g. "tree", "stone") and "relational concepts" (e.g. attraction "motion") respectively. We reduce the extensive multiplicity of the world by designating a plurality of phenomenon with one world. The intensive multiplicity of earth single phenomenon is overcome because we are able to subsume it with certainty under the meaning of a word. Even in prescientific discourse, terms denoting general concepts are constantly used. Communi-cation would be impossible without them. However, since they have not been formed with the intention to completely overcome the infinite multiplicity of reality in its totality, they merely simplify a limited universe of events for the practical purposes of everyday life. They do not have the special characteristics required by scientifically useful general concept. The latter have to be designed to completely overcome the infinite multiplicity of an unlimited universe of concrete facts. In natural science as defined by Rickert, the aim is the construction of a system of general concepts which leaves no phenomenon "unconceived". This is its specific way of attempting to overcome the infinity of reality. For instance, it is often impossible to decide whether to treat something as a "treat" or a "bush" a "mammal" or a "fish" (in the pre scientific meanings of the terms). For Rickert, the cause of this is manifest : he has described the content of concepts as "pictures" (or images or reproductions) of sensations which are thought as real. This description presents no problem as long as one dealing with individual mental content. Thus, having a concept of a particular tree may be adequately described as having a picture of tree-sensations in the mind. A general concept, however, cannot be said to be the mental image in this case, a general tree, For there are no general trees. Rather, what people have in mind when they think a general concept like "tree" is the vague image of some particular tree. What may seem to be a general picture merely is an undifferentiated and indistinct particular image. Thus, Rickert seems to be forced to conclude that concepts which are both general and unambigious cannot be formed.

If this were the last word on the matter, scientists might as well give up all hope of ever overcoming the infinite multiplicity of the empirical world by forming general concepts. It is Rickerts argument, however, that fortunately there is a way out of the dilemma. For he argues that it is possible to give a sufficiently precise statement of what is subsumed under a specific general concept through the procedure known as "definition". When such a concept is defined (in contrast to the term designating the concept), it is made explicit just what particular elements or parts have to be present in a specific combination in a concrete phenomenon for it to be subsumed under the concept. In other words, a general concept is the short, but vague, holistic version of what a person has in mind when he asserts, one after another, the occurrence of several things in a certain combination. These things are those component parts which are alike in all the concrete phenomenon comprised by the general concept. The concept and its definition are completely equivalent as far as the content of knowledge is concerned.

At this point, it is necessary to indicate an important implication of Rickert's characterization of general concepts. Obviously in his view, such concepts are summary representations of common aspects of many phenomena. Their definitions i.e. the sets of statements equivalent to the concepts, must therefore be interpreted as constituting descriptions of those features which many or all known phenomena have in common. The earlier statement that the conceptual content is facts, also supports this interpretation.

The process of forming general concepts, as it is described by Rickert, starts as a clarificaiton of the meaning of the terms occuring in everday discourse, ie. as a precise specification of the mental image evoked by the use of such a term. Basically, this procedure consists in providing an analysis of an already existing concept. It is clear, however, that such an analysis can be performed only because the conceptual elements have been previously combined in the mind. Therefore, it is really this synthetic process which determines the content of concept.

The synthetic process of concept formation may be described as follows: an observer is aware of a number of phenomena as really existing (e.g. elephants). The content of these concrete facts is complex (i.e. elephants have many parts common in diverse sizes and shapes, different shades etc). The observer forms a general concept by singling out from each particular content the partial contents which still are complex - which it shares with all the others (e.g tusks, trunk, hairless skin, herbivore, mammal). Of course he forms a mental picture which he treats as a unity ("elephant"). This is the general concept. Seeing now that the analytic definition of a concept consists in a series of judgments, we may infer from this that the synthetic definition, which we have described as the process of combining elements, also must consist of a series of judgments. The "content" of the general concept is the totality of the selected ideas of immediate sensations: these ideas represent the common component elements of those concrete objects which are subsumed under the concept. The total number of these objects (e.g. all elephants) constitutes the "scope" of the concept. The greater the number of concrete objects subsumed under the concept, the wider its scope its extension (i.e the greater the reduction of the existensive infinity of reality): the fewer the elements or parts which an object has to share with others in a certain combination, the smaller its content its intension (i.e the greater the reduction of the intensive infinity of realty): (EG

Indian elephants class have more features in common than elephants in general).

It must be indicated that Rickert's whole account of concept formation in the natural science, since it is focused especially on the justifiability of the ultimate aim (knowledge of what things have in common), rather simplifies the intricacies of the process as it actually occurs. Thus, very often it is not possible to define concepts by the constellation of elements which things have in common, since they do not simply share them equally - as is pre supposed by Rickerts argument but exhibit them in degrees.

2.3.3 NATURE OF CONCEPTUAL ANALYSIS

Analytical research describes and interprets the past from selected sources. With this methodology the researcher does not directly observe, measure, or experiment with current educational phenomena, nor are the findings tested statistically. Instead, the data of analytical research are traces of the past, usually documents preserved in collections. Rigorous techniques of criticism are applied to the documents. The validity of an analytical study lie in the procedures inherent in the methodology, which includes the research for sources, the criticism of sources, and the interpretation of sources. In summary, analytical studies provide knowledge and under-standing about past educational, historical, legal and policy events. Major ideas and concepts are clarified for meaning. Research questions focus on events (who, what, when where, how), how an event occurred (descriptive) and why the event happened (interpretative). This contrants with quantitative studies, which test hypotheses and ask "Is there a relationship between variable 'X' and variable 'Y' / or "Is there a statistically significant difference between the scores of the experimental and control group ?"

Analytical studies state generalizations as causal explanations for past events. Such terms as *cause, because, since, on account of and for the reason that* connote causal explanations. Causal explanations are implied with such statements as "*under the circumstances, it is not surprising that...*", " *naturally at this point,* ..... *"it was inevitable....?* Causal explanations are suggested with such nouns as *impossibility, necessity, influence, impulse, development, consequence*, and *motives* and such verbs as *lead to, result in, make, bring about, stimulate, force,* and *compile*

Analytical explanations differ from statistical and common sense explanations. The analyst first discovers the separate facts that assert that an event took place and then interprets the connection between the facts, that is, the causes. Cause and effect are not treated in an absolute manner. The researcher is interested in the particular circumstances may never be repeated again. Analytical explanations differ from common sense explanations because they require critical judgment using specialized knowledge about the era in which the event occurred the facts, and the connecting circumstances.

The validity of an analytical explanation differs from the validity of quantitiative explanations. Analytical explanations are not confirmed or proven by empirical testing. Analytical explanations are justified or supported by the facts stated in the study. Analysts will say, "If you do not believe my explanation, take a closer look at the facts". The specification of details - the who, what, when, where, and how - is precisely the feature of the explanation that differentiates it from statistical explanations. Analysts seldom claim, however, that they have all of the facts. Instead, a study contains that group of associated facts and ideas which, when clearly presented in a prescribed amount of space, leave no questions unanswered within the presentations, even though many questions could be asked outside it.

Generalizations are interpretations of facts. The more complex the events and the wider their spread intime and space, the greater the need for the analysts judgment. Usually, an event of any degree of magnitudes and complexity needs many generalizations to explain it. Explanations suggest multiple causes for any single event.

Analytical explanations are made from different points of veiw. The reason world - 1 occurred is, for example, answerable from the point of view of individual, human purposes, desires, weaknesses, and abilities, national policies, traditions of diplomacy and plans, political alignments, treaties and the international structure of Europe in 1914, and economic trends, social organization, political doctrines, and ideology. Each point of view is at a higher level of abstraction.

It appears that there are no absolute causes waiting to be discovered and offered as explantions by analytical researchers. Instead, analysts write at different levels of abstraction, at different chronological distances from the past events, for different purposes, in different contexts, and from different points of view. Not surprisingly, different studies suggest apparently contradictory but valid explanations of the past.

The type of analysis indicates the research purpose. A study may be an analysis of an educational concept, an edition or compilation of documents, a descriptive narration of an event, a comparative analysis of several events or periods, or a universal theory or philosophy. Each type of study differs in scope and level of generalizations.

Educational concepts are clarified by describing the essential or generic meaning of the concept, specifying the different meanings of the concept or describing the appropriate usage for the concept in a variety of instances. The analysis of an educational concept like professionalism may be the focus of an entire study. Clarification of the meaning of educational concepts has potential relevance for subsequent research.

The analysis of concepts clarifies the way people think about education. The focus is on the meaning of the concept, not on the researcher's personal values or on factual information. For example, the question, "What are the aims of education?" is not answered by collecting data to show that educators have aims or do not have aims. Instead, the analyst begins by asking, "Is having an aim an integral and necessary part of our concept of being an educator?" or "Can a person be an educator without having an aim?" Asking such questions allows the analyst to get at the meaning of education by carefully examining some ideas attached to the concept of aims as an aspect of education. The analyst assumes a neutral position while analysing a concept before taking a value position or collecting factual information.

Three strategies may be used to analyse such concepts as *education, literacy, knowledge, teaching - learning, equal opportunity,* and *due process*. Soltis (1978) illustrates generic, differential, and condition analysis. Each of strategies begins with a different prior question and applies specific techniques to clarify the concept. A generic analysis identifies the essential meaning of a concept. The analysis isolates those elements that distinguish the concept from other words. To clarify the concept academic discipline, one might, therefore, compare history, mathematics and physics as clear standard examples with home economics, animal husbandry, and water - skiing as counter examples in order to arrive at the generic meaning of academic discipline.

Differential analysis is used when a concept seems to have more than one standard meaning and the basis for differentiating between meanings is unclear. The prior question is "What are the basic (different) meanings of the concept ?" One could, for example, ask the question, "What are the different meanings of subject matter?" and analyse the concept of subject matter by intuitively classifying the topical uses with concrete examples, such as solar system, school subjects, knowledge and skills. The distinguishing charac-teristics of each type of subject matter is ascertained to clearly separate the types, and a typology is developed. The differential analysis distinguishes among the basic meanings of the concept and provides a clearer idea of the logical domain covered by the concept.

Differential analysis oftenleads to conditions analysis. The prior question is "under what context conditions would it be true to say that the concept present?" or judgment of whether they demonstrate implicit meanings in the language, meanings that are then rationally analyzed. Because different examples are frequently used, the analysis of educational concepts may lead to reanalysis and further conceptual clarity.

Analysis of educational concepts is applied is applied in the study of educational concepts and in historical legal and policy making research. A study of the public school movement, due process in education or groups that influence the passage of a law must first determine the meaning of public school due process and influential groups.

The present study of the concept of a university is a kind of generic analysis, identifying the essential elements which constitute a university. But before identifying the consti-tuent features of a university, the scholar must first determine the sphere of Higher Education under which the term "university" is covered.

2.3.4 ILLUSTRATION FOR CONCEPTUAL ANALYSIS

(I) JOANS F. SOLTIS'S CONCEPT OF KNOWLEDGE.

To illustrate the mode of conceptual analysis the scholar has taken Soltis's Concept of knowledge first. The conceptual analysis of the Concept of knowledge pertains to the domain of epistemology. Theories about what constitutes knowledge and how we arrive at it have perennially been central concern to both philosophers and educators. As humans, we are conscious that we know: and this consciousness of ours opens up a vast territory for human exploration nor otherwise available to us. It allows us to ask such questions as: By what processes do we come to know things (the psychological question): How can we be sure what we claim to know is true? (the philosophical question): or what use is this or that particular knowledge (the practical question): and what knowledge is of most worth ? (the traditional curriculum question). These and a host of other questions become possible because we know that we know. Moreover, and most important to educators, being conscious that we know also allows us as human beings to try consciously to help others come to know what we know. Because we can stand apart from our knowledge, we can think of how best to impart that knowledge. We call this most distinctive human enterprise of intentionally imparting knowledge "teaching" in its individuated sense and "education" in its collective social sense. In this fundamental way the concept of knowledge is inextricably intertwined with the concept of education and the answers we give to the host of possible questions about knowledge and knowing will have an important bearing on how we think and act as educators.[2.2]

J.F. Soltis has attempted to give an "organic" view of mind, a "transactional" view of learning, and a "contsructionist" view of knowledge, gradually moving away from a Cartesian view of mind, an associationist view of learning, and an absolutist view of knowledge. The earliest dominant philosophical view of mind, learning and knowledge was "ego centric", focusing on the individual and how one acquired true knowledge of the world external to oneself. The newer view is "socio centric" still considering the individual and the world but also taking into account the cultural nature of knowledge as a communal human construction that is both formed by and forms human beings. From a socio centric perspective knowledge must be viewed as both individual and social, personal and public constructions designed to make sense of and provide for effective action in a respective, malleable yet independently existing reality. Thus knowledge claim, epistemological inquiry and theories of education and human development need to take into account the complex reciprocal relations between an individual and

---

2.2 Soltis. Jonas.F. (edited by) Philosophy and Education, NSSE, 1981 part 1 Epistemology Character V. Education and the Concept of knowledge. (page 95) Chicago. Illinois.

his or her biological, social and cultural inheritance, between individuals and groups, between public knowledge systems and the structure of both the natural and social worlds, and between any relevant mix of these in multiple combination. Central to the development of the socio centric perspective in this century has been an increasing recognition that knowledge cannot be separated from knowers, that human beings construct different knowledge system, and that all knowledge is imbedded in the fabric of social life. The idea that this socially constructed world is the only one available to us is an important one in many ways and in one sense it could not be otherwise, unless at birth we are left to fend for ourselves in a world devoid of any human contact.

As social beings, we learn language and we also learn to participate in a social system that defines roles, manners, morals, institutions, and even develops formal fields of knowledge. To what extent are we locked into this socially constructed world and do what extent are we free to go beyond it or contrary to it? To what degree does formal education make us more of a prisoner of that social world or on the other hand provide us with the means to achieve our freedom to transcend it? By using the terms like"in one sense", to what extent' and to what degree, Soltis tries to convey the idea that this is not an all-or-nothing affair. We need to recognize the dynamic and reciprocal quality of the relationships between the world, individuals, collectives and the culture as a whole. At different times and under different conditions, we should expect the influence of individuals on collectives, collectives on culture, culture on individuals, and the world on all of these, to vary.

To illustrate these relationships and to demonstrate the educational power that can be achieved by becoming consciously aware of aspects of what we can by knowledge, Soltis suggests some of the limits and freedoms inherent in such human constructions as language, theories, skills, roles, and formal knowledge language is an enormously versatile human instrument. Does the language of our society lock us into a way of viewing the world? To a certain degree, this is so. There are words for mental things and other words for physical things, and through those words we see the world. But that does not mean that we cannot stand apart from those categories and ask if they make the best sense of the world, we experience. Gilbert Ryle's The Concept of Mind did just that. He argued that we make a philosophical blunder (a category mistake as called by him) with regard to the concepts of mental and physical things.

He said that this Cartesian way of dealing with the world misleads us badly in our ability to deal sensibly with ideas like knowledge and intelligence. He recommended that we rid ourselves of the "ghost in the machine" by recognizing that our mental language does not refer to the inner workings of some mysterious mind stuff, but rather to the ways in which we judge the performance of people as witty, intelligent, dull, stupid, and so forth.

Being made aware of the possibility that basic concepts or categories may distort or limit certain ways of thinking, however, does encourage us to seek ways to overcome this perceived deficiency. Thus, we are neither totally free nor totally restricted by the language inherit from our primary social group. On the conceptual and theoretical levels, language is constantly being reshaped by individuals and collectives within the group. Each person has the potential to engage in such activity in order to make more sense of the world, and educators have the obligation to make people aware of this fact. While it is possible for an individual to invent a unique way to think of the world, the advance of knowledge more ordinarily comes from refining or moving beyond what we now collectively claim to know. Thus knowledge making from the sociocentric perspective is more a communal rather than a private enterprise and educators play an essential role in insuring its continuity and success. Its development requires not only public expression and testing of knowledge claims by an individual or by a group but also serious consideration of the knowledge claims of others. According to this view, education has the obligation not only to transmit current knowledge and methods of inquiry but also to develop in individuals and groups the disposition to be willing to hear and test critically new claims in the future and to seek ways to improve upon methodology and instrumentation.

Besides learning the language theories and knowledge claims of our social group, we also learn recipes and skills for effective action and roles and mores that dictate "appropriate" conduct. The human capacity to do to invent, to create, to make, to develop skills, arts, crafts and dispositions in the service of "humanness" is part of human knowledge. From the sociocentric perspective, knowledge is not just what is contained in heads and books but also in hands and actions as take part in social living. Knowledge viewed singularly as truth about the world is too narrow a view. A sociocentric perspective invites our attention to those forms of human knowledge imbedded in human activities that embody the techniques and institutions we have developed to provide for our needs, satisfy our wants, and regulate our social lives. The mastery of skills and techniques, and of institutional and role-specific behaviour is too vast an area of human knowledge acquisition, development, and use to be overlooked by educators or scorned by philosophers. Knowing how to do something and how things are done are every bit as important as forms of knowledge as is knowing that something is true or false. This indicates the fact that our concept of knowledge has been broadened beyond what can be stated in words so as to include such legitimate categories as proper action and human skill . If we take skills and techniques to be knowledge, then we know that paper and pencil test will be inadequate in the evaluation of all but paper and pencil skills.

At the heart of formal education is the narrower but also highly important conception of knowledge as organized fields of inquiry and study. Here we have represented the organized efforts of collections of human beings through time to make sense of some aspect of experience. While we learn a common language quite easily and naturally as our children interacting with others, formal education in effect so includes the learning of special languages and special symbol systems for dealing with different kinds of experience/R.S. Peters, the British philosopher of education and his colleague, Paul Hirst, have made interesting use of the idea of education as initiation into the various public forms of knowledge developed by human beings to bring order to the several realms of human experience and to induct the learner into these various perspectives. For example, the appreciation of art calls into play a set of concepts, relations, and standards of judgment different from that employed in the appreciation of a logical argument or the development of an empirical claim. The concept of beauty is essential to art, the concept of truth to logic and the concept of evidence to factual assertions. Different domains of human experience call for different ways to justify a claim to know something.

Paul Hirst argued that the concept of a liberal education has as its central tenet the development of mind and that to have a rational mind requires experience structured under some conceptual scheme, some publicly developed form of knowledge that allows one to see the world with others as they see it. Thus, liberal education for Hirst becomes an education in the seven or eight distincitve "forms" of knowledge that he claims human kind has created to order and deal meaningfully with experience. His most recent list includes mathematics, physical science, knowledge of persons, of literature, and of fine art, morals, religion and philosophy. In Hirst's the justification for teaching the forms of knowledge becomes analytic and /or self-justifying just the Peter's like question "Why be rational?" presupposes being rational in the very asking of the question. Each of these "forms of knowledge" are "distinct worlds of discourse" that provide different "modes of structuring experience" and as such must therefore be the ultimate and fundamental components of any education. According to Hirst, they fully embody what it means to be rational and to know. Without them we are cut of from basic human perspectives on some essential part of our shared world. But Jane Martin opines that Hirst's view of knowledge and liberal education with its commission of concern for skills, attitudes, and the emotions. nevertheless, within Hirst's frame work, the idea that there are different worlds to see is an educationally powerful idea. We can view education as helping others to see the world from a new perspective in two ways. One way is to think of it as actually providing students with a particualr world view or interpretation of experience. The other way is to provide them with lenses to be able to see it, that is, with concepts, relational systems, and standards of judging whatever aspect of human experience is brought into focus by using that particular set of ideas.

Different conceptual systems are like different sorts of optical instruments that allow us to see, explore, and make sense of different visual phenomen on. The telescope and microscope point at and help us visually very different things, just as do aesthetic language and scientific language, for instance. Both open up new worlds invisible to us before. Content and form in human knowledge are at one and the same time independent while also being interdependent in important ways. As educators, we need to deal with form and content and the more consciously we do so, the more effective will be our educating. To transmit the content is only part of the job. To also provide a knowledge of and sensitivity to the concepts and standards of judgment in a domain of experience is to equip a person with the ability to use form to add to or after content and even to refine or change the form itself and to act reasonably in future encounters within that realm-of experience.

We know form and content are intimately intertwined. Dewey (Democracy and Education) reminds us that only in abstraction can we separate subject matter from method According to Polanyi, (Personal

Knowledge) in acting on the world we use knowledge "tacitly" that is, we do not focus our attention on the knowledge we are using to interpret the world or on the standards we are using to make judgments about the world. Our focal attention is on the objects being interpreted and judged not on what we are doing that with (our knowledge). Similarly, we focus on the meaning of what we are reading. In fact, we have to be able to see the letters not as simple discrete things, which is probably the way a child learning the alphabet sees them. We must be able to "see" the meaning that they convey. Being initiated into a "form" of knowledge, therefore, must be more than acquiring sense of its form and some part of its content. It must include being able to use both form and content tacitly to deal meaningfully and reasonably with phenomena appropriate to that form of knowledge. Knowledge is in one sense an artifact of collective social construction, but it is also intimately related to the everyday world we experience as human beings. At any one time, it represents the best individual and collective judgment of sensible and reasonable ways meaningfully to capture, represent, and deal effectively with some aspect of human experience in a world that exists to some degree independently of our shaping and knowing of it. From a sociocentric perspective, sense making and being able to act effectively are the social and individual purposes of knowledge. To achieve those ends, educators should help students see, appreciate, and gain skill in using the standards of reasonable judgment appropriate to the particular forms of knowledge being taught and learned.

Philosophically, the epistemological tradition generally has tended to view knowing "egocentrically", from the perspective of the individual knower. Too often this has led to a spectator or contemplative view of knowledge because the epistemologists are exploring the individual's acquisition and use of social knowledge skills, and standards of judgment in the various domains of human experience, Educationally on the other hand, we have tended to focus on the formal collective forms of knowledge in the traditional subjects and to treat them as highly organised stating collections rather than as dynamically growing and changing systems. The broader dimensions of knowledge include skills imbedded in all forms of human activity and values imbedded in ethical standards, institutions, arts and ways of life. They are also a central part of human knowledge thus broadly conceived at any single moment in the dynamic nexus between individual, collective and the world provides both the individual and the group with initial modes of communication, interpretation and understanding as well as with a basis for judgment and for skilled action but never without the possibility of critical reflection, modification, development and change. Such social and individual knowledge not only enriches and gives meaning to our experiences, but also provides the where withal, however tentative, to act effectively in the world and to seek more effective ways to conceive of it and act on it. In every immediate life situation in which we act as individuals or as collective, we draw upon our reservoir of developed knowledge, skills, beliefs and values and tacitly use them to diagnose and understand the situation, to choose appropriate ways to act, and to assess the consequences of our actions. In these many ways we see that knowledge ultimately gets its sense, effect and value in use and develops or changes as we test its fir in our common world. Knowledge seeking and using is both an individual and collective affair of trying to make sense of, appreciate and operate effectively in the world. It is only now we become more aware of this fact that we are also becoming more aware of both the problems and opportunities that are part of this conception of knowledge. Joans F. Soltis says "As we come to recognize and develop more fully) a concept of knowledge from the sociocentric perspective. We will become more sophisticated about such ideas as objectivity, relativism, learning, mind, science, art, judgment, and the like. Then we will be better able to invent educational strategies and practices that will help us fulfill an obligation to pass on human knowledge and to provide for its continual development in all its forms: (x)[2.3]

II) CONCEPT OF EDUCATION BY R.S.PETER

Another illustration for conceptual analysis can be cited from R.S.Peter's in his book Ethics and Education

Education is a term which we use for a family of procedures by means of which individuals are initiated into such forms of thought and awareness and into activities and modes of conduct informed by them. We call a person 'educated' who has been successfully initiated. It is possible for a lot of education to take place by people, picking things up when they are not in an explicit learning situation and when no one is setting out to teach them anything. But a great part of education takes

---

2.3 Solts, Joans.F. (Edited by) Philosophy and Education, NSSE, 1981 Part I, Epistemology, V: Education and the Concept of the knowledge (page 113) Chicago, Illinois.

place in more explicit contexts in institutions, devoted to it, where learning situations are intentionally contrived. It is obvious that the over all aim of education is the development of educated men and women. Determinateness to the notion of quality in education, therefore, can only be given by getting clearer about the criteria built into the notion of being educated. But 'quality' in education could also be taken to describe the efficacy of the procedure of initiation in the development of such educated men and women.

The quality can be thought of in the following two senses:

1) Product judgments of quality which related purely to the degree to which those who had been at a school or a college satisfied the multiple criteria involved in 'being educated'

2) Process judgment of quality, which took careful account of the state of students before they entered such institutions and measured the extent to which they had progressed towards being educated from a given base-line.

As an example, if quality was thought of only in the product sense, then a school with a highly selective intake which turned out a high proportion of students who reached university entrance standard, would exhibit it in a pre-eminent degree. However, it was thought of in the process sense, a school in a slum area, where the delinquency and illiteracy rate was high, would exhibit it if a fair proportion of its pupils obtained some kind of recognized school- learning certificate and if none of them was brought up before the juvenile court. The notion of 'quality' in the process sense could be applied without the notion of 'quality' in the product sense: for the efficacy of process of education could not be estimated unless we had an idea of their ideal outcome in the form of an 'educated man'.

What are the criteria built into this from which notions of quality in the product sense derive? What second, can be said about the characteristics of institutions, cirricula, teachers and procedures which encourage the development of quality in the product sense and hence give content to the notion of quality in the process sense? These questions provide a frame work for the discussion of quality in education: because multiple criteria are necessary to explicate what is meant by being educated. Attempts to formulate aims of education are nothing but attempts to emphasize or concentrate attention on criterial built into the concept of being educated. They are attempts to give specific content to the notion of an educated man. R.S. Peter, however, has set up a formal framework of criteria to systematize statements of aims under 3 main headings:

i) Commitment to what is regarded as valuable in itself

ii) Knowledge and understanding (together with the approp-riate effect)

iii) Wholeness

Crucial in this is the development of an autonomous attitude towards learning, together with concentration, persevance, absorption and a general attitude of spontaneous enjoyment. In terms of this criterion no special priority is given to purely theoretical pursuits, though traditionally these have been picked out as those which have supreme value in themselves. It is true that practical activities have additional value if they are also based on theoretical understanding rather than being mere exhibitions of know-how or knacks. Here comes the next criterion :knowledge and understanding. Being educated implies more than being just skilled even if the skill is exhibited in some worthwhile pursuit such as music. ballet or engeneering. It involves knowing that, not just knowing how. This requires in the early stages, the development of a basic structure of concepts and categories for distinguishing characteristics of the world from the product of wishes, fears and imaginings. The basic skills of reading and writing have then to be acquired so that the range of articulateness of experience can be extended and its expressions better controlled and communicated. Differentiated modes of awareness must then be developed - scientific, mathematical, moral, interpersonal, historical, aesthetic religious, philosophical. This must be done in a way which involves not an inert understanding but a concern for values underlying them, for example respect for truth and for persons, sensitivity to suffering and 'significant form'.

Within these forms of awareness the distinction has to be made between (a) knowing facts and mastering a body of knowledge (b) understanding principles and theories which provide backing to (a) and being able to interpret experience in the light of them: (c) familiarity with, and degree of mastery of, the procedures or means of which (a) and (b) have been acquired and can be assessed, criticized and developed (e.g. scientific method in the case of science). This permits some kind of autonomous problem solving exploration or evaluation in the relevant form of awareness. To be eduated, a person must at least have got as far as (b) and have some familiarity with (c) even if he lacks the mastery of such procedures. Quality in education based on this criterion would relate both to the level of discrimination and understanding achieved and to a multitude of virtue, exhibtied in these forms of awareness. Some virtues would be those very general moral virtues which are necessary pre-conditions for the pursuit of truth in any form, for example, respect for facts, for the giveness of materials, and for people as sources of argument, willingness to change one's opinion in the fact of facts and arguments, impartiality, humility tolerance. These are also other general virtues of a more intellectual sort-consistency originality, accuracy, clarity precision, sense of relevance, imagination. These would be the most general criteria of 'quality' shared by all forms of awareness. There would then be others which are more specific to the distinct forms of awareness for example objectivity and keeness of observation in science and rigour in mathematics.

Now a days the eduator's demand for 'wholeness' is understandable for being 'educated' rules out being confined to one form of awareness just as it rules out gearing knowledge entirely to extrinsic ends. We would not call a person who is narrowly specialized an educated man. It is implied that an educated person may be trained in something but being just trained does not mean 'being educated'. A trained artist, scientist or historian is not necessarily an educated man for he may have a deep but circumscribed understanding confined to one form of these spheres. To what extent a person has to develop in all the various forms of awareness in order to be educated would be difficult to determine. The main function of this criterion is to rule out narrow specialisation rather than to suggest positive requirement. Quality in education can therefore relate in someway to such a criterion of all round understanding. This, then is a framwork for classifying different criteria of quality in education, in so far as this relates to aims of education i.e. to our concept of an educated persons.

P.S Peters in his book *Ethics and Education* (1966) analyses the concept of education, probing to see whether any conditions that seem to be logically necessary conditions have been produced for the use of the term 'education' and puts forth counter examples to test this. Two types of conditions have been suggested for the use of the term education namely desirability conditions and knowledge conditions. Many appreciate that 'education' has something to do with the transmission of knowledge and understanding but they do not see any connection between what they think valuable and educative and have no specific word to differentiate the handing on of what they think valuable from handing on a lot of other things. Then understanding has not become differentiated to the extent of needing a special word for referring to the passing on of what they do think valuable. They have a concept of education which they use to refer to what goes on in schools and universities. But they have not our concept-the concept of the educated people who are professionally concerned with education. We are not in the majority of people who use the word 'education'. So it is doubtful whether the desirability condition of education is a logically necessary condition of the term that is in current use. It stands in this relation to a mere specific differentiated concept that has emerged.

Knowledge conditions are the only proper logical conditions and the desirability condition is dependent on them. On this view the fundamental notion involved in being educated would be that of having knowledge and understanding. Because knowledge and understanding are valued in our culture both for their own sake and for what they contribute to technology and to our quality of life. Generally, being educated has come to be thought of as a highly desirable state to be in-but not by everybody. Whether or not the desirability condition is fulfilled would depend, therefore upon contingent facts about the attitude of people talking about education to the passing on of knowledge and understanding. The desirability condition would not be a logically necessary conditions for the use of the term 'education'. It would rather be a contingent consequence of certain people's valuation. If they see that it may help them to run a farm or to cure a disease, they may accord a limited value to it- that of an instrumental type. Sometimes education would be called 'knowledge industry' without any importance. Poor or bad education would simply mark the efficiency with which knowledge was handed on or the worth of the type of knowledge that was handed on. The aforesaid analysis puts all the weight on the knowledge conditions.

The knowledge conditions include both depth and breadth of understanding. They rule out the process of specilization as well as the mere training of people in simple skills and folklore. In English, the word 'education' was originally used just to talk in a very general way about the bringing up of children and animals. The word was often used of animals and birds that were trained by human beings such as hounds and falcons. Now a days we sometimes use it in this general way as when, for instance, we talk about Spartan education or when we use in of our forms of training that are hardly connected with knowledge and understanding. But, with the coming of industrialism and the increasing demand for knowledge and skill consequent on it, education become increasingly associated with 'schooling' and with the sort of training and instruction that went on in special institutions. The large scale changes culminating in the development of compulsory schooling for all leads to a radical conceptual tightening up that we now only tend to use the word in connection with the development of knowledge and understanding. we distinguish now between 'training and education' in such a way that training is applicable to that to animals and birds.

The notion of 'educated' as characterising the all round development of a person morally intellectually and spiritually only emerged in the 19th century during which century the distinction between education and training come to be made explicitly. This was very much connected with instruction by means of which desirable mental qualities were thought to be produced as well as with the drawing out and development of qualities thought to be potential in a process. This term, 'however', continued to be used to refer to the meaning and bringing up of children and animals as well as to the sort of instruction that went on in schools.

Now a days especially, in educational circle, the concept of an educated man as an ideal has very much taken root. It is natural for those working in educational institutions to conceive of what they are doing as being connected with the development of such a person. They have become very sensitive to the difference between working with the ideal in mind and having more limited and specific goals for which they use the word 'training' (e.g the change in nomenclature from Training Colleges to College of Education, and the change from physical Training to Physical Education). In brief, because of the development of the concept of an 'educated man', the concept of 'education' has become tightened up because of its natural association with the development of such a person. We distinguish between educating people and training them because for us education is no longer compatible with any narrowly conceived enterprise.

Now in the analysis, connection was associated between education and the development of an educated man. In the case of older use of education, there is no such tight connection between various processes of bringing up and raring and the development of an educated man because many people still use the word 'education' to cover not only any process of instruction, training etc that goes on in schools but also less formalized child rearing practices such as toilet training, getting children to be clean and tidy and to speak with a nice accent. They may think these achievements desirable, though they have little connections with knowledge and understanding. At least the concept of education has shifted more or less universally in connotation inclining towards the development of an educated man. It looks therefore, as if the concept of education is a very fluid one. At one end of a continuum in the older and undifferentiated concept which refers just to any process of bringing up or rearing in which the connection either with what is desirable or with knowledge is purely contingent. There may be uses which link it just with the development of desirable states without any emphasis of knowledge there may be uses which pick out the development of knowledge without implying its desirability. The more recent and more specific concept links such processes with the development of states of a person that involve knowledge and understanding in depth and breadth and also suggests that they are desirable.

The general injunction to promote desirable states of a person that involves depth and breadth of understanding, would indicate only a general direction . It would offer no specific guidance. More specific guidance would have to be obtained by the teacher getting clearer about his aims in educating people. For the function of the formulation of aims is to specify more precisely what one is trying to achieve one's target in a metaphorical sense. This attempt to specify precise targets also takes over a further suggestion from the context of shooting and throwing where the concept of 'aim' has its origin namely that the end in view is not altogether easy to achieve. Distance and difficulty are endemic to ends that we would characterize as aims. Besides having the practicalities, the teacher has to be more specific then he is asked about his ideals. An educational ideal, for instance, might be that every child should learn out of the joy of discovery. A teacher's aim in the same context, might be a more specific and attainable objective such as that every child in his class should be brought to see some point in learning what had to be learnt.

Formulating aims in education must be distinguished from attempting to answer the general question what is the aim of education? In other words, if the foregoing analysis of the specific concept of education as the family process leading up to desirable states of mind in people involving depth and breadth of understanding is more or less adequate then it would be a conceptual truth that the production of this general end is the aim of education. It would be like saying that the aim of reform is to make men better.

Let us suppose that the teacher attempts to specify his aim in educating people or the aims of particular educational institution. What sort of answer could be given? Any answer that could be a more precise specification of what an educated man is considered to be: features would be emphasized e.g. critical thinking, specilized knowledge, autonomy aesthetic sensitivity- which would be part of the teachers understanding of what it means to be educated. Content would be given to the general form of an educated man provided by the analysis in terms of desirability and knowledge conditions. Much emphasis should be laid on some desirable qualities rather than others. Indeed this is one important respect in which educating people differs from curing them, when the aim of education is compared with medicine. For in education there is as much debate about the ends of education as there is about the methods to be adopted to promote these ends. The same is not true of medicine. There is much more consensus about what constitutes being 'cured' than there is about what constitutes being educated.

It is important to distinguish aims of education in these cases from aims of education when the more general undifferentiated concept of education is being used e.g. by politicians talking about the educational system. A politician or administrator, in an economic frame of mind, might think of education as the means by supply of trained manpower is assured. He might think of education purely in this way having no regard for the endeavors of educators who might in their turn be impervious to the economist's frame of reference. They might be concerned purely with the development of educated men and women. Looking at what goes on in school and universities from this economic point of view is not necessarily antagonistic to being concerned with the education in the more specific sense. Indeed a teacher might regard the development of responsible citizens who have the competence to fulfil same occupational role as his unifying aim as an educator. For him the civic consciousness might be the hall-mark of an educated person. He might, in his approach, concentrate on getting his pupils technically equipped to do certain jobs and attempt to make technical skills and knowledge the linch-pin of a person's depth and breadth of understanding as a citizen. Similarly teacher might teach a subject such as science with purely vocational or economic ends in view. He might regard himself just as equipping people for vacations or as serving a national need for trained manpower, without much thought about the development of the individuals concerned, as individuals, He might conceive of what he was doing just as contributing to economic growth. But teaching science with these limited ends in view should be distinguished from educating people. Teaching is not necessarily educative. On the other hand, though not unmindful of the nation's needs, a teacher might also teach science because he regarded this form of understanding as central to his concept of an educated person.

In conceptual analysis, We usually settle for making explicit defining characteristics in the weak sense. In attempting to make explicit the rules behind our usage of words and thus to get clearer about our concepts, Peter observes that it is important to distinguish logically necessary conditions from other sorts of conditions that may be present. Conceptual analysis consists in looking for logically necessary conditions for the use of a word and hence concerned with definition in loose sense. The concept does not depend upon the publicly observable criterion of the ability to discriminate and use word appropriately: it depends rather on how a human being conceives the concept. There is a kind of reconciliation between these two. In response to the view that there exist no logically necessary conditions for the use of a word, Peter maintains that thing brings out two important points which Wittgenistein himself made. The first is that we must not look for the defining characteristics in any simple, stereo typed way, with the paradigm of just one type of word before use. The second is that concepts can only be understood in relation to other concepts. We gradually make explicit the link between words which reflect our conceptual structure.

Word reflects the concept and the concept reflects the word. In Peters account, there is nothing for the concept to conceive and nothing for the word to articulate. When we understand concepts in terms of other concepts what we do is to pay attention to what we mean by using a word in the sense of the job that we conceive of the word as doing in the context in which we employ it. For words are not just noises or marks on paper: they are more like tools. They do specific jobs in social life. Peter speaks about the subjective side because the publicly observable criterion of usage to identify the possession of the concept is objective. The objective side holds that words would be just like noises or marks on papers. Peter maintains that words are employed for a purpose by the speaker and that purpose is their meaning. If understanding concepts must be done in terms of other concepts and the concepts themselves must be understood in terms of their purposes, in terms of the job we conceive the word as doing in the context in which we employ it, it must also be understood. Peter points out that the jobs, words do are and legion and that, moreover, many of these jobs are not to be understood merely in terms of other words.

Obviously one of the main jobs that words do is to convey information, to describe things and situations. But this is only one of their jobs. Sometimes we use words to warn people. At other times we use words to suggest courses of action to people. At other time we use words to express what we wish and so on. The use of words, in other words, is a form purposeful behaviour, but it has to be understood in terms of other non-linquistic purposes that people have on their social life In this human evdeavour, the quest rather than the capture of the logically necessary condition is of first importance. We must learn to trace ourselves to the realisation that the inability to emerge with a neat set of logically necessary conditions for the use of word like 'knowledge' or 'education' is not necessarily the hall mark of failure. The reason why it is not the hall mark of failure is that while engaged in the activity of clarification we should have become clearer about how things are and about the sorts of decision that have to be faced in dealing with them.

JONAS. F. SOLTIS'S CRITICISM ABOUT PETERS ANALYSIS OF EDUCATION

A search for the definition of education is a quest for a statement of the right or the best programme for education and as such is prescription for certain valued means or ends to be sought in educating. R.S. Peter's conceptual analysis of education in his book 'Ethics and Education' aims at expounding the goal of achievement. He sums up the results of his analysis of the criteria implicit in central case of education by claiming.

i) that 'education' implies the transmission of what is worthwhile to those who become committed to it.

ii) that 'education' must involve knowledge and understanding and somekind of cognitive perspective which are not inert.

iii) that 'education' at least rules out some procedures of transmission, on the grounds that they lack willingness and voluntariness on the part of the learner.

The first citerion points out the idea of transmitting what is worthwhile: worthwhile, in this context, means desirable, worthwhile is a perfectly neutral word until it is given substance. Regarding the second criterion, Peter tells us that the idea of education implies the acquisition of knowledge, understanding (ditto) and cognitive perspective (ditto) but these must be ERT and not inert according to Peters analysis. The latter requirement specifies a 'desirable' which is prescriptive. The 'must' in the sentence is the first clue, but the very idea of inert knowledge itself makes clean the prescription for a 'correct' or proper end of learning and, thus can hardly be considered a neutral idea. In the third criterion, we find that the concept of education rules out some procedures (both conditioning and indoctrination are ruled out as inappropriate or improper). Without such specificity in the statement under examination, it (ruling out) would seem neutral enough until it is so filleld in. But we are given the grounds for ruling out such procedures quite specifically and they are lack of willingness (consciousness-awareness) and voluntariness on the part of the learner. It is agreeable that it is important (desirable) to refrain whenever possible from these non-rational ways of educating, but it should be clear the lack of willingness and 'voluntariness' are not neutral ideas. They are put forward quide judgments about the propriety and justice of certain educational procedures and so carry an aura of positive value with them.

In sum, we have in Peter's critical definition of education a not so value free programme for educating which says in effect: choose that which is worth and transmit it in a way which insures that those who learn it will become committed to its values as you are. Be sure also that whatever worthwhile knowledge, understanding and cognitive perspectives which are learned by the student become a real part of them in an effective way so that they will use them to continually react with their world in reasonable ways. Let not what is taught become inert. Your students must be consciously aware of what you are about and what they must voluntarily come to learn.

Is all this to say that the conception of education offered by Peter's is worthwhile? faulty? or inconsistent with his claims for a 'detached' and clear-sighted view? The aforesaid statement is put forth to question the 'neutrality' of his analysis but it does not prove that Peter's has offered a poor conception of education. On the contrary, it may be a very important conception of education precisely because it does take some valuational stand with regard to the desirability of certain educational procedures and results. Without these it might be fairly empty defination of education fitting everything but saying nothing of worth.

J.F. SOLTIS CRITICISES PETER'S ON "EDUCATION" IN THE FOLLOWING WAYS:

1. Peter does attempt to rationally derive and justify these minimal criteria in his work.

2. The business of education is indeed a business of evaluating: Peter's definition is value laden and Peter's definition points out to desirable direction for educating and evaluating educational programmes. The value laden defination of education serve the vital function of pointing us in a desirable direction and giving us guide lines to be used in effectively educating people and making decisions of value. To know what you are after is very helpful in getting what you want.

The general concern of conceptual analysis is to achieve clarity in the use of concepts. The role of analytic philosophy of education is not limited to distinguishing the various meaning of concepts. Analytic philosophers of education view their concern with value as but an incidental aspect of their concern with concepts. Thus, as Richard Peter writes. "education" is different from ordinary case of tasks and achievements in that it is inseparable from judgment of value. And then clarifying the point, he elaborates: "Education" is like "reform": for it would be as much of a contradiction to say "My son has been educated but has learnt nothing of value" as it would be to stay "my sone has been reformed but has changed in no way for the better."This, by the way, is purely conceptual point. The connection between "education" and what is valuable can be made explicit without commitment to content. Thus, as Peter sees it the role of analytic philosophy is not to serve as an advocate of a set of values, but rather to show just how concepts like education' ential judgments of value. There are, however, two features in the actual practice of educational philosophy that complicate the relationship between values and the analysis of concepts. First, the strictly formal treatment of concepts such as "education" has been very difficult to maintain, and educational philosophers have often gone beyond the limits that one might expect world be imposed by the simple task of analysing concepts. Second; the treatment that is offered of "education" is almost always framed in terms that limit the analysis to single individuals or to an intended transmission between individuals. Thus, it provides few, if any, grudelines for understanding the relationship between education and other social institutions. It often appears as if the function and practice of education, as analysis defines it, is simple a matter of good judgment and conceptual clarity.

As understood by its practitioners in education, analytic philosophy does not stand as an alternative to the empirical tradition, but as a complement ot it and as a way to avoid confusing many of the noneducative functions of the school with education itself. Moreover, although the analytic philosophers proclaim a neutrality with regard to human values similar to that of the empirical researcher, their work attempts to aid our understanding of such values. These philosophers believe that although the enterprise does not and should not dictate which values people ought to choose, it can clarify what values are entailed in using certain concepts. Thus, whereas the empirical tradition attempts to avoid dealing with question concerning human values entirely, the ordinary- language tradition is quite willing to address such issues but it strives to do so in a neutral way. Rchard Peter illustrates the concern and methods of this approach in the following passage: Much of the confusion about "aims of education" comes about through extracting the normative feature built into the concept of "education" as an extrinsic end. Given that 'education" state of mind in a morally unobjectionable manner, it is only too easy to conceive of education as a neutral process that is instrumental to something that is worthwhile which is extrinsive to it. Just as gardens may be cultivated in order to aid the economy of the household, so children must be educated in order to provide the with jobs and to increase the productivity of the community as a whole. But there would be something inapropriate about this way of speaking: for we would normally use the word "train" when we had such a specifiable extrinsic object in mind. If, however, we do specify an appropriate "aim" such as the development of individual intellect and character, then the aim would be intrinsic to what we consider education to be.

The tradition that Peter represents begins with the idea that there are certain standards entailed by the concept of education itself that must be met if an activity is to be thought of as educative, and that at least in a formal sense these standards are to be derived independently from the perceived requirements of particular institutions. For example, whether schools are adequately meeting certain perceived "manpower" needs or whether they are providing for adequate mobility for talented members from all social classes is not to be confused with the question of whether they are fulfilling their educative function. Analysis is perceived to be value- neutral because it does not address the question of whether schools, or any other institutions, should have an educative function. Rather, if provides a set of guidelines for determining what schools, or any other institution, should have an educative function. For Peter, the first task is to analyses the kind of concept that "education" is and to then distinguish it from concepts of a different kind. He notes that the concept of education, unlike some other concepts, such as gardening, does not pick out or refer to any specific activity: people can educate themselves, they can be educated by tutors or by attending large lectures. In this sense he notes "education" is more like "reform" in that it picks out on particular activity or process. Rather it lays down criteria to which particular activities or processes must conform.

The approach is designed not so much to add to our knowledge but to remind us of and to underscore that which we already know implicitly. Most of the conclusions of this tradition are intended to high-light activities that can often go unattended in the daily pressures of school life. Peters, for example, reminds us of the need for the educated person to understand not just an array of facts, but also the principles behind such facts and he distinguishes the merely knowledgeable person from the educated one by the degree to which knowledge is used to inform everyday life. Thus, the works and much of the virtue in this traditions can be seen as providing a basis for discussing the values that the empirical traditions had taken as unproblematic.

One of the problems with conceptual analysis as used in education is that even as it attempts to isolate values and concepts that are to be thought of as belonging specifically to educations, it has not provided any explicit articulation of a domain that could properly be thought of as an object for educational understandings. A major difficulty that conceptual analysis has is to explain why some concepts are selected for analysis and others not. However, the mystery is dissolved when we remember that concept analysis is understood by its practitioners as a supplement to empirically oriented research. This has meant in practice that analysis will be exercised on either those concepts that are presently being employed on some (undefined) domain of education by practitioners of empirical research, or else it will be employed on commonsense ideas that are used in informal discussions about education. It is therefore not surprising to find, for example, educational philosophers treating psychological concepts in the first instance, such as "motivation" and "conditioning" or commonsense notions such as "play" and "work" or "freedom" and "indoctrination" in the second. Yet it is not at all clear whether these concepts are selected because they are somehow tied in an essential way to the domain of education or because they happen to dominate educational talk at the moment. For the most part, however, philosophical analysis in education follows school talk'.[2.4]

The fact that conceptual analysis begins by isolating its concepts from any specific institutional practice means that a certain critical potential is retained. Unlike empirical research, the ordinary- language tradition does not mistakenly assume that the domain of educational understanding is to be limited to a single institution such as the school and it does not take uncritically every school defined aim or problem to be an educational one. Education may occur in schools but then again it may not, and if it does not occur in schools, then it may occur elsewhere. Yet this points out the weakness as well as the strengths of the tradition. Empirical research is treated as problematic only if its basic concepts are unclear, confused or contradictory. There is, however, little impulse to move beyond these kinds of problems and to try to understand just why certain kinds of problems occur in certain research programmes and what the connections may be between these contradictions and deeply held social values.

Although ordinary language philosophy serves as a supplement to empirical research, its analysis of education is limited by its own

2.4 Feinberg, Watter, (1963) understnding education - Toward a reconstruction of educational inquiry (Page 99-100) Cambridge University Press, New York, USA.

approach to issues. That the concepts that are inspected by language analysis initiate from commonsense talk and from the work of other disciplines in education means that it is going to the lied in both its insights and its oversights very closely to those understandings and to the values that my rest on. In this sense it, take the empirical sciences, has difficulty in maintaining its claim to value neutrality.

The term "concept" is thus essentially a dummy expression or variable, whose meaning is assignable only in the context of a theory and cannot be independently ascertained. The chief advantage of employing it is that, once given determinate status within a theory, it enables the theorist to move systematically from one type of conceptual use (a) to know the meaning of the word `x', (b) to be able to pick out or recognize a presented `x' (distinguish non-x etc.) or again to be able to think of (have images or ideas of) x (or x) when they are not present, (c) to know the nature of x, to have grasped or apprehended the properties (universals, essences etc) which characterize `x' s and make them what they are. These descriptions of conceptual use are neither exclusive nor exhaustive, nor even particularly clear. In a sense, however, they are indisputable. No one denies that we can do such things as indentifying specimens of a kind or learning the meaning or words. But philosophers have differed long and often violently on two questions: (1) as to which (if any) of these conceptual uses is the fundamental one: (2) as to what sort of detailed account is to be given of them. The meaning of the term `concept' fluctuates accordingly'[2.5]

The answer given to question (1) determines roughly whether having a concept is to be given a nominalistic, mentalistic or realistic interpretation. The answer to question (2) comes down (again roughly) to a decision as to whether the chosen model of conceptual use is to be constructed as (a) a cognitive relation of somekind between a subject and an object or (b) the exercise of a function. Depending on this, the concepts involved, when disentangled from the having of them, will come to be regarded either as entities or objects (of which the word is the name) or, alternatively) as dispositions (capacities, tendencies etc.). Internecine disputes are therefore possible on this issue, even among those who agree on the answer to (1). Because of such disputes among

---

2.5 Edwards, Paul (Editors in Chief) - The Encyclopaedia of philosophy: vol. Two Concept the Macmillan Company and the Free Press, New York 1967.

the philosophers, it is very difficult to arrive at conclusive and definite ideas. Hence the term "concept" is essentially a dummy expression or variable and its meaning is always relative to the context of a theory. This is well reflected by R.S.Peters statement that the analysis of the concept must be viewed against a background of policy. Concepts cannot be dealt within an abstract and isolated way. They have a social and historical context which must be its account and analysis of them must have point related to some educational problem.

2.4 CONCLUSION :

The scholar reflects her own impression after having perused the methodological treatment for her study. Ideas in general serve as 'lenses' directing our attention toward important aspects of contextual background taken for the study - allowing us to locate and extract information that otherwise would be overlooked. Ideas educate attention so that we can access the rich information present in the socio- historical background of the study. Thinking, in fact is synonymous with the manipulation of information - its classification, organization, storage retrieval. Ideas function like perceptual schemata: They allow individuals to extract new information from the background study while at the sametime building upon existing knowledge.

Abstract understanding is rooted in experiences available in the form of information literature. Images provide us a kind of gestalt structure: Images play a key role in the social process. For they allow individuals to construct at least rudimentary understandings of what otherwise would be very abstract or complex ideas. Without this sort of resource, learning would be much less of a constructive process. Further, because images are based upon certain common experiences, they provide a "language" for talking about individual understandings. This, is turn, makes it possible for a community of learners to negotiate some sort to shared understanding among themselves. [2.6] If all representatives were indiosyncratic, it would be difficult to have any sort of fruitful research in the educational discourse.

Viewing from the aforesaid explanation, the scholar opines the concept is a kind of gestalt structure of varied impressions, expressed in

---

2.6 Educational Research Vol. 20 No.2 March 1991 - The Value of ideas: The Immersion Apporoach to the Development of Thinking. (Richard S. Prawat) (Page.7)

terms of functions and end - results, by the philosophers. The "wholeness of view" approach is well emphasized by J.F. Soltis who states that in recent years philosophers of education have been less inclined to build or interpret systems of philosophy and more inclined to provide elucidations, reflections, critical appraisals and conceptual frameworks for understanding what the bits and pieces of the complex educational enterprise are about.

3

UNIVERSITIES IN ANCIENT & MEDIAEVAL CIVILISATIONS

3.3 CONCEPT OF HIGHER EDUCATION

The term 'education' is used in a variety of contexts and with different shades of meaning. In its broadest sense, any act or experience that has a formative effect on the mind, character or physical ability of an individual can be called as educational. It is in this sense that travelling, reading, conversation or even living with someone can be an education. In the formal education of children, the school contributes only a limited share in the education of children: the other part comes from informal agencies like home, society, peergroups playmates and reading of books and magazines - in modern era, from mass media like press, radio and television. Education is thus a very broad term as far as individual is concerned. A basic character of education is that it informs a person and it enlightens him about things he does not know and thus initiates him into asking all sorts of questions about nature, about life, about society and its organisations. One is made capable of thinking for himself and finding answers to the questions which one considers important or significant for one's life. In this sense, education is said to be a liberating force. It makes the individual free and capable of ordering his or her life according to his or her own choice or playing a more active role in his or her society either to preserve it or to change it. This basic feature of education has led, throughout history, to education being used as an instrument of struggle, for liberation or for suppression both by the individual and by the society.

However, education may also connote a system of institutions organised by society to deliberately transmit its cultural heritage - its accumulated knowledge, values and skills - from one generation to another. The educational system of a society would, accordingly, comprise institutions such as schools, colleges, universities including teachers, administrators, curricula and courses, examination and certification procedure, and so on. Formal arrangements for the education of individuals in present day societies is conceived in term of stages arranged in a hierarchy. Our own educational ladder commencing at six years of age, comprises the elementary, secondary, higher secondary and higher education stages. Since 1968 when the Parliament approved a National Policy on Education we are committed to a structure symbolically called "10+2+3". This means ten years high school education including five years of primary, three years of upper primary and two years of secondary of college or university education culminating in the Bachelor's Degree. The new National Policy on Education approved in 1986 reaffirms the 10+2+3+ structure and most of the Indian states have adopted this structure although a few states are still in the process of adopting it.

Higher education, refers to education in post higher secondary institutions, colleges and universities. It is higher education, firstly because it constitutes the topmost stages of formal education and more importantly, because it is concerned with process in the more advanced phases of human learning. The entrants are about eighteen years of age and therefore, they are mentally mature and capable of performing at the abstract level. They can analyse, synthesise and grasp concepts and ideas of all kinds. Their creative faculties are also developed adequately. Naturally the content of course, methods of interaction and organisation of work have to be very different from what they are at the school. In the Concise Dictionary of Education, Higher Education refers to "education beyond secondary school that is viewed as intellectually more rigorous and sophisticated than that of the secondary level, and that either leads to academic degree or is on a comparable intellectual level." [3.1] Higher education is also described as "instruction offered to persons of considerable intellectual maturity usually requiring previous preparation through the secondary school. In terms of the institution common to the United States, higher education includes all education above the level of the secondary school given in colleges, universities, graduate schools, professional schools, technical institutes, teacher's colleges, and normal schools. The junior college is considered an institution of higher education by some authorities and by others it is considered a part of secondary education." [3.2]

3.1 Hawes, Gene R, Lynne Salop Hawes, the Concise Dictionary of Education: Higher Education, (page 107), A Hudson Group, Published by Van Nostrand Reinhold Co. Inc. New York, 1982

3.2 Good, Carte. V, and Winifred R, Merkel (editor) Dictionary of education: Foundations in Education, Higher Education (page 267) Mc Graw Hill Book Co. Inc. New York 1959

Three aspects of higher education are relatively of recent origin. One of them is that social, economic and industrial development have created a pressure towards greater specialisation. The tendency has been strengthened due to expansion of knowledge also, since within given time it is not possible to include vast areas of disciplines or subjects in the curriculum. Whereas two centuries ago, students could study philosophy mathematics and medicine in their university's programmes, today these subjects are studied usually by different student in different faculties or institutions. Philosophy gave birth to psychology and many specializations including various sciences. History led to the new area of political science, geography led to a specialization in geology and so on. Because of specialization today's student in higher education knows more and more about less and less and sometimes special efforts are necessary to create a broader understanding of subjects and disciplines. The second aspect is that as societies grew more complex, more selective and efficient means of cultural transmission evolved. The result is the formal, institutionalised system of education. The curriculum, due to specialisation and paucity of time has crystallized into clear-cut papers or courses. Formalism both in structure and content have crept in. The need of producing students of comparable base of knowledge and standard of achievement by a large number of institutions, has led to formalism in evaluating or examining of students. Thirdly, research has emerged as one of the most significant dimensions of higher education today. Creation of knowledge is a tangible output of the educational system because of which the universities have acquired a new social status, particularly in the developed countries. In fact, there exists a symbiotic relation between research and specialisation of knowledge and skills. Much research is a team effort of collaborate nature in which the combined intelligence of large numbers is brought to bear on the solution of a problem.

3.4 HIGHER LEARNING IN ANCIENT AND MEDIEVAL CIVILIZATIONS

Higher education as we have it today, is the outcome of a long socio-historical process of evolution. In a brief presentation such as this kind of theoretical build-up, we can only highlight some important aspects of the character of education and its development. Society is an organised entity and education must prepare individuals to fit into a variety of jobs and responsibilities. The role of higher education in relation to knowledge has been so predominant in history that higher education has come to be equated with production and dissemination of knowledge. In fact, the emergence of higher education as a distinct state of education with its own aims, content and pedagogy was due to the substantial increase in the fund of knowledge and even more to man's increasing desire, and need to know more and more. The medieval ancestors of the modern universities started Universities (corporations), communities of scholars committed to the search for dissemination of knowledge.

All of man's achievements have depended upon the application of existing physical and mental powers. The use of tools promoted the development of techniques for their manufacture and employment, leading in turn to further development forms of social life in which tools became essential instruments. The organization of society around the making and use of tools marked the beginning of culture - that accumulation of instruments, ideas and institutions by which social life proceeds. In man's early culture improvements in the techniques of tool - making were accompained by the appearance of abstract conceptions, evidenced by the incision of designs on tools and rocks and the execution of cave paintings, the famous paleolithic art of Lascaux in France currently being dated by radio-carbon methods to a period around 13,000 B.C. Such paintings mark a major development in man's capacity for thought. In due course man was able to abstract visual design from the environment and give it graphic representations. A further effort of abstraction was achieved, with the development of speech. Through its use ideas emerged, were communicated and transmitted through time. Speech and graphic representation provided the two elements from which the symbolisms of writing and reckoning were made, and these formed the basis of civilization. With them man was able to develop the many instruments and processes by which he pursued his activities: they enable the transcendence of time and space, the liberation of man from the immediate and fortuitous. By these symbolisms the world of ideas was constructed and its exploration sustained.

The constant search for control, liberation and expansions characterized man from his first appearance, and part of his success in devising effective mechanisms rested in his ability to secure the perpetuation and refinement of such skills through the procedures of education. For education includes that cultural process by which techniques for control' of the environment are transmitted.

3.4.1 SCRIBAL CULTURE IN MESOPOTAMIA

The world of early oriental man was pantheistic: he had not achieved an intellectual separation of subject and subjects. He was in blissful ignorance of the mystery of the universe. The temple emerged to assist man in propitiation and the high priest became mediator between man and God.

The Calender and astronomical observation was linked with prediction and propitiation: from those activities astrology developed as a study of the influence of nature on man, and it remained a significant element of Mesopotamian thought. Writing and reckoning had their beginnings in this context. Later Mesopotomian mythology attributed the origin of writing to the great god- scribe Nabu, and throughout several thousand and years of high civilization in the region the peoples of Mesopotamia continued to cultivate a reverence towards writing. The earliest use of graphic symbols and the wedge- shaped impressions, known now a days by the Latin name of cuneiform (L.cuneus, wedge) were developed to express ideas. A cuneiform script of thousands of complex symbols was developed by the Sumerians. That script remained in use for almost 3000 years and throughout that time was adopted by numerous other peoples for writing their respective languages.

The Sumerians dominated the lower, south-easter part of the Mesopotamian valley during the first half of the third millennium and their culture gave the pattern to early civilization of the Ancient Orient. Both Sumerians and Akkadians developed the cuneiform script into more phonetic forms, decreased the number of symbols, and improved the calligraphic quality of the script. By 2500 B.C the Akkadians were the dominant people and Sumerians had become relegated to the status of an ancient and scholarly language, employed almost exclusively in the temples. In the centuries the growing religious literature was recorded in Sumerian. On the other hand, Akkadian became the language of everday life: it was the public language. So developed a dualism in language which was to have parallels in later history - the co-existence of a scholarly and a common tongue.

Social and political life continued to be organized around the temples, and by the time of Hammurabi (the Babylonian king) these had become architecturally and functionally quite complex, reflecting the extension of sovereignty into the religion: as Hummurabi became king, so Marduk (the chief god of Babylon) became chief god. By virtue of this office the king remained high priest but much authority had to be exercised through delegated offices. The minor priests and temple staff, in addition to religious tasks attended to the numerous social and economic functions of the temple, and among their number were the scribes and teachers.

Learning in the third millennium was distinctly a priestly prerogative and closely related to either the temple or the palace. Writing itself was held in some reverence and awe, and in Babylon the priestly study of words, with the relationship to their objects, was of some importance. The priests considered themselves the guardians and conservators of knowledge:

Regarding training of the scribes, all the scribes had to specialize in one branch of the bureaucracy - the temple, law, medicine, commerce, the army, or teaching itself and underwent, in consequence, two periods of training. The first in basic literacy was given by group instruction: this was followed by appointment to the particular government department where higher and more specialized instruction was obtained through a system of apprenticeship and individual tuition.

General supervision of the edubba (Tablet House) was exercised by the ummia, a term meaning authority or expert and referring to the function of the principal. He was assisted by a deputy the adda edubba, literally, father of the Tablet House. Instruction was given by the teacher, the dubsar (or table writer) assised by the seshgal (or big-brother), the latter being an intending teacher gaining his specialized training in teaching by apprenticeship to the dubsar. The basis of all instruction was writing given by the dubsar keṅgira, the scribe of Sumerian.

After mastering the instruction given in the Tablet House the novice became a junior scribe and his new status carried with it the title of either dumu edubba or dubsartur and he was ready to proceed to higher specialised studies.

The House of Wisdom, which operated as a place of advanced instruction during the second millennium, was attended by some graduate scribes, and studies proceeded there at a higher level. The House of Wisdom was not concerned with higher thought in the sense of speculation. In Babylonian period considerable advances were made in notation and recknoning. Theoretical speculation did not become highly developed: The scribal occupations were connected closely to craft traditions, especially in the sciences, and overwhelming preoccupation was with solving specific problems.

The whole tradition of scribal literacy demanded obedience and compliance by the student: there was virtually no scope at all for creative thought or speculation. By the end of the Second millennium the creative vigours of the Mesopotamian peoples was exhausted. The oral tradition remained honoured, but in literature rather practice: The inventions of speech and writing were potentially great instruments for developing the object subject relationship. Consequently, the vigour of the oral tradition was diverted into written literature, which in turn became formalized and conservative, and its study heavily tradition- bound. The civilization of Babylon and Assyria after it, developed into scribal cultures in which the possibilities of a wider public literacy were not realized. Throughout those millennia similar developments were occuring in Egypt where a comparable scribal culture had emerged.

3.4.2 THE EGYPTIAN SCRIBAL CULTURE

Contemporaneously with summer, but largely independently the great and historically influential culture of Egypt was forming in the valley of the Nile. Although the palace was the most important early Egyptian institution, the temple, as in Summer played a very important role. The temple, was concerned with regulation of the calendar and that the king owed some of his authority to that of the Nile made prediction emergent. In Sumer the king was archpriest: in Egypt, the king was himself god and the son of the sun-god, Re. The office of the king was charged with the profoundest of functions, that of mediating between the gods and the people.

In Egypt recknoning preceded writing, Egyption writing comes into history as a fully developed script and like Sumerian it was originally pictographic although, unlike cuneiform, the Egyptian script retained much of its original pictorial.quality.

Travelling in Egypt around 499 B.C. the historian Herodotus reported that the Egyptian had two sorts of writing, the sacred (hira) and the common (demotika). The Greek writer Plutarch (A.D 46-C 120) is responsible for introducing the term hieroglyphics (Greek hieros + gluphe, sacred carving) which ever since has given a false etymology to the script. None the less the classification remains : the pictorian monumental, carved form is hieroglyphic, the corresponding cursive is hieratic, and the latter, degenerate form is called demotic.

The nature of writing materials influenced the form of the script and was responsible for changing the monumental pictorial form into the simpler everyday hieratic cursive. The almost universal materials were three papyrus, limestone flakes and ostraka). Of these, the papyrus became the most common for official records and was written on with a calamus made from an abundant rush.

By the end of the second Dynasty (people of Nagada II who brought writing into Egypt) C.2700 B.C which was also the beginning of the Old Kingdom, scribes were made members of a permanent civil service, initiating a tradition of more than 3,000 years. So literacy was difficult to acquire, and in practice it never became a public possession. Instead, literacy remained the prerogative of a privileged class and served as the agent: not of liberation and creativity, but of conservation and formalization.

Two basic forms of literature emerged, written in Middle Egyptian -' Wisdom Literature' and another, on diverse topics and in varying styles; myths, fables, songs, poems: mortuary, legal and historical texts: rituals, incantations, prayers, hymns, letters. This literature included fanciful romances and short stories. In the period of the Memphite Theology literacy was valued more for the social advancement and prestige it conferred than for any intrinsic intellectual qualities. The so-called Wisdom Literature constituted the major part of instructional writings used in the training of the apprentice scribe, providing both preceptive and edifying advice, and material for calligraphic practice. Of this literature, three pieces enjoyed long use in scribal training, the Hyman to the Nile, Instruction of Duauf and Instruction of Amenemhat. During the Middle Kingdom (c.2050-1800 B.C.) individuality and eloquence were valued qualities in the educated man, and that search for the good life was pursued through the literature used in the training of the scribe.

In the second millennium Egypt developed numerous relationships with Mesopotamia including the inter charge of scribes and related aspects of literacy. From such stimuli and from further internal growth and consolidation both cultures continued to move-towards developing a more institutionalized and systematic process of education. The Akkadian vernacular of Babylon was that of international discourse: diplomatic despatches were written in that language, and Egypt hired scribed from Babylon for her rapidly growing civil service.

TRAINING OF THE SCRIBE:

The priest and the scribe were the two main members of the Egyptian literate. In the Old and Middle Kingdoms a distinction was not clearly drawn: high priests and officials were connected closely with most, if not all, scribal activities. During the Empire, a considerable separation occurred between the two occupations. Although the higher sacred and scribal tasks were discharged by priests, the majority of scribes belonged to the Civil bureaucracies, differentiated into many and complex hierachies, and as the Empire became consolidated, the division between the priest-scribes and the civil functionaries widened.

The boys learned at least the rudiments from their father or relatives. Direct apprenticeship to a department of the civil service was used in respect of the numerous minor offices requiring minimal training and little understanding. The son or nephew of a scribe would first be given the simplest elements of literacy, after from a private teacher, and then employed in a marginal capacity in the department of his relatives. Direct apprenticeship was used extensively too for advanced training in the youths specific vocation. In the course of his duties he learned the routine function of the department: and when the opening for promotion came, after the demonstration of suitable skill, the apprentice was advanced to the appropriate scribal rank. Once the scribe was so placed he remained, generally, in that particular calling throughout his life, although advancement in the bureaucracy was possible for exceptional youths.

Scribes were connected closely with the ruling classes, and the prestige attached to the higher scribal, and priestly, rank was great. The Egyptians were more strongly motivated by the social advantages of the scribal calling than by the intrinsic liberalizing qualities of the valuable books. Training in the School of Books was permitted with operations of its priestly associations and disciplined demeanour:

The background of the scribe's training was permitted with rigorous moral conditioning: equally so was the content of instruction given in the school of Books. Since the writing of hieroglyphics is extremely difficult, considerable time was spent in exercises with calamus - the study of the art of calligraphy.

Instruction was given in recknoning, by empirical and routine procedures. As in Babylon, Egyptian reckoning was directed to specific problems, especially those of measuring areas, rectilinear and circular, calculating volumes, notably of grain storage, and enumerating tallies. It was those empirical procedures that were transmitted to the apprentice scribe. Some ones, once they had acquired an efficiency of skill, were then appointed to the particular governmental office of their speciality, there to learn the necessary skills and knowledge that would confer the professional qualifications entitling advancement to the rank of scribe. Yet others, a small minority, progressed to even higher studies: teaching, medicine, astrology (including astronomy and calendar studies) and the more secret aspects of the crafts. At least some of them were related to a special institution of higher learning known as the House of Life.

HIGHER LEARNING: THE HOUSE OF LIFE:

The exact function of the House of Life is difficult to be determined. This institution was not primarily a school. It included a scriptorium for the production of documents on religious and cognate matters and it was, in addition, quite possibly a centre of learned discussion and composition. It is assumed that the House of Life functioned as the integrator of all Egyptian learning, that is, as an institution for maintaining the social and personal continuity in after - life that was sought and believed in so fervently. It provided the model for other aspects of higher learning. Such higher learning was itself of the craft variety: it considered in customary activities, practices and beliefs transmitted without specific reference to experience. Experimentation was not a strong aspect of Egyptian life in the Empire:

In marked contrast to the increasing rigidity and cultural conservation of Egyptian state during the Empire were the creative developments occuring outside Egypt. In terms of thought, and the development of education, two of those creations were the invention of the alphabet, the Hebrew doctrine of monotheism.

Through the possibilities opened up by this great invention men's conceptual development was carried forward to a new era of creativity, in Greece.

In an environment relatively free of cultural paralysis that had gripped the Orient, the Greeks were to develop a culture of surprising vitality and novelty, In so doing, from the immense period of protc- literacy and pre-philosophic thought, they moved towards the development of a theory of education.

3.4.2 HIGHER LEARNING IN GREECE

Of the 5,000 years of Western man's historical continuity the first 4000 from 3000 B.C to A.D 1000 were entered in the lands bordering the eastern Mediterranean. In the Ancient Orient man first achieved literacy and civilization: the cultural heritage of the Mesopotamians and Egyptians was transmitted to others - Hebrew, Greeks, Romans, Byzantines, Arab as - who in turn were to give their own distinctive contributions. Although Mesopotamia and Egypty invented literacy and developed a scribal culture they did not extend these beyond a special class of literate. The process of education, initiated in those two ancient cultures, was given its first major development by the Greeks who came to civilization quickly, during Iron Age, demonstrating a remarkable vigour. They did not create their culture simply out of native genius and inspiration: they drew in part of on the traditions of the Ancient Orient and their relations with Egypt and Mesopotamia were marked as much by continuity as by discontinuity. However, the Greeks made some radical breaks with those traditions particularly with regard to their conceptions of the world, physical, social and intellectual.

The Athenians were the first people to deal consciously with process of education: to it they gave the name paideia. The state was the overmastering institution: from it the individual drew his identity. The state had to be served first: the individual came a necessary second. The great speeches of Athens were given in the assembly: it was there that policy was made and action initiated. Both serve to the state and success as a citizen required skill in speaking and the ability to capture the interest of the audience. At the sametime the demands of the state could be served best by citizens who were properly informed and able to give eloquent voice to wise decisions. In fifth century Athens there was little that could be called organized higher learning to meet this need. Beyond elementary literacy there was mousike, which included some kind of practice in effective speaking as well as cultivation of the mind and character. This was not universal. There was a real need for a system which would train young men to learn the arts of effective citizenship and to provide further studies for the number of leisured sons of wealthy fathers who wanted to pursue intellectual question.

Athenians legal and political procedures also contributed to this growing need. Each man had to plead his own case before the court since advocacy was not practised professionally. The speculative philosophers were no more successful in court than less learned citizens. Daily life in Athens - in the court, the assembly, the gymnasium, the political clubs or synomosia - was not so abstract. In such locations the environment became, part of the argument: persuasion, emotional appeal and rhetorical fluency were as potent as logical sequence in determining the issues. The orator was the overwhelmingly influential figure. So a new occupation appeared in Athens, that of the "Professor" of higher learning. These new teachers were the sophists (sophistai), their name being derived from the word `sophia' which means wisdom, skill or even cleverness. Included among the sophists were also the sceptics, who doubted or denied the possibility of knowledge and so professed to teach only practical skills, especially the art of persuasion which had a ready application to public life. In this group also were the rhetoricians who were concerned with the use of words and not with values except plausibility, expedience and political or legal success.

In the absence of legal profession some sophists developed the practice of legography, the writing of speeches to be delivered in the courts by their clients. Growing out of this practice was the compilation of set of speeches which were sold either for use or for study in the growing schools of rhetoric and the writing of handbook of instruction in the art of rhetoric. The handbook of rhetoric (GK rhetorike the art of speaking) consisted of rules of speech composition and guiding precepts, in distinction to the collection of actual speeches. The handbook, or techne, sought to give a theoretical basis of instruction in rhetoric.

In the fifth century two thinkers Gorgias (483-375 B.C) and Protogoras (485-411 B.C.) became concerned with teaching of rhetoric: Rhetoric was brought to Athens by Gorgias (C 483-375) from his native Sicily. According to Aristotle, Gorgias made his pupils learn by heart rhetorical speeches and questions and answer on both sides of prepared arguments.

Despite the reputation of Gorgias and Protagoras the greatest sophist of the later fifth century was Socrates (469-399 B.C.), who excercised a considerable influence on the development of education in Athens. In mature life, in the company of a circle of friends, Socrates developed the intellectual style for which he became famous and this was, basically, a concern for the assumptions underlying moral and ethical behaviour. In examining any issue, Socrates usually himself disclaimed knowledge the prior step of irony - as a means of beginning an inquiry of some moral quality. Usually the respondent in these dialogues - the sole form in which his teachings survive - would be forced after a number of fruitless attempts, to confess his own ignorance. Thereupon Socrates would try to lead him to a better understanding of the problem, usually by suggesting particular instances and showing what common characteristic they shared. This, expressed in words was definition. His two great contributions to the development of logic, then were induction and definition.

The Sophists brought higher learning to Athens, offering a wide variety of subjects of instruction ranging from Rhetoric to the scholarly studies of grammar and mathematics. By the fourth century Athens had become the undisputed centre of Hellenic culture and learning: to it went the interested sons of the wealthy and aristocratic families of the Greek world. Some sought knowledge for its own sake: most were attracted to it for more utilitarian ends. The schools of sophists continued to grow, offering instruction beyond that given by the elementary teachers. All teaching was given privately: the Athenians never developed a system of public education, although it was recommended by Aristotle later in the fourth century. The influence of Socrates continued to be felt, although he offered no positive educational goals, and his teaching embraced no systematically ordered body of knowledge.

Athenian life did not demand an exhaustive philosophical study of ultimate values: Knowledge adequate to the purposes of daily life was well established, and it was generally accepted, particularly by many of the sophists. Two distinct approaches developed in the fourth century, each offering a way to higher learning: one continued the Socratic method of critical examination and inductive logic in the school of Isocrates (436-338 B.C.)

Public eulogies were a well- established Athenian institution, and Isocrates teaching, like that of other sophists, gave instruction in such a useful civic accomplishment. Furthermore it was a patent fact of Greek Public means of directing the course of affairs. Socrates and Plato had illustrated with the childbirth analogy in Theactectus their belief that intelligence needs to be stimulated and brought to development through the process of rational questioning. The view was accepted by Isocrates who pointed out that philosophy - and he meant rhetoric with a little political theory - had been devised as the discipline for training the mind, thus paralleling gymnastic as the discipline for training the body. Plato, (428-348 B.C.) however, was much closer to Socrates and continued his master's philosophical investigations, particularly those related to the nature of truth. Throughout his career Plato showed a great interest in Pythagorean studies and remained in fluenced by them. During his travels (to Egypt, to the Greek Colony of Gyrene on the coast of North Africa, and across to Sicily and Southern Italy) he abandoned the intention of a political career: he returned to Athens sometime after 398 B.C. and began teaching in or near the gymnasion some two miles north-west of the city in the grove dedicated to the early hero Academus. The gymnasion was known popularly as the Academy, (the First University of the World) and the name was attached in turn to his school, which was founded at the time Plato began teaching in Athens. Supported by his belief in a higher good than that of the public will, and rejecting the Protatorean humanism - man is the measure of all things - he asserted a belief in an absolute measure, justice, which is beyond human manipulation. The best of all possible worlds is that in which social and political harmony is obtained, secured by the operation of justice. And that in turn cannot be achieved until government is based upon the rule of justice, administered by enlightened men. He began to develop a systematic theory of education, extending it to encompass the whole of an individual's relations to the State. This theory was not, however designed necessarily for immediate application: at most it was an ideal to be kept constantly in view, and this, in fact, raises an important distinction that must be made between Plato's two means of spreading his thoughts. One was through formal teaching in the Academy, the other through the literary dialogues.

Now all of the dialogues are concerned in some way with dialectic and many of them deal with education, some, chiefly The Republic and the Laws, being concerned explicitly with education as a dialectical activity. So it is inferred that the method of oral question and answer must have been employed in the Academy: and since all of the dialogues deal with philosophical points, that these must have been the content. In the Republic Plato said that it is dangerous to teach the skills of dialectic argument to youngmen for they will simply misuse them and get lost in the mere verbal quarrelling or eristic (GK. eristos, a matter for contest or argument). In the Republic he says, quite specifically and emphatically, that dialectic should not be taught to persons under thirty years of age. From the writings of Aristotle, the most distinguished student of Plato, it can be inferred that the studies in the Academy were concerned primarily with mathematics, particularly plane and solid geometry and number theory and , at the advanced levels, stereometry. This is consonant with Plato's expressed preoccupation with the search for truth. This is apprehended through the study of Being which is best grasped, in the first instance, though mathematics. In essence mathematics are concerned with eternal qualities, unlike the natural sciences and physics, which study the process of Becoming. Certainly there would be no place for rhetoric as it obscured the view and pursuit of the Good. Further more, Plato asserted rhetoric is directed to the most suspect of ends: social and political success, shallow speech-making and the defeat of justice.

Throughout his mature years Plato kept improving his doctrines and correcting the difficulties his theories had encountered. Throughout his writings, Plato represents the quest of man for knowledge as the central concern of life itself: the cultivation of the harmony of the soul yields an insight into absolute being, into truth itself. Thus the key to Plato's thought is this concept of knowledge which was the end product and goal of a process he called paideia (education towards the Good). Since Plato was the first thinker to propound a serious theory of education, naturally he enriched the content of the term and gave it a decidedly intellectual significance.

After the death of Plato in 347 B.C. control of the Academy passed to Speusippus (Plato's nephew) a mathematician of importance and a person highly esteemed by Plato. Meanwhile Aristotle had already left the Academy which he entered in 366 B.C. and where he had studied for a period of twenty Years. Aristotle was invited by Philip of Macedonia to be a tutor to his son Alexander. As Philip was assasinated in 336 B.C. he was succeeded by Alexander, then in his twentieth year. With the ascent of Alexander to the Macedonian throne and to political domination of the Greek world, one era was ended and another initiated.

Macedonian ascendency did not end Athen's pre-eminence as a centre of higher learning. On the contrary, throughout the brief career of Alexander and the century immediately following, known as the Hellenistic era, Athens continued to exercise an influence. The intellectual decline of Athens was slow, even imperceptible: in fact, the reign of Alexander was accompanied by the foundation in Athens of a school of higher learning which rivalled the Academy of Plato and was destined to be equally influential in the course of human affairs and the development of education. That school was Lyceum (Lykeion), founded by Aristotle. The aim like that of Plato's Academy was to reduce the finite world of experience to a set of basic, immutable categories, to seek the fundamental principle. So Aristotle continued the philosophic quest initiated by the Milesians centuries before. In Plato's time techniques had not been developed whereby the generalizations themselves could be scrutinized, except dialectically: the procedures of empirical investigation were unacceptable to Plato and his school. Plato, in fact, had criticized quite stringently any reliance on the evidence of the senses and in the Academy offered his students little encouragement in direct observation. This was one significant area in which Aristotle began to diverage. In one major respect, then, the Lyceum differed from the Academy. The studies of the later were those directly accessible to reason, that is, studies with a mathematical and abstract basis: in the Lyceum, inquiry turned to biology, physics, ethics, politics, rhetoric and logic. Aristotle approach depended in the first instance upon the collection of the minutiae of daily occurrence and the multiplicity of existential forms. Gradually, through stages no longer known, the studies of the Lyceum developed into two major categories, the natural and the normative sciences. Aristotle rejected the entire basis of pre-mature generalization upon which the Platonic views depended. Aristotle argued that of the primary tasks of a philosopher is to secure his theories on a firm basis. However, with the Platonic theories as the starting point, Aristotle's inquiries open up a further sequence in intellectual development.

GARDEN AND ACADEMY: HELLENISTIC SCHOOLS OF HIGHER LEARNING

After Aristotle, development in education became complex, occuring in a variety of ways and in a large number of places. In Athens additional schools of higher learning were established, all expounding different philosophies, including stoism and Epicureanism, while the Academy, Lyceum and various schools of rhetoric continued with their own particular teachings. Learning became systematized, methodologies and critical cannons were established, and the schools of higher learning entered into scholarly and philosophic controversies. The occupation of professor flourished, and to their schools were attracted numerous scholars seeking training so that inturn they might establish schools of their own. The notion of teaching as a vocation began to develop: the demand for professors and schools of higher learning in scores of new Greek cities throughout the Orient provided an additional stimulus. Many schools based upon the sophistic and rhetorical models sprang up in Athens and returned as rapidly to obscurity. In addition to the Academy and Lyceum which continued in operation only two achieved major significant and historical endurance- the stoa and the Garden. During the Hellenistic era these were to rival in popularity the schools of Plato and Aristotle. Zeno of Citium (C 336-264 B.C), a young merchant from Cyprus was attracted towards Cynicism- mistrust of all knowledge, a doctrine developed by Diogenes of Sinope. He established a school of his own (between 310 and 300 B.C) in one of the colonades (Stoai) of the market -place in Athens, and according to the custom of the time it took the name 'Stoa'

The foundation of the Stoic school was accompanied by the establishment of another Athenian school of philosophy by Epicurus of Athens (342-270 B.C.). After a period of teaching philosophy at Mytilene he returned to Athens in 306 B.C and there set up a school of philosophy in his own home in the Suburb of Melite. From its cultivated grounds it became known as theGarden (Kepos): it was modelled on the Pythogorean prototype, operating as a society of scholars that welcomed all persons including women: the Garden, in fact, was the first organized school of philosophy to do so. After fourteen successive directors, the Garden was closed in 79 B.C.

3.4.4. LEARNING IN THE ROMAN EMPIRE

In the establishment and maintenance of the dominion of Rome over the nations that came under her sway education played a most important part. Following the example of Alexander the Great, the Romans from the last days of the Republic made it their deliberate policy to introduce their institutions and culture among their subject peoples.

Schools of grammar and rhetoric were set up for the children of the country. In all parts of the Empire, the process of Romanizing through the schools went steadily on, and by second century the Roman schools were practically universal

For the most part, the rules in the First Century took little interest in the educational concerns of the Roman world outside Italy. The chief exception was made in favour of Alexandria, which, under the patronage of Augustus and his immediate successors, who sought to emulate the achievements of Alexander and the first Ptolemys, became for a time the chief seat of learning in the Empire.

In accordance with the demands of the age, rhetoric and philosophy became the chief subjects of study, and with the coming of large numbers of students from over the seas she deveveloped into a great centre of instruction more like Athens than the earlier Alexandria. In interesting contrast with the encouragement of Greek learning in Alexandria was the establishment of Latin schools in the north of Africa and in Gaul which continued to flourish and to produce worthy scholars.

Upto the beginning of the Second Century the edcucation activities of the emperors after Augustus were mainly inspired by their personal interest in learning or by their desire for popularity, rather than by any clear conception of the needs of the Empire or by any broad considerations of policy. With Hardrian (117-138) Antoninus (138-161) and Marcus Aurelius (161-180), the method of occasional intervention ceased and a great system of education, was created. In Hadrian's case, the moving impulse was a passionate admiration for everything Greek which won for him the epithet "Graeculus". The Greek philosophers and teachers everywhere were the objects of special care. In Rome he established the Athenaeum, as a meeting place for Greek and Roman men of letters and a centre of the higher learning. In Alexandria he gave his patronage to the Museum and nominated several of his scholar friends to its membership. But it was Greece, and above all the beloved Athens that stood highest in his favour. Thus Athens became the chief "University" for the Roman world.

The work begun by Hadrian was continued in the same generous spirit by Antoninus. The contribution made to educational progress by Marcus Aurelius, the next ruler was more limited but still considerable. His main interest, like that of Hadrian, was in the schools of Athens.

When the great Roman Empire finally collapsed in the West its secular, intellectual and cultural achievement had virtually disappeared. By the year A.D 600 literacy and learning had reached their lowest levels ever. The learning that did survive was, in general, conservative, encylopaedic and degenerate, and apart from a few exceptions in Italy, was maintained almost exclusively in monasteries and cathedrals. It persisted throughout the seventh century into the eighth and by the middle of the later century showed no signs of improvement until the advent of Carolingian rulers. Their new dynasty initiated some reforms, and when the Frankish Prince Charlemagne succeeded to the throne in 771 he brought with him a burning enthusiasm to make his kingdom the vehicle for a rebirth of Latin Christian civilization (Byzantine Culture). Charlemagne invited two Irish clerics who came across to Gaul at the time when the pursuit of learning was almost forgotten throughout the length andbreadth of the kingdom. He gave one the direction of new school which contained a great number of boys chosen not only from the noblest families but also from middle class and poor homes: the other priest was given a similar charge in monastic school near Padua.

In order to sustain the desired high calibre of thought and ideas, Charlemagne stregthened and expanded the palace school (schola palatina). This had been in existence for half a century, having functioned as a training centre in courtly procedure for the children of the palace. As an early move towards the upgrading of the schola palatina its direction was offered to the English scholar, Alucin of Yark, who Charlemagne had first met in 781 as the Englishman was engaged in a mission for his king, Eanbald. Sometime in the late 780s Alucin became more closely involved in the daily conduct of the palace school: At the time of his appointment the palace school, was neither scholarly nor cultivated. His work at the school, in which he was assisted by tutors, began with instruction in simple writing and reading. From that foundation the student was enabled to proceed to the study of grammar and rhetoric.

The destruction of the Roman Empire by the northern bar-barians in the Fifthe century A.D threatened to make a complete end of the culture which flourished in the Mediterranean lands during the previous millennium. The municipal schools of grammar and rhetoric which had been vigorously at work throughout the Empire only a century before vanished almost entirely in the course of a generation or two, and with the disappearance of their teachers a dense cloud of ignorance settled over the greater part of Europe. In conquering Rome, the barbarians themselves came under the sway of the Christain Church and under the protecting care of a religious faith that had retained its vitality in an age of disintegration sufficient of the ancient civilization was preserved to keep learning in feeble life till the new-comers had grown able to appropriate some of the knowledge of the past and to advance beyond it in accordance with their own genius."

The church did not step immediately into the place of the municipality and the state as the provider and the director of education. The old literary and rhetorical education had been pagan in spirit, and the profound distrust it inspired in a considerable section of the Christian community, still lingered. Nevertheless, it was not long before the church was compelled by force of circumstances to concern itself with education and out of its cultural needs there ultimately grew a system of schools which by the end of the Dark Ages was almost complete and as comprehensive as that which had passed away with the Roman Empire.

The church undertook the business of education not because it regarded education as good in itself but because it found that it could not do its own proper work without giving its adherents, and especially its clergy as much of the former learning as was required for the study of the sacred writings and for the performance of their religious duties. In the first instance, there was not thought of instructing the young in preparation for the needs of ordinary life. As time went on, however it became necessary for the church to extend the scope of its educational interests. Here and there were churchmen who advanced their scholarship beyond the limits of what was directly valuable for religious purposes and cultivated learning for its own sake. In some parts of Europe too, where the Latin language was unfamiliar,schools for laity and particularly for the ruling classes were established sided by side with the churches in order that the principles and practices of the church should be comprehensible. This step was more easily taken because from the first the spread of education was encouraged by the more enlightened kings who saw that the prosperity of their states depended on the diffusion of at least the elements of learning among their peoples.

In spite of its borrowing from the old, the new education was very different in spirit. The aim of the Roman schools had been quite difinitely secular. Their finest products had been well versed in literature and masters of the oratorical arts, which enabled them to play their parts in the law courts and in the service of town and state. With the transfer of educational authority from the state to the church the studies of the schools had changed their character with their purpose. The aim was now essentially other-wordly. The ultimate reason for any form of education was the advantage it brought to faith. The typical man of learning was no longer the cultivated man of the affairs but the educated clerk: and all the secular business of society which required the highest learning for its performance fell as a matter of course into the hands of churchmen.

The clerical mopnopoly of education established in the age of transition from the ancient world to the modern lasted for more than a thousand years, and its effects on the intellectual life of Europe were tremendous. The most obvious result was the general restriction of learning within the boundaries fixed by the Church interests and doctrines. The suspicion with which secular literature was regarded in the first Christian centuries gradually passed away, as the pagan faiths with which that literature had originally been allied dwindled into mere memories of a remote past. But even when the church had broadened its ideals to permit studies not strictly religious in character or in aim, it frowned persistentlyon all ventures in philosophy and science which seemed likely to be inconsitent with the central articles of its faith; the consequence was that intellectual inquiry was compelled to spend its forces for serveral centuries in the rediscovery of the classical learning. and in the systematizing and re-statement of it in terms of comformable with the Christian religion as interpreted by the church. The time came when this enforced limitation of thought imposed a serious check on the forward movement of the human spirit. But for the Dark Ages (5th Century A.D) it proved an almost disguised blessing. It was an admirable discipline that the peoples which were the forerunners of the modern nations had to undergo in extracting the knowledge that met their needs from the intellectual achievements of the past.

The commonly accepted belief is that the monks were the pioneers of education in Europe after the fall of the Roman Empire. Monascisn was a movement which attracted to itself earnest men of the most diverse character and attainment and the forms it assumed were correspondingly diverse. But the ascetic spirit which dominated the movement was generally inferable to educational work. Men who had left the world to seek salvation in seclusion from their fellows were little likely to be interested in learning for themselves or to be desirous of imparting it to others. In the Fourth century there were men like St Jerome who clung passionately to their books after renouncing everything else, and found satisfaction in the imparting of secular instruction as part of their religions duties. A notable case of the kind is that of Cassiodorus, who attempted maintenance of learning. In addition to certain commentaries on the scriptures, he compiled for the benefit of his monks a treatise entitled Institutions divinarum et saecularum lectionum, the first part of which was devoted to sacred literature and the second to the libral arts. The idea that all secular knowledge was comprehended in seven arts had found expression in the treatise of Martianum Capella, but the pagan atmosphere of Capella's book had prevented its general adoption. The work of Cassiondorus emphasized afresh thesevenfold grouping of knowledge and gave it sanctity by connecting with the text that "wisdom had builded here house she hath hewn out her seven pillars" Hence forward the seven arts constituted a standard part of education, and the work of Cassiodorus became one of the texts commonly studied.

But though the example of Cassiodorus did something to encourage the scholarly side of monastic life, the general tendency of monasticism in the sixth century was antipathetic to learning. After seeing the evil effects of literary study on some of his fellows in Rome, in his youth, Benedict (a well born Roman) deliberately renounced all worldy learning choosing to be knowingly ignorant and wisely unlearned. "In 529 A.D he founded his famous monasteries on Monte Casino on the site of an old temple of Apollo. Certainly there is no indication of any provision for study in the Rule he drew up for his monks. "Idleness is the great enemy of the soul" he declared in the forty-eighth chapter of the Rule, In order to ensure this, he prescribed seven hours of manual work and at least two hours of reading as part of the daily rountine. But no monk was to be allowed a book or a pen of his own. The inclusion of reading among the tasks prescribed for those who followed the Rule presupposed a supply of books and the ability to read them. And this in course of time led to the copying of manuscripts being made a common part of the work of monasteries, and to the teaching of monks and the young boys given by their parents to be brought up as monks. But though both of these practices were of considerable importance for education, they give no warrant for the view that the monasteries provided instruction for the people outside their walls.

The common attitude of the monks of the sixth and seventh centuries to all learning except that concerned with sacred writings is aptly illustrated by the educational policy of pope Gregory the Great (504-604 A.D) one of the ablest and most distinguished men who ever filled the papal chair. His chief contribution to education was the establishment of the Song School the schola Contorum, in which scholars received a training in singing and in the elements of Latin and reading to fit them for taking part in the choral services of church. (The song school, in due course, became a permanent institution in connection with the churches and subsequently developed into a school for elementary institution). He certainly opposed thesecular literature and, pagan classics as they were regarded as contrary to the very spirit of Christianity. To considerable extent, Gregory's great influence did much to impose the Benedictine Rule in its original narrow form on the monasteries of the Western Europe. This is borne out by the fact that with one exception there is no certain evidence of any considerable degree of scholarship, outside the sphere of religion, in any of lands under the papal jurisdiction till the end of the Eighth century. The one exception was Spain, where intellectual life was kept vigorous by the Arian controversy. The orthodox side at its best was represented there by Isidore (570-636 A. D) Bishop of Seville, the most learned man of his age. Isidore did not differ greatly from Gregory in his estimate of secular learning. In the Rule he imposed on the monks in his diocese, he prohibited the reading of Gentile or heretical works and thus excluded all the writers of antiquity from the monasteries.

Regarding the educational position of the monasteries in the Sixth and Seventh centuries, all that has been said about the neglect of learning on the part of the monks applies as much to the whole of the Dark Ages. The monasteries which paid no attention to learning at all and even in those distinguished for their culture the educated monks usually formed only a small section. Such education as there was moreover, related mainly to sacred subjects, and was confined to those who were going to follow the monastic life. It is sometimes said that the monasteries had two schools attached to them, one in the cloister for their own novices and one outside for the pupils (externi) who by the common rule of the monasteries were not permitted inside the cloister.

While monasticism on the continent from the sixth to eighth century was sunk in ignorance and was indifferent to education a very remarkable revival of learning was taking place in the monasteries of Ireland which made Ireland the best educated country in Europe during this period. In the Fourth century Christianity was established among the Scots (as the people of Ireland were then called) by the missionaries from England and from Gaul. Instead of a system of dioceses ruled by Bishop subject to Pope such as prevailed on the continent, there were scattered throughout the land a great number of independent monasteries, whose members combined the functions of both secular and regular clergy for the districts in their immediate neighbourhood.

The character of the learning which was imparted in these monastic schools is not exactly known. Probably theology formed the most important in it. But even if that be so, the Irish schools differed in certain essential respects from the monastic schools of the continent.

In the first place, they were not confined to those in Holy order, but like those of their predecessors, were open to the laity.

In the second place the Irish scholars were at an early date students of the classics. At a time when the Western Church was ignorant of the literature of Greece and distrustful of the literature of Rome, the Irish monks were enthusiastically studying both. The missionaries who crossed over from Ireland to Gaul towards the end of the sixth century were well versed in literature and wrote much purer and better Latin than any of their contemporaries; and throughout the two following centuries their successors enjoyed a great reputation as Greek scholars.

In the third place, unlike the Roman clergy who generally confined their attention to Latin and ignored the vernacular of the peoples among whom they worked, the Irish monks maintained a lively interest in the native language and literature.

For fully two hundred years piety and learning flourished in happy union inthe Irish monasteries. Then in 795 the storm of Viking invasion broke violently over the country and the peace and security which Ireland had enjoyed while the greater part of the Europe was in confusion, vanished, to return no more. But all was not lost. In the heyday of Irish prosperity a great many missionaries, impelled by the Wanderlust of their race, had crossed the seas and had settled as preachers and teachers in the northern parts of Britain and Frankland and Gaul and still more followed as the terrors of the Norse ravages increased. In their new homes they formed a numberof little colonies in which they clung pertinaciously to the language and cult of their native land, and their zeal for learning and teaching suffered no abatement. In later times these scions of Irish monasticism went still farther afield, reaching through Germany to Poland and Bulgaria. As late as the Twelfth century quite a number of monasteries were established by them in different parts of Europe where the Irish traditions were in large measure maintained.

THE BISHOPS SCHOOLS

The real successors of the old Roman schools were not those of the monks whether Celtic or Roman, but those of the bishops. As early as the third century, schools for the training of the clergy was conducted by the bishops: but so long as the public schools of grammar and rhetoric existed, the instruction they gave had reference for the most part to theology and to pastoral duties. With the disappearance of the public schools, however, it became necessary for the episcopal schools to wider their scope so as to include the elements of a more general education. At first, the extension of their functions met with considerable opposition from those who were still prejudiced against the old literary studies and who saw more danger in educating the clergy than in keeping them ignorant. The letter written by Pope Gregory to Bishop Desiderius was a protest against one of the earliest attempts to make the bishops schools a schools for grammar as well for theology. Gregory was indignant because grammar was being taught by the bishop's fraternity to "certain persons" not specified. It was in England, that new schools first made their appearance. According to Bedes History, the king of East Anglia (631) wishing to imitate what he had seen well arranged among the Gauls he instituted a school in which boys might be taught grammar. In this enterprise he was assisted by Bishop Felix, Burgendian Bishop, sent as a missionary to England by Gregory who came to him from Kent and brought with him ushers and teachers after the fashion of the Canterbury people. The Canterbury school was not really a grammar school at all but one that limited its instruction to the knowledge required for the understanding of the church services. The English people were in different position from that of their continental neighbours in that they were totally ignorant of the Latin tongue in which all the church services were conducted. The missionaries had to come with the Latin service book in one hand and the Latin grammar in the other. Not only had the native priests to be taught the tongue in which their services were performed, but their converts atleast of the upper classes had to be taught the elements of grammar before they could grasp the elements of religion. So the grammar school became in theory the necessary ante-room the vestibule of the churches. But as there were no schools any more than the churches in England, Augustine had to create both and in doing so, he presumably took as his model the ordinary grammar schools which still existed though in decadence in Italy.

There was also a song school at Canterbury when peace was restored and the number of the faithful increased. James the Deacon taught many people church chanting in which he was highly skilled, after the fashion of Rome or Canterbury. From this it is evident that the conjunction of song school and grammar school in the great churches which is a constant feature of medieval education had been made in Canterbury at the beginning of the seventh century. The same forces which were at work in the creation of the English schools were active elsewhere about the same time. According to social needs, the progress was unequal in different parts of Europe and there were many local variations.

In the Western church as a whole, the instability of political conditions and the passions engendered by the conflict between Christianity and cultured paganism undoubtedly put obstacles in the way of education and retarded its development. At any rate in the Eastern branch of the church the obligation of the clergy to undertake the work of education was firstly assumed.

About a century later (797) the responsibility of the Church for the maintenance and conduct of elementary and grammar schools eveywhere was definitely recognized in a long series of enactments of church councils. The General Council of 826 under pope Eugenius for example, enjoined that in bishop's sees and in other places necessary care and diligence should be exhibited in the appointment of masters and doctors to teach faithfully grammar and the liberal arts, because in them especially God's commands are made clear and explained.

These decrees presuppose the existence of Church schools. Their object is not the creation of new system, but the improvement and extension of one already estblished. By the end of the Eighth century (when Theodulph and Charlemagne were prescribing universal education) all the cathedrals and collegiate churches had a song school and a grammar school associated with them, and that the song school was no longer a purely professional school for the training of choristers, but an elementary school as well and the grammar school in like fashion no longer merely preparatory for theological study but an institution in which future clergy received a general education in company with all the professional classes. In many of the humbler parish churches, further there were song schools sometimes taught by the priest themselves which served for the popular education.

This expansion of the functions of the Church schools naturally brought about very considerable changes in their organisation. At first the bishops were themselves the teachers. By the Eighth century the bishops, whose duties compelled them to move about from place to place had begun to delegate their teaching duties, to members of their councils permanently in residence in the Cathedrals. The care of the song school fell in the first instance to the official who was called cantor in Eleventh century statues. The grammar school was entrusted to the school master (variously named schoasticus magister scholarum archischola), who was also the lawyer of the chapter and was consequently called at a later date the Chancellor.

At this stage no sharp distinction was made between ordinary school studies and the subjects of higher instruction. The basis of the curriculum was the seven liberal arts as expounded in encyclopedic fashion in the works of Martianus Capella, Cassiodorus and Isodore, in combination with law and theology.

The influence of Charles the Great (768-814 A.D) on English education in the Ninth century was specially marked. Even greater was the effect of Charles's example of Alfred at the end of the century. Like Charles, Alfred began his reforms by encouraging educaion in the church and it was stated that he expended an eighth of his income in the maintenance of a Palace school, which was attended by many boys of noble birth and even by boys of humbler rank. But his aim throughout was the uplifting of the whole people. He not only encouraged English learning but also recommended the knowledge of Latin for those who wished to continue their studies and rise to a higher rank. To this his chief personal contribution was the translation from Latin into English of some of the best books of the time Gregory Pastoral Care, Boethius's Consolations of philosophy, Orosius's Universal, History of the world Bedes

Ecclesiastical History. Legend connects his name with the foundation of Oxford University: His real glory is that by precept and example he brought a new life into English learning and so prepared the way for the renaissance which manifested itself in the rise of the English Universities two hundred Years after his day.

THE PASSING OF THE DARK AGES

The impulse given to education by the work of Charles sufficed to maintain the continuity of learning in Europe till the greater revival of the Eleventh and Twelfth centuries. There always remainded monasteries and cathedrals where learning was cherished and the losses which took place through the failure of some centres were constantly being made good by new efforts in others. Thus in the tenth century when Otto the Great, attempted to recreate the Empire of his famous ancestor, the educational ideals of Charles were once more revived by the scholarly movement. But in spite of all this, education was undoubtedly in a precarious state in these centuries. From the Eighth to the Eleventh centuries, the Norsemen laid waste all the lands on the Western sea-board especially Ireland, Britain and Northern France. About the same time Saracen Conqueror's of Africa poured over the straits of Gibraltar brought all Spain under theri rule; Towards the end of the Ninth century, while the Moors were still active in the south, the Magyars a Mongolian race remotely akin to the Turks of a later day, overran Germany, Southern France and Northern Italy, until finally defeated by the Emperor Henry the Fowler in 933. In Ireland, the ancient schools almost wholly disappeared and the schools of England only escaped the same fate because there the work of destruction was never so complete, and because Alfred was ready to undertake the work of restoration as soon as he had forced his terms on the invaders. Even in a more favoured lands men were too much preoccupied for any but a cloistered few to give thought to books and study or to care about education. Under these circumstances, many of the schools came to an untimely end.

3.4.7 THE EMERGENCE OF THE UNIVERSITY SYSTEM IN EUROPE

In the end Europe emerged safely from the great ordeal. By the Eleventh century the Norsemen had been absorbed and christianized. The Moors and Magyars had been pushed back, and rendered incapable of working serious mischief. Prosperity speedily returned and civilized conditions established themselves more firmly than ever. The DARK AGES were over and the Middle Ages proper were ushered in with the promise of a moral and intellectual awakening, thebeginnings of which are dated from the millennial year (1000). But the civilization of the Eleventh century was very different from that of the Eighth: Out of great evil great good had come. The life of Western Europe had been enriched both directly and indirectly by the long conflict through which it had passed. The sturdy barbarians from the north had introduced into the populations of all the countries a new strain of manhood, with a vigorous mentality that responded readily and freshly to the influence of culture. The Moors, with their Moham-median faith and a learning which owed a great deal to Greek science and philosophy successfully resisted absorption and compelled Christendom to rise to a higher intellectual level in defence of its own faith. Even the Magyars who had little to give in the way of new knowledge or inspiration produced far-reaching changes in the social life of Central Europe and more particularly of Italy by causing the rise of fortified cities. These cities were destined to be the birth places of the univeristies.

Apart from this historical circumstances, the cities of Italy were in no way unique. As a matter of fact, the formation of large defensible towns had taken place everywhere and it involved a momentous transformation in the mental attitude of Europe. In the preceding age individual enterprise and initiative were almost wholly shifted by the greatness and remoteness of the institutions under which ordinary men had to live their lives; only the few responsible for the exercise of secular and religious authority could properly be said to enjoy any real freedom. The rise and growth of the towns altered all that. Within their wall the citizens acquired an ever increasing measure of independence. They formed councils for the management of the common affairs and guilds for the protection and regulation of their crafts: and with progressive autonomy they gradually freed themselves from the more irksome of the restraints imposed on them by their over-lords of church and state.

The new civic movement quickly made itself felt in the sphere of education. One effect was a great increase in the number of schools. With the coming together of people into the stimulating atmosphere of the towns, there arose a demand for education, and it was not very long before there were few towns of any size without schools of their own. To all appearance, indeed, these schools did not differ in any essential respect from the older foundations associated with cathedrals and the collegiate churches. Like them, they were administered and staffed by the clergy and then courses of study closely followed the established tradition. In spite of clerical control, they inevitably became more and more secular in character. Towards the end of the Middle ages some of them even passed out of the hands of church and became purely municipal institutions.

It is not the grammar schools or the humbler song schools, however, but the new schools of higher learning, first called studia gereralia, and subsequently known as "Universities" which show the most remarkable effects of the development of the medieval towns on education. It is impossible to assign an exact date to the origin of the universities, for the simple reason that the first of them grew into being over a considerable period of time. The most that can be said is that sometime about the beginning of the Twelfth century students had begun to flock in considerable number from different lands to certain town which had acquired a reputation for the instruction their schools gave in some particular subject like medicine, law or theology. Some of these towns more fortunate than the rest in the possession of great teachers or favoured by some peculiarity of geographical situation succeeded in maintaining their attraction and their schools began to organize themselves as permanent institutions with forms of government that afforded security to masters and students, and won definite recognition from the civil and ecclesiastical authorities. Such among others more obscure were Blongna, Paris, and Oxford, the great "mother" universities which served as models for the universities which sprang up in every part of Europe in the course of the next few centuries.

The intimate connection between the universities and the growth of civil independence is shown by the fact that it was in those part of Southern Europe where the municipalities were freest and most vigorous the university movement extended with greatest rapidity. In Italy no fewer than nine universities established themselves by spontaneous growth or by special creation in the first half of the Thirteenth century and as many more were instituted in the next two centuries. In Spain, where also municipal life was active the joint interest of the municipalities and the kings resulted in the founding of twelve universities during the Middle Ages: In the South of France the towns took a smaller part in the educational affairs of their people than those of Spain or Italy, but there were one or two ancient studia (the chief one at Montpelier: and the Italian influence led to the establishment of half a dozen more in the

North of Europe, where feudal conditions generally presented a serious obstacles to municipal progress; on the other hand, the universities were slower to develop. France had many great schools notably one at Charles, which so far as scholarship went had as much claim to become studia generalia as their Italian fellows, but except Orleans and Angers, where law was the main subject of study, they were all overshadowed by Paris, and never attained University rank. Much the same thing happend in England where the predominance of Oxford and Cambridge was great enough to crush out attempts made to institute universities in other centres. Germany and the low countries again, though sending large numbers of students to Bologna and Paris and other universities, had no universities of their own till the second half of the fourteenth century and the first of the four Scotish universities (St. Andrews, 1411) was not founded till the following century. Altogether there were seventynine universities in actual existence in Europe by 1500. The universities of Italy and southern of North Europe generally took Paris as their model. Underlying this difference was the difference in the educaional traditions of the two groups of nations. Education in the North was everywhere in the hands of the church and young churchmen formed a large proportions of the pupils in the schools. Hence it was a matter of course that ecclesiastical studies should predominate, and that the church authorities should claim a large share in university government. In Italy, on the other hand, the secular view of learning had always held its ground. There were church schools in Italy as elsewhere, but the old literary studies which had commonly become ancillary to religion in the North were there pursued for their own sake even by the clergy: and what is even more significant, the teachers in many cases were laymen. In consequence of this, ecclesiastical studies played but a minor part in the Italian universities: the subjects of prime interest were medicine and law, especially law. With the development of the towns a new value was added to the study of law. A knowledge of law now became of the greatest service not only for the maintenance of their rights as against outsiders, but also for their internal regulation. For this reason it came to have a place in the schools as a branch of rhetoric: and with the decay of the Latin language the reading and writing of law; Latin became a common part of grammatical instruction. The next step beyond this diffusion of law studies as part of a general education was a wise of specialists in law. But at a critical moment in the context of the cities for scholastic superiority, the appearance of great lawyer named Irnerius (circa 1050 - 1130) gave a new impulse to legal studies in Italy.

During the centuries in which law was growing into a special study in Italy a similar movement was taking place in the North with the respect of theology. In both cases the starting point in the development of learning was the liberal arts but whereas in Italy the needs of practical life made rhetoric the art of most importance and the legal applications of it the main concern of scholars, the clerical monopoly of education in the North gave supremacy to dialectic or logic. Of the three branches of the trivium, grammar was suspect because of its associations with the paganism and rhetoric was regarded with a certain indifference in an age of low literary standards. Logic was the one subject free from obvious objection which was open to the student eager for knowledge that would satisfy the intellect.

Not only had the cathedral schools grown in efficiency but schools had sprung up everywhere in the towns which were the centres of resistance to barbarian invasion. Consequently when peace returned to Europe, with the Eleventh century there was a more numerous company of students in all countries than ever before to whom the philosophical and theological discussions of the scholastics appealed. It must not be thought that logic was the only interest of these scholars. At a later time, indeed, it almost monopolized the attention of the schools of higher learning: but even at the beginning of the Twelfth century there was a famous school at Charles in the north of France, where the study of the ancient literatures flourished under the inspiration of Bernard Sylvester, as it did nowhere else till the renaissance of the fifteenth century. So long as the great schools were isolated in stitutions and depended for their reputation and for the special character of their studies, on outstanding teachers, there was very considerable variety among them.

With the rise of Paris to a position of pre-eminence however the age of great teachers passed, and the tradition of learning became localized in enduring institutions greater than their greatest teachers. And with this went a standardizing of the subjects of study and a certain narrowing of educational interest. This change took place sometime about the beginning of the Twelfth century. Before then Paris had only been one of several French towns frequented by students. It only needed a man of outstanding genius to complete the ascendency of Paris, and in due season the man appeared in Peter Abelard (1079-1142). But it was not Abelard's philosophy which gave him his extraordinary popularity and made his teaching an abiding influence in the educaional life of

Paris, and through Paris, of all Europe. It was his treatment of theology as a subject for philosophical discussion by means of disputation. In the prologue to the book he entitled Sie et Non (Year and da) he sets forth quite boldly the need for a critical examination of doct ne. For this purpose he selected 158 disputed points in Christian doctrine, and drew up the counter arguments used by St. Paul, St. Augustine, and the Fathers. The first topic, was the query: should human faith be based upon reason or no? "The others covered a wide range of subjects. For example "Is God a substance or no? "Is God the author of evil or no? "Do we sometime sin involuntarily or no?" Once introduced by Abelard the method of quotation form opposing authorities speedily became the accepted method of dealing with all kinds of questions. It was applied, for instance, to the law of the church by Gretian, a monk of Bologna, in his Concordia discordantium Cannonum (1139-1142) which became one of the standard works on canon Law. But its effect was the greatest in the sphere of theology. It was its free employment by all parties in discussing the burning questions concerning church doctrine that made the scholastic theology the central interest of the students of Paris for over three hundred years.

THE CONSTITUTIONAL DEVELOPMENT OF THE UNIVERSITIES

There was a fundamental similarity in the academic conditions prevailing at the beginning of the Twelfth century in Bologna and Paris. In both cases, certain schools of the liberal arts gradually concentrated attention on interests and attempted to give higher instruction in them. In both cases, again, the appearance of a great teacher had a decisive effect on the development of the schools: in the first place, by so extending the scope of the subjects studied and changing the methods of study that it was no longer possible to consider them merely as parts of a course in the arts, and in the second place, by attracting great numbers of students and accustoming the scholars of Europe to think of a particular city as the place where specialised instruction in certain subjects could best be got. Here in fact, were the beginnings of the universities. The schools had become studia generalia : that is, generally recognised places of study open without local restriction to the students of Europe. But these studia generalia were not yet universitates in the proper sense of the word. At this stage we look in vain for the peculiar features which distinguish the medieval universities from the ancient schools of Athens or Alexandria. The qualifications that entitled a man to teach had not yet been settled. In Bologna any scholar who could get students to come to him could teach. In Paris, the teacher only needed the permission of the Chancellor of Notre Dame, the head of the Cathedral school. Nor had the masters or students any of the rights and privileges they afterwards enjoyed in their corporate capacity. The chief difference between the studia and the schools out of which they had developed lay in the fact that among the pupils of the studia were many who had come from other lands to get instruction which their own land did not afford. It was these difference which led to the rise of the universities.

The "universities" in the original meaning of the word were simply societies (or guilds) of masters or students, formed for the purpose of mutual help and protection, after the manner of the guilds of craftsmen which were rising into prominence with great impulse to corporate life which made itself felt through out Europe in the Twelfth century. In the Middle Ages a man lived in a foreign country at his own risk. He had no claim of any kind on the contrary into which he had ventured, and his best chance of security lay in associating himself with his fellow countrymen in that country. It was for this reason that in the seats of learning the various groups of foreign scholars banded themselves together into a number of separate "Universities". The first societies of the kind both in Paris and Bologna were those of the masters. (the beginnings of a rudimentary organisations of masters between 1150 and 1170 and therefore the beginnings of Paris University of masters. In the scholar's guild as in the other guilds, the student had to qualify himself for mastership by an apprenticeship lasting from five to seven years as the disciple of a recognised master and at the end of that time he was formally introduced to the society by his master and entered its ranks by a ceremonial "inception" at which he delivered a probationary lecture. At this stage the master scholars had no written statutes and had not yet become a legal corporation with an official head. Conerning the Bolognese masters even less is known. Though therre is no documentary evidence for their existence before 1215 it is understood that they also had formed a society about the same time as the Parisian masters.

The master's societies followed the general precedent of the trade's guilds. The "universities" of law students which arose in Bologna in the last decade of the century belonged to a different category, since their members had only the status of apprentices. Their position was more like that of the societies of merchants who combined in national companies when living in a foreign country in pursuit of their calling. They were foreigners who needed to cooperate in self- defence and their associations followed the same principle of emotional grouping. They were merely private societies concerned with the personal interests of their members. The object of the guild was declared to be the cultivation of fraternal charity, mutual association and amity, the consolation of the sick and support of the needy, the conduct of funerals and the extirpation of rancours and quarrels the attendance of escort of their Doctorandi to and from the place of examination, and the spiritual advantage of members. Even at this stage, when the societies of masters and students were still feeble and under developed, the scholars in cities like Paris and Bologna occupied a favoured position. In Paris they were recognized as a section of the clergy and allowed such privileges as the right of trial by the ecclesiastical courts. In the Italian cities they formed a class by themselves on whom the cities for their own sake were willing to confer special advantages. Over and above that they enjoyed the favour of the superior secular powers almost from the beginning. In 1158, before there was any definite university organisation at all, the Emperor Frederick Barbarossa issued a decree, granting special legal standing to all students of Bológna in the Lombard Kingdom, in the case of legal proceedings the students were allowed the option of bringing their case before their own masters or before the bishop of the city in which they were studying. The students of Paris received a similar charter of privilege from Philip Augustus after a quarrel between citizens and students in 1200 in which several students were killed. In these royal favours there was no recognition of the studia at Bologna and Paris as such, the privileges conferred had reference only to the masters and students as individuals. And the reason is plainly obvious that the studia were still in a loosely organised conditions. But with the thirteenth century came great changes. The several "universities" of scholars developed into corporate bodies with well-defined administrative functions, and the particular stadium of which they formed constituent parts became the entity known at a later time as "universities Studi" or even "Universitas" without qualification.

Both in Bologna and in Paris the amalgamation of the serveal "universities" into one university was the out come of a conflict with the local authorities. By the middle of the thirteenth century the various groups had united into "universities" each with a rector chosen from its own members, whom every student had to swear to obey under penalty of being declared perjured and treated as outcast. Early in the next century the two "universities" had practically become one. Though there were still two rectors, the universities had common statutes and met in one congregation. Ultimately they became the governing body in the university. The members of the numerically weaker faculties of arts and medicine were as much under their jurisdiction as their own members though having no part in them.

As the medieval universities had no permanent buildings and little corporate property, this practice of migrating from one city to another to set up a studium was common in all the centres of study throughout Europe. (Cambridge, for example was raised to university status by a migration from Oxford in 1209, and Oxford itself was greatly benefited twenty years later by a migration from Paris. The victory of the students in their dealings with their teachers was still more complete. In the twelfth century academic matters were under the control of the doctors' guild but by a ruthless boycotting of recalcitrant doctors and of the students who attended their lectures, the student "universities" brought their teachers into entire subjection. They were forced to swear to obey the rectors and to regulate their classes according to the instructions of the students officers. They could not be absent without leave even for a single day. They must begin and end their lectures punctually. They had to arrange their courses so as to cover the ground at a proper rate without evading difficulities or omitting anything. Any infringement of the regulations was punished by a fine proportionate to the offence: and persistent contumacy ended in expulsion from the guild to which they were compelled to belong, but in whose affairs they were allowed no share.

In the long run the very strength of the "universities" proved their undoing. In the second half of the thirteenth century the city began to pay the salaries of the doctors in order to propitiate the students and keep up the reputation of the university and by this arrangement it gained a certain responsibility for the appointment and supervision of the teachers through a board of reformations studii. With the reaction against the tyranny of guilds in general, this board became the real controlling power in university affairs, and the student "universities" lost all but a fraction of their former strength. With some modifications they continued to exercise their diminished authority till they were finally away in the great European revolution at the end of eighteenth century.

The development of the university of Paris took place under quite different conditions from that of Bologna. The opposition between students and teachers was never of the least consequence, since the students in the faculty of arts, which was much the largest faculty were too young and too poor to assert themselves as the law students of Bologna had done. Even the opposition between the scholars and the civil authorities was at most times comparatively unimportant. The real struggle with the constitution of the university was that which went all through the thirteenth century between the masters' guild and the Chancellor of Notre Dame as representing the Church of Paris.

The constitutional effects of the century of struggle were very great. At the beginning of the century there were only groups of masters and students, loosely combined according to faculty, but without any common ties beyond what was implied in the fact that every teacher had to receive licence from the chancellor of Notre Dame. At the end there was a closely knit and powerful corporation in which all the faculties were represented, with the rector of the arts masters the virtual if not yet the legal head. The common opposition to the chancellor had welded the several "universities" of masters into one, and had given the chief position to the inferior (that is, preliminary) faculty of arts. To understand how this had come about it must be remembered that it was the masters of arts who had been the brunt of the struggle. It was they as the youngest group of masters who were most affected by the oppressions of the chancellor, and who consequently were forced to organise first. It is worth mentioning Pope Gregory IX 's Bull Parens Scientiarum (1231) which was issued in the interests of the masters, had been called the Magna Carta of the University. Following the example of the Bolognese law students, they ranged themselves the early in four nations - the French, the Normans the Picards (from the low countries) and the English (including the Germans and the other northern students). To the officers of these four nations with their common rector fell the chief control of the arts steadily increased and the nations with their rector became the main upholders of university privileges,. partly because the artists (as they were called) were by far the most numerous section of the masters and were therefore the largest contributions to the expense incurred in the constant litigation, partly because most of the masters in the other faculties were also masters in the faculty of arts and had a joint deliberations of the faculties: and had a share in its affairs, their officers took a foremost place in the joint deliberations of the faculties: and their rector from being on a position of equality with the rectors of the other masters societies, came to be recognised as the head of the seven "companies" (the four arts nations and the three higher faculties of theology, medicine and law) comprised in the university.

ORGANISATION OF UNIVERSITY SYSTEM

All the while the development of university government was going on, an equally distinctive organization was the institution of degrees sometimes about the beginning of the Thirteenth Century. Before that time a student qualified for mastership in much the same way as the apprentice became a master craftsman or the page became a knight. He attended the lectures of a member of the masters guild, and after a number of years (four or five years) in this capacity, if he were studying in Paris or in any of the other northern towns, he applied to the chancellor, or to the corresponding church official for a licence to teach, and was presented to the other masters by his own master as a candidate for admission to their masters, he himself became a master. In Bologna and the South, the procedure was very much the same, except that at first there was no need for the ecclesiastical licence. It was not till Pope Honorius III in 1219 required all candidates in Bologna to receive licence from the Archdeacon of that city after the manner of Paris, that the church's licence became a necessary condition of mastership also. As time went on, however, the honour of mastership was sought even by those who had no intention to devote themselves to teaching, and a distinction came to be made between teachers and non-teachers. Mastership thus came to signify the successful completion of a special course of study, and it became necessary to define the qualifications for it with greater precision.

As an illustration, we can cite the way adopted by Bologna. In the Middle Ages a knowledge of law meant the knowledge of certain texts and the recognized commentraies on them. The attendance on lectures on the standard texts and some kind of examination on their contents were therefore obvious requirements for a degree in law. After devoting five years to study, the student in Civil Law might apply to the rector for permission to lecture on a chapter of one of the law books, and a year later on a whole book. After delivering a course of lectures, he became a Bachelor without any examination. Two years later, at the completion of seven years study, he was entitled to apply for the Doctorate. Before examination he had to appear before the rector, affirm on oath that he had fulfilled all the statutory requirements, and swear obedience to him. Having received the rector's permission to go forward, he was then presented for licence to the Archdeacon of Bologna by his own Doctor or by another who gave testimony concerning his fitness. Next came the private examination. The candidate came before the college of doctors and was given two passages to study. Later in the day he gave an exposition of the passages and was subjected to examination, first by two doctors appointed for the task and then by any or all of others. If on a rote of the doctors present his candidature was approved, he became a licentiate and graduation was completed by his appearance at the public examination, which took place with much ceremony in the cathedral. The final act which marked his admission into the ranks of the doctors was the delivery of a lecture on some question of law and a disputation with selected students on the points which had been raised. He was then presented to the Archdeacon and received from him the licence to teach. Thereafter he was formally installed as a teacher. He took his seat in the magisterial chair (cathedra), one of the law texts was put in his hand, a gold ring was placed on his finger (perhaps to show that he was the equal of a knight), the doctor's cap was placed on his head, and finally he was escorted through the town by the two "universities".

A similar system developed in Paris in imitation of the practice of Bologna. As early as 1215 we find a definite curriculum of study for the degree in arts. The basis of the course was the seven liberal arts in a much modified form. Logic as set forth in Aristotle's Organon, and Porphyry's Introduction was the main subject of study. Grammar was pursued in a narrow way with reference to the treatises of Priscian, and did not include literature. Rhetoric and philosophy were regarded as of secondary impor-tance and only read on feast days. The books specified on Rhetoric were the Barbarisms of Donatus and the Topics of Boethius. Philosophy included Aristotle's Ethics and the four subjects of the quadrivium. Modifications were subsequently made at various notably by the addition of those works of Aristotle on Metaphysics and Natural philosophy, recovered at the beginning of the Thirteenth century, but prohibited at first as dangerous to faith. By the middle of Fourteenth century the course fell into three parts : (a) for the baccalaureate - grammar, logic and psychology: (b) for the licence - natural philosophy: (c) for the mastership - moral philosophy and the completion of the course on natural philosophy.

By the end of the Thirteenth century there were examinations on the prescribed work at the various stages of the course. The candidate for the baccalaureate had first to give proof of his capacity by a disputation with a master in logic and grammar. He then appeared before a board of examiners appointed by his own nation. If the examiners found that he had attended the appointed lectures for the proper period and was familiar with the contents of the books he had studied, he went on to determine - that is, to expound a thesis and to maintain it against opponents for several dates. If he came through this ordeal successfully he ranked as a bachelor. After he had given further attendance at lectures till he had gone over all the books at were to be known and had himself lectured and disputed he applied to the Chancellor licence, and again was subjected to an oral examination and had to lecture and dispute, this time in the presence of the Chancellor and four examiners. If approved he was now a licentiate, but he had still to be received by the masters at the ceremony of incep-tion. After being approved by his nation and taking the requisite oaths he finished by conductin a disputation before the regent masters, and formally became a master himself by having the master's cap put on his head and taking his seat on the master's chair.

The degree arrangements in the three higher faculties were similar to those in arts. Usually, after some study, but not necessarily graduation, in arts, the candidate for a mastership in theology, medicine or law had to undergo a prescribed routine of study over a fixed period of time, examinations in which disputation figured largely and a ceremonial admission to magisterial rank.

At first the degree system of the universities was regarded as simply a part of their internal economy. But with the rise of new universities from the very beginning of the Thirteenth century the question of the relative value of the degrees conferred soon became of some considerable importance. At this stage even the univesities of the best standing were only well developed in one of the higher faculties and had either no teachers or only inferior ones in the others: and it was necessary for students who wished an all round education to go to serveral studia in quest of satisfaction. Hence the frequent wandering of both masters and scholars from university to university, was one of the characterstic features of the early Middle Ages. Such changing from place to place inevitably raised the question of the standing of the masters in different universities. The case of the older universities was comparatively simple.

On the strength of the reputation, they claimed for their masters the right to teach everywhere in Europe without any prelude of new examination or apporval or any duty of beginning again, or obtaining anyone's leave", and claim was generally, but by no means always, admitted. Regarding the new universities which lacked the standing of the old, the king of the country in which they were situated might grant them special privileges, as was done in Spain and it was important that they should receive these privileges if they were to attract students from other countries. Such recognition was merely local and it could not affect their relations with other universities. The solution of the problem was indicated by the fact that the beginning of the Thirteenth Century universities began to be founded by monarchs and popes for reasons of policy. Gradually it came to be recognised that the only way in which a university could get proper standing was to get its charter of foundtion from a universal sovereign. That meant that either the Pope as the religious head of Europe or the Emperor as the secular head of the Empire must give a university his imprimatur to make its degrees of general validity. This is why most of the universites other than the first law were founded either by an imperial gegree or most commonly, by a Papal Bull. So well established was this principle by the end of the Thirteenth century that even the older universities like Paris and Oxford sought to strengthen its position by seeking from the Pope an express recognition of the jus ubique docendi (the right to teach everywhere in Europe) for their graduates. In this way the universities of Europe were brought directly under the jurisdiction of the Pope, and the licence to teach which had originally been conferred by the Chancellor of Cathedral or some other Church dignitary for purely local purposes came to be given on behalf of the pope as a universal qualifications.

3.5 INDIAN HERITAGE

In Ancient Indo-Aryan literature, we can come across three or four words which roughly correspond to the modern word "education". Firstly the word "sicksh" is to be found in the Vedic hymns which means "to learn to recite". In the Brahmanic, Upanisadic and Sutra literature the word "adhyayana" is to be met with which literally means "to go near" and expresses the idea of pupils going to some teacher for education. Thus the initiation ceremony "upanayana" was instituted which literally means "taking near". Young children were taken near a teacher for their education. In early vedic times instruction was confined to particular families where the father generally taught his sons and there was no such initiation ceremony; but later on it came to be regarded as the preliminary to school life. Thirdly, the word "Vinaya" is to be met within classifical literature which comes from a root meaning "to lead out in a particular way." Thus it literally means "an action in which (inborn faculties) are led out (i.e. trained) in a particular way "or" an action in which (one) leads (oneself) in a particular manner". The first meaning is identical with that of "education" and the second expresses the idea of the formation of character. Kalidasa carries the credit of having used it very often in that sense. Here is a reference to the "development theory" of education: the inborn powers of man are to be drawn out and developed "probodha" is used by the same poet to express the results of education. It means "awakening" or "enlightenment". indeed an idea of the allsided development of man conceived by the Indo-Aryans and this will be further evident from the following passages:

> "Learning brings on Vinaya (development of inborn power or modesty) which in its turn enhances the worth of man" (Hitopadesa)

Whoever learns by heart, writes, observes, asks questions (to get difficulties solved) and waits upon the learned, has his intellect developed like a lotus by the Sun's rays. (Subhasita)

> "Just as well secured learning brings on enlightenment and leads to the formation of characters "(Raghuvamsam)

But an all-sided development of man cannot be complete unless he is prepared by the education he receives, not only for this life but also for a future existence. The harmonising of these two purposes in due proportion has always been a difficult task for educators. Thus in the Middle Ages in Europe stress was laid upon preparation for the world to come. while modern European systems often tend unduly to ignore this side of education. But the ancient Hindus attempted a happy synthesis of both these purposes. Thus a young Brahmin was prepared by the education he received for his practical duties in life as a priest and teacher but the need of preparing him for the life after death was also included in the education he received. The same may be said of the young Kshatriyas and Vaisyas who were required not only to fit themselves for their respective vocation in life but also to study the Vedas and give heed to the teachings of religion.

The technical name for the study proper i.e., Vedic study is "Swadhyaya". The object in view was the three- fold knowledge, that of Rg. Yajur and Saman. Besides the three Vedas the branches of knowledge cultivated the Hindus included not only literature, both sacred and secular with its accessories, Grammar, Phonetics, Exegetics and Metrics but also Logic, Philosophy, Itihasa, Vartta (Economics), Dandaniti (Science of government), Dhanurveda (Science of war,), Astron-omy, Law, Medicine and Mechanical and Fine Arts of all descriptions.

Besides these we find innumerable references to the supreme or highest knowledge, technically called para-vidya, as distinguished from all other knowledge termed apara, as is done in the Mundakopanisad. The Mundaka defines aparavidya as comprising the four Vedas and the six Vedangas. By the paravidya the Mundaka understands that knowledge through which the ultimate Reality is known. All knowledge para or apara, is opposed to ignorance, avidya. Paravidya however, is extolled as Sarvavidya pratistha, the foundation of all arts and sciences, as Vedanta, the final and highest stages of Vedic Wisdom, and as verily the science of sciences wherein lies the implicit knowledge of everything.

It is obvious, however, that all men are not physically and mentally fit for the acquisition of paravidya, nor can they be fit for it, all at once. It was to meet this difficulty, that the ancient Hindus considered education as a life process and divided the life of an individual into four stages to each of which different duties were assigned in such a way that their due performance in any stage might prepare the individual for the next higher stage. Thus the ancient Hindus did not ignore this mundane existence but on the other hand prepared the people for it by providing education on a caste basis so that on the completion of their education they found no difficulty in obtaining a means of livelihood.

A singular feature of ancient Hindu Civilization is that it has been moulded and shaped in the course of its history more by religious than by political or economic influences. Religion, as understood by the ancient Hindus, practically dominated every sphere of their national life. The foundamental principles of social, political and economic life were welded into a comprehensive theory which is called Religion in Hindu thought. Practical attitudes thus followed theoretical orientations. The total configuration of ideals, practices, and conduct is called Dharma (Religion, Virtue or Duty) in this ancient tradition. Thus it is Religion that regulated ancient Hindus and even their economic activities and pursuits. Ancient Indian Education is also to be understood as being ultimately the outcome of the Indian theory of knowledge and a part of the corresponding scheme of life and values.

As the individual is the chief concern and centre of this Education, Education also is necessarily individual. It is an intimate relationship between the teacher and the pupil. The relationship is inaugurated by a religious ceremony called Upanayana. It is not like the admission of a pupil to the register of school on his payment of the prescribed fee. The spiritual meaning of upanayana, and its details inspired by that meaning are elaborated in many texts. By upanayana the teacher, "holding the pupil within him as in a womb, impregnates him with his spirit, and delivers him in a new birth. The pupil is then known as a Dviya, "born afresh", in a new existence, "twice born". The education that is thus begun is called by the significant term 'Brahmacharya', indicating that it is a mode of life, a system of practices."

The Upanisad mention three steps of eduction called (1) Sravana (2) Manana and (3) Nididhyasana. Sravana is listening to words or texts as they are uttered by the teacher. It is the system of oral tradition by which India has built up her whole culture through the ages; the system was called Guruparamparya or Sampradaya as the uninterrupted ideal succession of pupils and teachers, by which knowledge is conserved and transmitted. Thus, the Book of knowledge in those days was called Sruti what was heard. This character of knowledge also fixed its form known as Mantra or Sutra by which the maximum of meaning was compressed within the minimum of words, of which the crowning example is the letter 'OM' containing within itself a world of meaning. Another point to be noted in this connection is that Sabda or Sound by itself has its own potency and value, apart from its sense, ans its intrinsic attributes, its rhythm, and vibrations should be captured. Sabda is Brahma. "The word is God"

In short, the system of education adumbrated in the Rigveda concerns only with the acquisition of the highest knowledge and saving wisdom and not of ordinary secular knowledge or intermediate truths for purposes of worldly life. The method of this learning is determined by its aims and content. The method of attaining the knowledge of the Absolute "Parabrahma jnnane," is not the method of acquiring a knowledge of the objective sciences, arts and crafts. It is the method of realization of the highest and ultimate truths called Rita and Satya by inhibition of the senses and objective, the method of meditation (dhyana) sustained by a life of austerities, tapas or yoga. in a Rigvedic passage, Tapas is described in a literal sense as "the most radiant effulgence coming from the highest knowledge " (tapah uttamam mahah), where the worshipper prays for the highest gift, the light of supreme knowledge or Tapas (the opposite of Tamas or ignorance). The vehicle, the language, of this learning, too, is different. The Rigveda describes the popular speech, the spoken tongue as "imperfect" (papaya vacha) and untrue (alaka) because it cannot serve as the vehicle of Truth or Supreme knowledge. It is the language of the field and factory, a fragment of Vak or Brahma (Brahmayam Vachah) which cannot express the truths hidden in the depths of the soul. These highest and ultimate truths are revealed by a different language, the language of the Vedic Mantras evolved out of the popular speech by means of Tapas and Yoga by learned men called Vipras, Vedhasas or Kavis, Rhishis, Manishis, and Muni's who live in a state of trance and in the subtle body and are worshipped by the gods themselves. We are further told that these learned men and seers developed Vedic knowledge and speech by their discussions at Assemblies or Conferences meeting on occasions of sacrifice where this knowledge and speech were attained, mastered, collected and distributed. "It was these Academics and learned Assemblies which were thus the agencies for the formulation and propagation of Vedic learning". The members of these bodies are described as Sakhas i.e. those who come together by the bond of fellowship in learning, and are fellow seekers after truth.

3.5.1 *CENTRES OF HIGHER LEARNING IN INDIA*

i) Brahmana - Sanghas, and Parishads of Vedic Era

The highest stage of education is represented in what are called the Brahmana- Sanghas, the Assemblics or Academics where the more successful students flocked together for the advancement of knowledge by discussing their respective contribution to it. Thus the conference method for the promotion and diffusion of learning, the method of discussion in seminars and academics, was first evolved in India, as evidenced by the Rigveda.

The learned meet in their Assemblies where through their discussions language is refined into the language of the Veda, like groats through a sieve. As fellow seekers of Truth, they are bound by a community of ideas to which they give expression in that language, the source of the highest good and knowledge.

Thus the Vedic Sanskrit was hammered into shape out of spoken Sanskrit of the times at learned Assemblies where it was the vehicle of philosophical discussions. It may also be inferred that the Rishis used to gather in these Assemblies to disclose and discuss the hymns they had themselves individually attained as the result of their tapas and meditation. This may be called the Conference method, the method of discussion, for the development of the Vedic Language and knowledge.

These learned Assemblies were held at the sacrifices. These sacrifices are therefore described as opening up the way which the wise tread for finding speech. The Rishis were repository of such speech and they revealed it at such sacrificial gatherings of learned. Their words thus acquired were then collected and spread far and wide. The system adumbrated here is that at the Yagna-Assembly each rishi brought forward his individual contributions to speech and then these were collected and codified. Then this standardized speech was suitable for being imparted to pupils and was thus propagated through the whole country. The different processes in this method of learning and evolution of Vedic Sanskrit are indicated by the words ayan, avindan, abhritya and adadhuhi i.e. "attainment, mastery, collection, and propag-ation" of the words which were originally confined to the Rishis and brought to light by them at the learned assemblies accompanying the sacrifices. The manner of learning and teaching this Vedic Sanskrit is also indicated here.

IT WAS TO BE LEARNT IN THE FORM OF METRES.

The Brahmanas united in fellowship in Vedic learning come together for the purpose of developing further the truths they had realized in their hearts or reached by their minds. They excluded from such assemblies the ignorant who cannot follow their discussions so that they may have full freedom to wander about unhampered in the realm of speculation and work out their own conclusions.

Rigvedic Education proper being religious and literary in its character, was for the few who were fit and eager for a dedicated life in quest of the highest truths and supreme knowledge. It was thus not meant for the many or the masses. And yet Rigvedic India did not present a one-sided development. There was a considerable amount of secular non-religious education to build up its economic life. It is known for its progress in all departments of national life, economic, political or religious, its progress in the various arts and crafts of civilized life, in Agriculture, Industry and Trade. All this economic progress was built up by the talent and training produced by schools of craftsmanship, the existence of which we can only infer in the absence of any direct evidence from the Rigveda.

The other Vedic Samhitas show the trend of learning and educational development as influenced by the trend of religious thought. The three later Vedic samhitas of Sama, Yajur and Atharva usher in the age of Brahmanas, a different type of literary activity. In the Rigvedic Samhita, the order of the hymn has nothing to do with the order of sacrifice. The order two Vedic Samhitas were compiled exclusively for purposes of ritual application. The fact is that in their time the old Rigvedic religion showed considerable developments of ceremonial and priesthood out of their beginning in the Rigveda. Higher education now related itself to the requirements of this priesthood and ritualistic religion.

The relations between the teacher and the taught were of the happiest kind. The pupil looked up to his preceptor as his father. He (the teacher) is to possess the highest moral and spirtual qualifications. "The truths is not grasped when taught by an inferior man" says the katha. The Mundaka requires him to be well versed in the sacred lore (strotriya) and dwelling entirely in the Brahman (bramanishtha). He must have a conviction based upon realization of the unity on which he is to enlighten his pupils; otherwise it would be like the blind leading the blind. It is the duty of the teacher, when a fit pupil approaches him to teach him the truth exactly as he knows it without concealing anything from him, for such concealment would spell ruin to him. There are on record certain cases of learning kept secret and revealed only to special persons. Where the teacher found that he was not quite fit to teach a subject, he considered it to be his duty to send up his student to a fitter teacher. The conscientiousness on the part of teachers was, however, consistent with their desire for securing as many pupils as they could teach. This desire was natural in teachers who felt that the truths they had discovered should live after them in their pupils through a succession of teachers, guruparam parya, keeping up the continuity of culture and an unbroken tradition in knowledge. Every teacher was anxious to assure the continuity of his school of Thought and for pupils who could contributed to that continuity.

Regarding the educational conditions of the period broadly speaking, there were evolved three different types of institutions for the spread of learning (1) Homes of teachers as Schools (2) Debating circles and Parishads (Academies) and (3) Conferences.

Firstly, there was the normal system under which the teacher, as a settled householder, admitted to his instruction pupils of tender age who, on the first dawn of consciousness, leave the home of their natural parents where their body was cared for and nurtured for that of spiritual parents where their mind and soul would be nourished. This entry into the preceptor's home was a sort of spiritual birth and hence a rebirth where the brahmacharin become a dviya and an antevasin. The admission of the pupil was formally made by the clebration of the specific ceremony of initiation. A typical instance of this institution may be again conveniently cited of Satyakama Jabala going to his preceptor's house as a young boy where he spends several years tending his cattle and later on he himself as a teacher, admits to his house as his pupil Upakosala Kamalayana who tends forces for twelve years.

Secondly, there was another type of institutions which ministered to the never-to-be satisfied needs of the advanced students whose quest of Truth and Knowledge did not cease with the period of formal studentship and necessarily elementary education but was continued into the hoseholder's state. Such students improved their knowledge by mutual discussions or by the instruction of renowned specialists and literary celebrities in search of whom they wandered through the country.

In this connection that the Upanisads themselves are in a sense to be regarded as the record and outcome of such academic disputations, the transactions, of the philosophic societies or circles of the literary celebrities of the times. They represent the results of the researches of advanced scholars with whom the pursuits and quests and who frequently met together to discuss and compare the results of their independent investigations.

They constitute a kind of knowledge a body of truths which could not usually and naturally be attained in the preliminary and preparatory period of formal pupilage under a system in which the student was to "sit down near" (upa+ni+sad, to sit down) his teacher for instruction. The various discussions of philosophical problems now embodied in the upanisads originally took place during the celebration of a great sacrifice. Literary disputations have always been the characteristic feature of such festive occassions. It was during such sacrificial sessions that Sukadeva recited the Bhagavatam to Janamejaya and Suta recited other puranas to Rishis.

Max Muller says that according to modern writers a Parishad ought to consist of twenty-one Brahmans, well versed in philosophy, theology and law. But in early periods a smaller number was considered sufficient. Gautama says that a parishad shall consist of at least the ten following members, namely four men who have completely studied the four vedas, three men belonging to the three orders enumerated first, and three men who know different institutes of law. In Vasishtha and Baudhrayana it is said that it shall consist of four men who each know one of the four vedas a student of the Mimasa, one who knows the Angas, one who recites the works on the sacred law and three Brahmans belonging to three different orders.

The ideal in ancient times appeared to have been that the parishad should consist of at least ten persons, but a smaller number might be regarded as suficient in case of necessity. Thus Parasara another ancient authority says that four or even three able men from amongst the Brahmans in a village who know the veda and keep the sacrificial fire, or three who have studied the vedas and the vedangas and know the law may well form a parishad. Or if they do not keep the sacrificial fire, five or three who have studied the vedas and the vedangas and know the law may well form a parishad. Of old sages who possess the highest knowledge of the divine self, who are twice born to perform sacrifices and have purified themselves in the duties of the vedas also may be considered as a parishad.

Although the exact composition of the parishad varies from place to place, the growth of specialization in studies is evident. The representatives of the three orders were a student a householder and a hermit or according to some authorities a student, a householder and an ascetic.

These Parishads were in some respects like judicial assemblies and in others like ecclesiastical synods, but as those who composed them were, most of them, also teachers, they correspond to a certain extent to the associations of teachers in the Middle Ages of Europe which developed into universities. Thus not only were different faculties represented but even a student was a member of the parishad. The settlement of Brahmans proficient in different branches of the ancient learning in various centres must have meant the gathering together also of a number of students who were receiving instruction from them, and thus these parishads would form the nucleus of something corresponding to a university.

This would be specially the case in some places where a large number of Brahman teachers were gathered together like towns or monastic institutions. An instance of an early brahmanic intellectual centre is Takshasila (or Taxila). It was a strong hold of Brahmanic learning as early as the fourth or fifth century B.C. and perhaps earlier. Here at the time of Alexander's invasion the Greeks first came into contact with the Brahman philosophers and were astonished at their asceticism and strange doctrines. Many other centres of learning, as for example, Benares and Nadia, became famous in later times. In Buddhist system of education it was the monastery which was the centre of learning. Monasteries have never had such an important place in Hinduism as in Buddhism but they have existed, and are still to be found.

We can understand well that Parishads (lit. sitting round) developed for the cultivation and propagation of learning. The term, as used in the Upanishads, means an assemblage of advisers in questions of philosophy. It was a settlement of Brahmanas, a community or college to which members of any charana might belong. It therefore rested on a broader basis than a charana which signified an ideal succession of teachers and pupils who learn and teach a certain branch of the Vedas. Thus member of the same Charana might be Fellows of different Parishads and Fellows of the same Parishad might be members of different Charanas. (The Charanas were practically the schools for the cultivation and propagation of particular texts of the Vedas). To sum up, we may say in modern pharaseology that a Parishad corresponds to a university comprising students belonging to different colleges called Charanas.

The Parishads lead to the third type of institutions developed for the spread of learning in these ancient times viz. Conferences. Besides the small circles of philosophical disputants and parishads or academies of different localities, there was occasionally summoned by a great king a national gathering or Congress in which the representative thinkers of the country of various schools were invited to meet and exchange their views. One such Congress of Rishis (the first of its kind in history) is reported in the Brihadaranyaka upanishad, the Satapatha Brahmana, and the Vayu Purana. King Janaka Videha performed a horsesacrifice to which he invited all the Brahmanas of the Kuru-Panchala country. The king offered a special prize of great value. (1000 cows with horns hung with gold) to the person "the best read." "the most learned in sacred writ" and "the wisest" and the prize was at once appropriated by Yahnavalkya. This was the signal for the great tournament of debate to begin, and Yajnavalkya's assumed superiority was challenged by seven representative scholars of the age who began to put a series of perplexing problems to Yagnavalkya requiring him to explain a large variety of points concerning the ritual, the gods, the soul, thesupreme cause of the world and the soul of all, good deeds, bad deeds, etc. The satisfactory answer that Yagnavalkya was able to give to each and all of the numerous questions by which his boasted and assumed supremacy was questioned at once won for him a country wide fame and demonstrated the versatile character of his learning and wisdom whereby he felt quite at home in problems ranging from the domain of the most abstract and subtle philosophy and eschatology. But he was challenged by the wise Gargi - the learned Brahman lady to state and describe the nature of unveiled Brahman the Atman which dwells in everything. The language of these debates, the medium of instruction in these times, was Sanskrit which was a spoken language then.

3.5.2. THE BUDDHIST MONASTERIES OF ANCIENT INDIA

Higher studies and teachings went within the limits of the Buddhist canon - Vinaya, Abhidharma or sutta. Generally speaking, the scope and nature of higher education in the monasteries were determined by the particular Buddhist school to which they belonged. The higher studies consisted of not only studying the advanced texts of religious and philosophical importance, but also conducting debates and discussions on the various doctrines of different creeds.

The viharas were the chief seats of education and centres of culture of the time. They were all residential colleges consisting of numerous students and teachers who partook and promoted a wide, collective academic life in them. They were the educational agencies of the time, through which education and culture were spread intensively and extensively throughout the land. They were sometimes called Sangharamas, to which, temples,libraries and schools were attached and in which dwelt wealthy communities of monks, who were allowed to hold property in land.

Besides the famous Buddhist universities at Nalanda, Taxila and Vikramashila Vanci, Puhar, Kanchi, Uragapuram, Bhutamangalam, Nagapattinam were some of the important centres of Buddhism in South India which produced outstanding schools and debators. Of all the centres, Kanchi deserves special mention in this connection. Kanchi was as old as Buddha himself which was the birth-place of Dharmapala. Hicum-Tsang gives a graphic account of Buddhism at Kanchi during the 7th century A.D. According to him, in the Pallava country, there were 100 monasteries and 10,000 brethren. The most important fact is that Dharmapala of Kanchi went to Nalanda University and becoming victorious in disputations, he rose to the position of the Head of the university.

As a general rule, along with Sanskrit, other subjects of Buddhist philosophy were taught to the students. The Chinese traveller Hieun - Tsang and I - Tsang refer to the study of secular subjects in the monasteries. They were the subjects like medicine, astrology, arts and crafts and other useful arts.

According to Hieun-Tsang, in the monasteries of India, there were many students entrusted to the bhiksus and they were ordained students (brahmacharis) of the Order. Besides regular students, there were unordained students called manavas. They were given instruction in the Buddhist scriptures. Both the manavas and brahmacharins were permitted to be in residence in the monasteries or could attend the classes as day scholars. Thus, the remarks of the traveller throw some welcome light on the catholic and generous attitude of the monks towards the progress of education in the country. They imparted education not only to persons belonging to their creed and way of life but also to one and all who came from various walks of life with a longing to learn something from the Buddhist monks.

As in the case of Jaina and Brahmanical systems, the instruction consisted mainly of "giving recitation, holding recitation, making e xhortation and explaining dharma. There were special lectures on specific topics.

The relations between the teacher and the students were cordial and affectionate. The teacher and the student moved so affectionately that they looked like father and son. As in the Brahmanical and Jaina system, the student was expected to do service to his teacher. The students in the viharas were also in charge of keeping their residential places very clean.

DISSCUSSIONS AND DEBATES:

Discussions and debates were also methods of education. In fact, Buddhism, being more proselytizing than other religions, was keen on cultivating its leaders and votaries, of the powers of debate by which, it could spread and win converts from other rival sects. Buddhist education made dialectic skill and ability in argumentation, a most important part of intellectual equipment essential to leadership. But these intellectual debates were practised not only by the Buddhists but also by the scholars belonging to different creeds from the days of the Upanisads.

Thus academic debates brought together scholars from distant and different parts of India and even from outside India and paved the way for the promotion of active intercourse between monasteries representing different schools of thought. There are instances which proved the scholarship and debating power of certain great Buddhist scholars of South India who went all the way to North Indian monasteries and gained victories and likewise many scholars from North came to the South. To mention according to Hieun Tsang, Nagar juna with the permission of his master went to the monastery called kukkutarama in Pataliputra, where, in a twelve day discussion, he defeated the tirthikas of that place. Another victory achieved by South Indian monks was that of Dinnaga at the Nalanda University and Hieun-Tsang on the merits of Yoga schools of philosophy. Commenting on the Buddhist system of education, Mookerji writes that not confining their sympathies and valued services within the limited boundaries of their own church and faith, they (the monks) thus became the Directors of Public Instruction in the country.

3.5.3 ARABIC MADRASAHA OF MEDIEVAL INDIAN

Muslims from very early time held education in highest reference. Muslims consider diffusion of learning as a sacred duty. With a motive of expanding Islamic religion, Muslim teaching was imparted. The spread of education was regarded as religious act and the money spent by the state for the cause of education was considered to have been spent on charity.

During the Muslim rule in India, education was imparted through (a) maktabs and madrasas, (b) mosques and monasteries and (c) private houses. Discussion method was adopted as a method of disseminating knowledge in those days. Mosques had schools attached to them. These schools were supported by state grants or by land-holders and nobles. The primary education was to be imparted through the maktabs and secondary through the madrasas.

In Islamic times education was thus diffused in the country by three fold means of maktabs and madrasas, mosques and monasteries, and private houses, typifying three forms of education viz: 1) university or higher education with undergraduate and post-graduate courses : 2) secondary education, which obtained in grammar schools, high schools and private academies: and (3) primary education imparting elementary knowledge.

The schools or colleges meant for the secondary and higher education of the Muslims were called madrasas. These madrasas were often attached to mosques, sometimes the tombs of Muslimem perors, nobles and dervishes had also madrasas attached to them. The madrasas grew up even before the beginning of the 12th century. These institutions had a strong religious bias, and the state sometimes patronized them. The religious creed and dogmas of Islam were preached through these institutions. Each seat of higher learning was meant for specialisation in a particular branch of knowledge. The students used to migrate constantly from one place to another in search of suitable teachers. Teachers and students were in constant and intimate touch with one another. Thus the pupils imbibed the methods of their teachers for widening their knowledge. Except in certain parts of India like East Bengal, Muslims were mainly urban people during the medieval period. So, unlike the Hindu Pandits, the Muslim scholars worked mainly in towns. Madrasas were established in both imperial and provincial capitals. As a result, Agra, Delhi, Lahore, Jaunpur, Gujarat, Sialkot, Ahmedabad and other cities became the main centres of higher education for the Muslims.

S.M. JAFFAR Education in Muslim India (1973) - .pp 27-28) asserts: "In the spiritually minded countries of the East, the chief aim of education has been to produce religious men. In Muslim India, it was to bring out the latent faculties of stuedents, to discipline the forces of their intellect and to equip them with all that was essential for their moral and material improvement. It was, in other words, the formation of character. Education was regarded as a preparation for life and for after death. Hence it was that religion was at the root of all study: Every maktab and madrasa had a mosque attached to it, and in every mosque there were separate classes for the instruction of students in science other than religious, so that secular education might go hand in hand with religious instruction."[3.3]

The subjects of the study were classified into two groups namely science and non-science. The subjects that required the exercise of intellect were included in the science group. Such science subjects were philosophy, astronomy, geometry, astrology, arithmetic and mechanics. The remaining subjects required the excercise of memory. In Muslim institutions, the course of study comprised of grammar, rhetoric, logic, theology, metaphysics, literature and jurisprudence. Astronomy, mathematics and medicine also were included in the syllabus.

METHODOLOGY OF TEACHING

In Muslim institutions, educations was imparted through the medium of Persian. In course of time due to the mixing of the Muslims with the Hindus, a new language (Urdu) was born: and this language for conversation in urdu became common in Northern India but it was not used as the medium of instruction during the sultante or the Mughal period.

Both teaching through prescribed books and learning by rote were in vogue. At the beginning of the Muslim rule the method of teaching was mostly oral, because of the want of convenient writing materials. It was Akbar who emphasized on the writing of the alphabet first for effective teaching. Seminars and discussions among students were also held for better understanding of the subjects; though the madrasas were residential institutions, yet day schoolars also were admitted and allowed to attend lectures. A good library was attached to every madrasas for the benefit of the students. The relation between teacher and taught in Muslim educational pattern also was like that of the old Indian system. It was based on mutual feelings of reverence and love. Such filial relation-

---

3.3 JAFFAR,S.M. (1973)Education in Muslim India (1000-1800 A.C) IDARAH - I ADABIYAT - I DELHI

ship as well as personal touch in education was in accordance with the social requirements. Teacher paid individual attention to the pupils. The mutual contact had greatly influenced the life of the students and facilitated the development of his capacities and abilities. Able and brilliant students got ample opportunities to display their worth.

The intimate relationship between them inculcated the spirit of discharging their duties in the right way. The students while rendering services to the teacher, learnt to behave properly and respect the learned.

Moral and manners, sincerity, good habits were to be cultivated and its sole responsibility was of the ustad. Performance of daily prayer was essential for the moral improvement of the disciple. The students in the medieval period were well behaved and disciplined.

In the spiritually-minded countries of the East, the chief aim of education has been to produce religious men. Quran prescribes the path of well-being in the present world and well-being in the hereafter. Muslim education in India envisaged for people a discipline for the material as well as spiritual progress. Through education Islamic faith and beliefs were communicated to all the sectors of society. That is why, Muslim education touched not only the spiritual but simultaneously the material needs of people as well as a minimum necessity, irrespective of their individual temperament.

Hence it was that religion was at the root of all study. Every maktab and madrasa had a mosque attached to it, and in every mosque there were separate classes for the instruction of students in science other than religious so that secular education might go hand in hand with religious instruction.

Jaffer says (Education in Muslim India 1973) that "Religion the backbone of Indian culture and civilization, was once the root of all study."

3.5.4 GHATIKAS, SABHAS AND AGRAHARAS, MATHAS AND SALAI AS CENTRES OF HIGHER LEARNING IN SOUTH INDIA

Education in South India in ancient and medieval times was generally religious and based largely on Sanskritic and Tamil learning in its scope and orientation because of the fact that the ancient literature, particularly the four Vedas and their auxiliaries were believed to contain all the essence of true knowledge and the acquisition of such knowledge was considered necessary for equipping oneself for leading a good and full life. Education in those days was not exclusively literary for the study of subjects like fine arts, technical and other useful arts also received equal attention and patronage and enjoyed a status equal to that of literary studies.

Education was largely a private concern of the people, though kings and others of power and influence gave encourage-ment to the prevailing system of education and learning. The aim of education in South India as in North India was not only intellectual, moral, religious and spitritual but also to equip people for different persuasions and service to society.

The sources which supply information about education in South India fall mainly into two groups: (1) epigraphical records and (2) the contemporary literature. Of the two groups, the former supplies the bulk of the material. The epigraphical records of the period from the 4th to the 13th centuries contain much information, particularly about the establishment and organisation of Ghatikas, Temple, College and other types of institutions which worked for the preservation and spread of education in South India. In ancient and medieval South India, education was promoted mainly by institutions like the Ghatika, Matha, Agrahara Temple and Salai. These institutions served as great residential colleges and provided facilities for the study of religious literature and secular subjects.

A) GHATIKA:

Ghatika was identified with Gosthi and was stated as an establishment consisting of groups of holy and learned Brahmanas in each case founded by a king. Of all the ghatikas in South India. the one which existed in Kanchi during the days of the Pallavas was more important from the point of view of education and politics. Ghatika had been a centre of advanced studies - a centre of Vedic learning Famous Ghatika like that of Kanchi attracted scholars and teachers from different parts of the country. Sanskrit learning with religious background (e.g. Sanskrit learning and Vaishnavism in Ghatika at Sholingan hill of North Arcot Distt., Tamil Nadu was the characteristic feature of Ghatika. Thus a Ghatika was a centre of learning and religion and small in size.

B) SABHAS & AGRAHARAS:

The cause of learning and culture was not confined, however, to these Schools or College. Accordingly the public benefactions established educational institutions of a wider scope, serving as centres of post-graduate advanced study under sevants devoting themselves completely to the pursuit of knowledge for its own sake. These endowments of higher learning research sought to establish entire learned settlements or cultured colonies, made up of households of pious and scholarly Brahmans, in select areas.

These learned settlements (sabhas) were centres of light and life, showing how theory and practice should go together, how precept should be supported by example, ethics by conduct, learning was to be lived, and truth or religion was to be realized in the activities of daily life. The cause of learning was thus very well served by these endowments supporting advanced scholars in a life of research and religion and pursuit of Truth for its own sake, to the exclusion of all other pursuits.

Sometimes, advantage was taken of these learned settlements or Sabhas to judge of literary works of authors. The Sabha met under a royal order and heard the work of a poet recited. On its verdict, the poet was granted land as reward of his merits. It was a relic of the old and famous Sangams which judged the works of Tamil poets and upheld the standard of Tamil Literature.

The Tamil Academy was also regarded as a kind of educational institution. The first Academy was held at Madura, the second at Kavatapuram and the third at Uttar Madura. These associations of learned men summoned by kings from time to time to set the standard in Tamil style, to regulate the state patronage and to set the stamp of approval on works conforming to the standard. They remind us of the Babylonian Academy (the Metibta) which convoked a general Assembly (the kalla) twice a year, when a treatise previously announced was brought and discussed. Among the titles bestowed by the Tamil Sangam we find Asiriyar (Sanskrit, acarya) Pulavar (pandita) and Kavi chakravarti (prince of poets). It also made gifts of land and money. Mysore was abundant in wider cultural institutions which were known in three distinct varieties called Ghatika, Agrahara and Brahmapuri.

(C) AGRAHARAS

The gift of tax-free village or lands given for the maintenance of the Brahmanas is called brahmadeya. The brahmadeya villages are also variously known by other names agrahara, agaram, caturvedimangalam and brahmapuri, proclaiming that they mainly contained Brahmana population. The Brahmana villages are called Caturvedimangalam in the inscriptions mostly coming from the Tamil country. The term brahmapuris was widely prevalent in the Karnataka country to mean a Brahmana village or a settlement of Brahmanas in cities and towns. Big cities and towns had several brahmapuris: For instance, under the patronages of the Hoysalas, a number of brahmapuris were created in Talkad and Manyapura. The agrahara and caturvedimangalams were generlly named after the kings, queens and other distinguished persons whose benefaction caused the formation of these villages.

The main purpose of the establishment of numerous agraharas by successive generations of kings of various dynasties in South India was to accelerate the progress of Vedic learning and culture in the country which ultimately resulted in the downfall of rival sects like Jainism and Buddhism. The agraharas were considered as centres of higher education and served as abodes of learned scholars and profesors. They consisted of educational establihments like ghatikas, Salais, kandikas, mathas and temples besides being themselves repositiories of knowledge and learning. In the words of R.K. Mookerji an agrahara was a wider institution a whole settlement of learned Brahmanas with its own powers of Government and means of maintenance granted by generous donors who founded them.

It this is so of the Brahmanas, the Sabha in the agraharas also availed of the opportunity and did what all was necessary to encourage the learned scholars by way of organising celebration of plays, entertaining the visiting Mahajanas and scholars, arranging of disputations, expositions and interpretation of new and conflicting doctrine by the learned besides discharging their normal duties. In the record, it is stated that the Sabha met under a royal order and heard the work of a poet recited and, on its verdict he was granted land as a reward for his Sangams which judged the works of Tamil poets and upheld the standard of Tamil literature.

Thus these learned settlements were centres of light and life, showing how theory and practice should go together, how precept should be supported by example, ethics by conduct, and truth or religion was to be realised in the activities of daily life. Referring to Karnataka, Vatapi, the capital of the Chalukyas was a flourishing agrahara, adorned by the presence of several thousands of Brahamanas, who were proficient in the "fourteen vidyas" during the time of Vijayaditya (end of the 7th century)

C) MATHAS:

The interest of education and learning were served by a variety of institutions supported by religions endowments. The College proper sprang up as annexes of the Temples, while their work received a wider scope in a more extended sphere in institutions like the Mathas and settlements of learned men functioning like the Academies of science of modern times. The Mathas specially are indigenous Indian examples of educational organization by which different and distant centres of culture and religious life, religious brotherhoods of different localities, are affiliated to a central and common seat of the authority at head quarters and regulated and controlled by it. The temple and the matha were two of the great gifts of medieval Hinduism to South India. These mathas gradully spread all over South India and secured a position of ascendency over the Buddhist viharas and Jaina pallis. Both Saiva and Vaishnava mathas were founded by the followers of the respective creeds throughout South India. But the process of establishing mathas gained momentum only during the 10th century and afterwards it became a common feature to attach mathas to temples. It may even be said that almost every temple had one or more mathas functioning in close proximity to it.

These mathas just like the monasteries of medieval Europe were important religious institutions, maintained by the wealth, they possessed. They also recovered royal patronage. In the most cases, the mathas were located within the precincts of the temples or very near them.

The mathas were founded not only by the ruling sovereigns and their chiefs but also by some communities and by private individuals who came from various walks of life. The establishment of mathas was in those days considered as an act of religious merit and found encouragement even at the hands of foreigners.

Mathas were also built to perpetuate the memory of certain great acaryas. Some of the Saiva Nayanmars are also said to have founded mathas and encouraged learning. The religious life and culture of the Tamil country were very largely influenced by numerous Saiva Mathas which acquired great power and popularity under the Chola Kings. The Mahas of Sivayogins or Mahesvaras were also great cultural influences in those days.

The mathas were each presided over by a sanyasin or a pandita who was invariably a cultural ecclesiastic and whose duty was not only the management and administration of the matha but also encouragement of learning. They were not merely sanyasins or religious heads but also scholars well versed in various branches of knowledge. Since the heads of the mathas were learned scholars, they played a vital role in society as spritual guru in the propagation of dharma as well as literacy among the people. They not only expounded the Saiva or Vaishnava tenets but also propagated the message of moral condut to their disciples and those who thronged in numbers to hear them.

The members of the matha were called here madattu cattapperumakkal (the learned elite of the mathas). The educational activity of the matha lies in the the inscription of learning viz. Mimamsa, Vyakarna and Paurohitya in addition to the Veda and vested with the management of the entire properties of not only the Salabhoga but also of the devadana of the temple attached to the salai.

Kanchi has been considered as one of the earliest religious centres in the South, the history of which is woven with the growth of many cultural activities right from the days of Patanjali. The existing monuments of both the Saiva and Vaishanava creeds (temple and mattas) together with the contemporary literature and chronicles, especially of the Chinese Traveller Hieun- Tsang including a few place names like Jinakanchi bear testimony to the religious and cultural importance of this place which was undoubtedly connected with Buddhism, Jainism, Saivism and Vaishnavism. It was this place which felt the wonderful touch of very great religious personalities of South India like Appear, Sankara and Sri Ramanuja and attracted scholars and religious teachers both from the rest of India and abroad, a fact which remains undoubted and of India and abroad, a fact which remains undoubted and unchallenged even today. It has been pointed out earlier that it was here that we find the existence of one of the earlier mathas in South India.

The Advaita philosopher Sankara is said to have founded a matha at Kanchi after having won the Buddhists in a controversy. Later literary works which deal with the life and activities of Sankara also speak of the establishment of Kamakoti Pitha in Kanchi (8th century A.D.). For the conversion of the common mass Sankaracharya is said to have founded Vidyapithas with a great teacher presiding over each. One such was the Kanchipuram Vidyapitha. Others were at four important corners of India Sarada (Badrika) in the North, Puri in the East, Dwaraka in the West and Sringeri in the South, In theory the Vidyapitha was an expansion of the old Gurukulas but in practice it was modelled on the Saiva mathas. Logic and Grammar were taught free as also Vedic and Vedantic lore. Students were fed free of cost in most cases by liberal endowments made by the generous public.

The Tamil Saiva mathas concentrated on the development of religious literature and took special interest in training students in the art of reciting religious texts like the Tirujnanam and Tirumurai. In some of the mathas, provision was made for reciting the Tirumurai and Tirujnanam and reading the Agamas.

Though mathas appear to have been primarily seminaries for imparting religious education, they at the same time disseminated secular knowledge as well.

D) SALAI:

The word 'Salai' is referred to as a feeding house either attached to a temple or as an independent one carrying out the task of feeding Brahmanas and students and servants of the temple. It is also referred to as aracalai (dharmasala) and named after kings and queens besides religious personalities. Students admitted into this institution were called catar which suggests that they were all learned scholars pursuing higher studies or imparting lessons to advanced students. Further , the members of the institution both, teachers and students, were all called by the same word 'cattar'. If a student desires to become a member of salai, he must satisfy the following qualifications:

1. He must duly be certified on earth by five catar that he is proficient in Vyakarana, Mimamsa and Paurohitya.
2. He must be free from the fault of forgetfulness.
3. He must have knowledge or learning necessary to acquaint himself with the affairs of the three kingdoms.

The particular portion of the record clearly suggests that the scholar who got admitted to this salai were really proficient in several branches of learning and well versed in the method of varam recitation. Therefore, it may be said that the salai at the place was not an ordinary institutes of learning but a centre of higher education.

3.7 CONCLUDING REMARKS:

A glance through the evolutionary process of education in many a civilization of world be it occidental or oriental , the seeds of education were laid on the soil of religion of the people Religion formed the basis for the development of educational process. In short, 'faith' was the beginning of intellectual pursuit. In terms of phiolosophy, ontological background was the first and foremost background for developing education. Gradually, in the intellectual pursuit of faith man acquired more and more information to supplement his quest which ultimately land him in the pursuit of knowledge. The quest for knowledge made him thirsty of more and more information which might be more abstract and universal. This unquenchable thirst for knowledge made him resort to highly sophisticated mental proceses which were the results of his rigorous mental training. Although religion inspires the pursuit of truth it also constricts it and academic freedom becomes a demand asserted against religion. Slowly man drifted away from the pursuit of faith to the quest for knowledge.

In brevity religious pursuits were tinged with secular interests which unravelled the wonders of the phenomenal world to man. Secular interests were socialised and institutionlised by man for the posterity and hence appeared the agencies of education to transmit the rich heritage to the furture. Social agencies like home, society and state systematised the transmission of rich heritage and formal agencies of education appeared in the society to teach the younger generation in gradation. Love of learning made man go higher and higher the educational ladder and his devotion to academic pursuit resulted in the innovation of a centre exclusively for advancement in learning.

From this chapter it has become evident that the universities were institutions of adult and higher learning and such institutions developed only after the appearance of settled civilization. According to Basil Fletchei the first of these institutions of adult learning were the Forest Ashramas of India, the origin of which is traced back to as far as 1500 B.C by the Hindu. In comparison to the Forest Ashramas of India there were other early centres of civilization which had their own forms of higher education. It has been observed that in Mesopotamia there had been institution of higher learning connected with temple and libraries where subjects such as astronomy, medicine, architecture and engineering were taught and wherein qualified youngmen were required to undergo periods of internship under a master of his chosen profession. In Egypt Heliopolis had been a popular centre of higher learning. Excavations have unearthed a ruined building the bricks of which are stamped with the words "THE HOUSE OF LIFE (the Egyptian term for university) along with lists of names of regency professors of that university.

It has been inferred that the university refers to an educational institutions designed for instruction or examination or both of students in all or many of the more important branches of advanced learning. Conferring degrees and other academic distinctions, often embodying colleges or similar institutions, members of this collectively representing a university. The term contextually includes institutions of higher education similar in status and purpose to those referred to a universities in the Middle. Ages as seen earlier in this chapter. However, the very term university had not risen in the educational horizon until the beginning or the thirteenth century. Etymologially the word 'university' means whole. In the Middle Ages it was used to mean every trade guild of mechanics or artisans or every corporation of men associated together in a common enterprise. Literally the word "University" means a union of persons with a common interest.

The universities could be seen as organisations, as institutions or as communities. They exist to achieve concrete ends which on the whole, are capable of rational analysis. The university's main objective is the advancement of learning and thought. The arts and sciences liberally conceived at the centres of the university's concern and enterprise feed actively into searching thought. They tell us what the best of men have thought and felt and discovered in their forthest reaches of mind and imagination. They bring us into touch with those great currents of thought and understanding. Part of this pulse and life is the spirit of free rowing critical inquiry coupled to an open view about the nature of truth. And it follows that a root of function of a university is that it be dedicated stubbornly to the pursuit of improved knowledge, understanding light, in all of its teaching and all of its research.

4

THE CONCEPT OF A UNIVERSITY

4.1 INTRODUCTION

Education is a social institution for regulating the life of mankind. Education has always played an important part in preparing men for life in society and moulding them accordingly. Whether directly or indirectly, overtly or covertly, educational purposes, content of education, processes by which education is imparted and the institutional system of education are at any point of time, shaped according to the needs, demands and aspirations of society. Vice versa, society is deeply influenced by the education which is provided for its members.

Educational institutions are generally considered to be highly conservative. This is because cultural reproduction is one of the primary effects of formal systems of education. In fact one of its essential functions is that of repetition, to repeat to each generation the knowledge that the previous generation has inherited from its forebears. It is therefore normal for educational system to be given the job as in the past of handing down the traditional values. However, education may also connote a system of institutions organised by society to deliberately transmit its cultural heritage, its accumulated knowledge, values and skills from one generation to another. The educational system of a society would, accordingly, comprise institutions such as schools, colleges, universities including teachers, administrators, curricula and courses, examination and certification procedure and so on. In fact, educational institutions are considered key instruments of social purpose in most modern societies and education, from the point of view of society, is a process of transmission of culture.

Of all the educational institutions, the university is esteemed as the prestigious institution in the hierarchy of the formal educational ladder connected with higher education. The university is undoubtedly a unique social institution. It is unique social institution. It is unique because of its role as "social critic". Universities do not create new knowledge only but also subject all social, economic, political and philosophical matters to scholarly scrutiny and so provide new insight into every aspect of our life. Therefore, this "social critic" role of the universities has emerged as one of the important roles in society.

4.2 THE UNIVERSITY-AN INSTITUTION OF HIGHER EDUCATION

The university was an institution which was universal in as much as it gathered students or scholars from many lands (territorial universality) and pursued knowledge of various kind (intellectual universality) at the higher levels within a single unit. The universal milieu in terms of people as well as knowledge conducive to free enquiry, to fertilisation of ideas across disciplinary boundaries and to research as well as teaching. According to the concise Dictionary of Education by Gene R. Hawes. Lynne Salop Hawes (A Hudson Group Book published by Van Nostrand Reinhold Company Inc. New York, 1982), university is an institution of higher education; in actual practice, institutions with the term university in their names, range from small enrollment colleges, awarding the bachelor's degree to large enrollment institutions with many constituent undergraduate and graduate schools offering programmes of bachelor's, master's doctoral and post doctoral study. Generally it is thought that the term applies most approximately to an institution with several constituent schools, broad undergraduate offering and graduate offerings through the doctorate.

Schools and Colleges are not something apart from the social order to which they belong. They are that order trying to prepare its youth for participation in its own activities and a society can only teach the hopes, the knowledge, the values and the beliefs which it has.

Alexander Meikkyohn, while discussing the Experimental Colleges, states that the universities are recognised symbols of cultural traditions, cultural tradition still conceived as a directing force, representing a wisdom older than modern civilization and having an authority that should check and control the blind drive onward of material and mechanical development with its human consequences.

According to the Dictionary of Education, Foundations in Education, editor Canter V. Good, Winifred R. Merkel, McGraw Hill Book Company Inc. New York, 1957, university is an institution of higher education consisting of a liberal arts college, offering a programme of graduate study, and having usually two or more professional schools or faculties and empowered to confer degrees in various fields of study; (2) an organisation that includes the recognized secondary and higher educational institutions of a state and certain other institutions for education for e.g. the university of the state of New York; (3) the institution of higher education that grew up in Europe in the later Middle Ages, from which all modern forms of higher education are descended provided instructions in the seven liberal arts, medicine, law and theology.

The word 'university' comes from the Latin Universities magistrorum scholarium univarsitas may is trodom et sko-lare-dm) meaning a company of masters and scholars. It refers to a national group of students attending one of the larger medieval universities in Europe. In short, university is a community of scholars who are in search of intellectual pursuit. This is well evident from a glance at the educational history of the Medieval Europe. During this period inspite of a political and military turmoil which largely yoked mens endeavour to the barest practicalities of life, a collection of cathedral schools came into existence, becoming in time the soil in which universities could grow. In the 12th century a collection of intellectual endeavour- editing, collecting, systematizing culminated in bands of scholars setting up studia generalia. These were places of learning which, by virtue of the fames of their teachers, could attract students from all over Christendom; it was precisely this universal significance which made such studia also generalia. The two centres which became by virtue of considerable distinction the models of later foundations were Paris and Bologna; but they were rapidly succeeded by many other centres so that the network of such institutions soon stretched in Europe from Spain at one end and to Poland to Bohemia at the other. In Paris, the scholars, and in Bologna the students found it advantageous to band together into a legal corporation and consequently acquired the term 'universities' a term which was used of any kind of legal association towards the end of the middle ages; it was restricted to what we now call universities. This organisational character of universities is in a number of respects just as important as their intellectual distinction for it is here that we find the secret of that astonishing longevity, that capacity for decay and revival which has marked the university out as distinct from any of the other scholarly institutions of other times and other civilization. In words of Rashdall, universities were products of that instinct of association which swept like a great wave over the towns of Europe in the course of the eleventh and twelfth centuries, until political sovereignty began to impair their independence, they excercised the corporate freedom of feudalism to the full.

Universities have been founded for all manners of reasons: to preserve an old faith, to proselytize a new one, to train skilled workers, to raise the standards of the professions, to expand the frontiers of knowledge, and even to educate the young. Max Weber views these as four models, known as "ideal types". These four models are: the university as a Sancturay of Scholarship; the university as a Training Camp for the Professi-onal; the university as a Social Service Station and the university as an Assembly Line for Establishment for Man. The first model is drawn from the history of the university; the second model reflects its present character; the third is a projection of the present trends and thus is a prediction of the shape of the university, an anti-model, as it were.

Whatever may be the model, the university is a part of the society. It can play a role in changing society by changing the thinking of young people, by putting new findings about the society before the society, by creating new knowledge which may call for new products, services and even new modes of management. This intricate relationship requires the higher educational system to be a living and dynamic entity. If it turns passive and only carries out the orders of those who at anytime are at the help of affairs in society, it fails in providing positive impusles for changing the society for the better.

From the view-point of society, education is a process of transmission of culture. By culture, here we mean a great deal more than mere art, music or literature. It refers to the total way of life of a society- its knowledge, beliefs, attitudes, values, skills and behaviours patterns. Education can be considered as mechanism by which society inducts its members into its ways of life and beliefs. It is partially responsible for the transfer from one generation to the next of society beliefs, values, sentiments, knowledge and patterns of behaviour. Apart from transmitting the best in the culture, higher education functions also as the creator and critique of culture. A major contribution of higher education has been refinement of culture leading to differentiation of knowledge into various desciplines and specialization. Advance-ment of the frontiers of knowledge, discovery of newer technologies and their application in industry, business and agriculture to make man's life better have also been the contribution of higher education. Further, higher education acts as a critique of the society. It is only free and fearless thinking of the intellectual elite that has generated new ideas and banished prejudices and irrational beliefs. Colleges and universities are centres of creative thought and discovery and all contemporary educational institutions disseminate new knowledge and values to younger generations. Because they disseminate new knowledge and attitude, educatio-nal institutions can be used to create new elite strata or promote greater social equality. They can both modify and transform traditional institutions and become bases of rebellion or revolution. Higher education in this respect, stimulates and encourages cultural change in traditional socieities.

4.3 THE FUNCTIONS OF THE UNIVERSITIES IN GENERAL

The university, as we know it, evolved in the Middle Ages in Europe. There were, other more ancient forms of higher learning in China, in India, and in the Islamic world. But of the various types that emerged only the university grew, adapted itself to new conditions, survived and flourished. The university is one among the oldest of institutions in Western society. Its durability and its success relate, in part, at least, to the mission, the organisation, the ethos that evolved in the early European universities some eight hundred years ago. In some respects the Middle Ages did not provide the most fertile soil for the growth of universities. Elements of Dark Ages violence superstition, license, barbarism remained deeply embedded in the European society.

But there were other conditions that favoured the growth of higher learning. One was economic development: all material indexes moved upward from the eleventh century on. Economic development was accompanied by the growth of cities, the spread of commerce, the creation of a new social class of men involved on trade and commerce, increased wealth and increased leisure. A new society was emerging which required trained administrators, lawyers, physicians and theologians. These needs called for a higher learning than was provided by the many cathedral schools which flourished in the eleventh century. A form of post secondary education was required and the universities emerged to meet the need. Incessant thirst for knowledge that occured in the early centuries approximated an explosion of knowledge from Arabia, the rediscovery of Roman Law and the translation of Aristotelian logic. This new knowledge was to stimulate and nourish men's natural interest in learning and to provide new content and purpose for the early universities. The changing economic, social and intellectual climate made the creation of universities possible and indeed necessary.

The early universities were informal unstructured and spontaneous organisations. Individual teachers and students associated, joined forces and read and studied together. Only gradually did these "gatherings" became structured and grew into formal organisations which at some uncertain date were incorporated and recognised as universities. The first universities were those of Bologna, Paris, Salerno, Oxford and Cambridge, formally organised in that order and all began in the later eleventh or early twelfth century. These are the universities from which the modern university derives its most important heritage. It is often said that these early universities were centres of pure scholarship and humanistic study by which it is usually meant that they were concerned with what is now called Liberal Arts. But the great university historian Rashdall says that the rapid multiplication of universities during the fourteenth and fifteenth centuries was largely due to a direct demand for highly educated lawyers and administrators. In a sense the academic discipline of the Middle Ages was too practical. It trained pure intellect, encouraged habits of laborious subtlety, heroic industry and intense application, while it left uncultivated the imagination, the taste, the sense of beauty in a word, all the amenities and refinements of the civilized intellect. From a more practical point of view their greatest service to mankind was simply thus that they placed the administration of human affairs - in short the government of the world - in the hands of educated men. Here the scholar is bound to recall Plato's utterance Philosophers are kings. Belonging to one of the oldest and noblest families of Athens aristocracy whose members used to take part in governing the state, Plato also felt a leaning towards statemanship. For Plato was convinced that any state must perish if its rulers were not philosophers, and philosophy meant to him the ability to perceive the world of Ideas, immaterial, Forms which contain the true and ultimate realities while the world of sensible things is only a vague transitory and untrustworthy copy. Only the cognition of the Ideas enables man to act with wisdom. The rules of rightful conduct of human life were derived by Plato from the laws that rule the universe.

The early universities were indeed vocationally oriented to create leaders for the state and the church and practitioners in law and medicine. But as the institutions evolved, marked differences appeared. The Italian universities tended to emphasize the practical: the professions of law, medicine, theology and administration whereas Paris, Oxford and Cambridge were soon dominated by doctors of theology who taught what became known as the seven liberal arts : grammar, dialectics, rhetoric, geometry, arithmetic, astronomy and music. It is this latter form and tradition which took root in England and later spread to the United States and Canada. It is universally accepted that the threefold purpose of liberal education is to learn to know nature, society and ourselves, to acquire certain skills such as clear expression and grasp of the scientific method and discipline and finally to embrace certain values such as intellectual honesty, tolerence and the capacity for wise judgement.

Universities are criticized for their devotion to the academic ideal. This criticism is not only of modern origin but of historical tradition. From the seventeenth century to the twentieth there has been a continuous tradition of attack on universities which takes the form of regretting their isolation from the world and which despises their monkish erudition. This tradition stretches from Leibnitz's desire that universities should become centre where savants and students should participate as much as they can with other people and in the world to the twentieth century demands that universities should become more relevant to the present time.

Now the university is one of few places where the individual can be greater than the group and his imaginnings given free play. The university is a place, where, if teaching is sound, students learn to do their own thinking and their own reflecting. Robert F. Goheen describes the human nature of a university thus: The Modern University is involved in no less than the survival of our civilization and the future of the human race. No other institutions or agencies in our society are so particularly designed and dedicated to the large and essential task of searching for clarity and understanding of trying to see the requirements of our civilization steadily and whole, of developing the root knowledge on which wise action depends; It is he universities who are engaged in preserving and re-examing ideas and knowledge, always looking to the relation between the individual and the state. It is universities who insist on man's duty and right to think otherwise, and to say so and who habitually seek to bring the light of reason to the understanding and conduct of human affairs. Robert F. Goheen uses the pronoun 'who' rather than which deliberately to understand the fact that persons, not places perform these functions and that the university is a human institution. As an institution in time and space, the university cannot be immune to the effect of turbulence in the general society. It has, further more, the fundamental obligation to put the power of critical intelligence to work on society's problems - through both research and teaching.

In the Society of Man, Louis-Halle presents an image of the scholar's role which expresses the most critical function of the university in relation to society. The scholars business is direction. He is like the navigator of a ship who does not himself take the wheel but makes the calculations on the basis of which the actions of the man at the wheel can be addressed as opportunity serves, to a purpose beyond the immediate moment. If the sea is chaotic the man at the wheel will have to be preoccupied with every looming wave that threatens the ship, and will have to act quickly either to evade or meet it, even though this means acting with apparent inconsistency, turning first in one direction, then in another. But these waves are not the navigators business and he will only confuse himself and the helmsman if he tries to make them his business. His business is to see beyond "the transient and the complicated" and to make known what he sees, so that ship can, in the long run realize a purpose beyond that of survival in the present so that it can have direction.

The arts and sciences, liberally conceived at the centres of the university's concern and enterprise feed actively into searching thought. They tell us what the best men have thought and felt and discovered in their furthest reaches of mind and imagination bring us into touch with those great currents of thought and understanding. Part of this pulse and life is the spirit of free-moving, critical inquiry coupled to an open view about the nature of truth. And it follows that a root function of a university is that it be dedicated - stubbornly dedicated to the pursuit of improved knowledge understanding light in all of its teaching and all of its research.

Literally the word "University" means a union of person with a common interest. Knowledge and professions divide into branches, specialists, sub-specialities and sub-sub-specialities. In some measure at least, the modern university has helped to create the restless currents of this era. It has done so by its searching inquisitive spirit and the change it has helped to effect- especially through science and technology in the ways in which men think, work, communicate and spend their leisure. In other ways too, what happens in universities these days has great consequence outside their classrooms and laboratories, Industry, government and the professions all depend heavily upon the knowledge, insight skills and talents which are cultivated and made available in universities. From the aforesaid realities, it is understood that the cardinal function of a university is to be a place where searching, inquiry and sober reflection, are the order of the day. All other activities of a university properly grow out of these. It is the university's responsibility to bring about sound innovation in every field, and this includes its own: that is the field of higher education. Of the aims of a liberal education, the most critical is that of providing the impetus or momentum that makes an individual want to go on inquiring and learning long after his formal education ends.

As seen from the development of the university, the scholar feels that the role of university is not static but dynamic. Universities are adaptable to the dynamic changes in the society and rise up to meet the demanding situations and requirements of the society from time to time. This is very well reflected from the views of Rogen Dillemans: the universities in terms of their two main tasks - research and education - and above all focuses on the essential link between the two : the education given in universities and which should be part of a general plan for education and training differs from other types of higher education because it is scientific; in other words it is based on long term willing to share the research they undertake and feed the results into the educational process.

Through these two functions and above all by combining them effectively the universities are already taking their irreplace-able position in preparing for the third millennium, and will have a decisive impact on the first decades of the twenty first century. Around these two axes, they are rapidly emerging from the long tradition of the medieval universitas studiorum having passed through the era of von Hum Boldt and Newman, and decades of isolation devoted to training in the few major and much sought - after liberal professions. Now, after years of direct hard and critical confrontations with society some of them are finally becoming true centres of excellence in Europe, North America and recently in Japan. At this point in their history, the universities are discovering new tasks and responsibilities towards society and are deploying new techniques and methods of teaching that are beginning to operate alongside the traditional forms : correspondence course telecasting Open University etc, aimed at new groups (as in the case of continuing education or at the whole community).

The definition of the vocation of the university is complex as far as the objectives are concerned. Briefly they could be described as "having a vertical and a horizontal mission : pursuing deeper knowledge by bringing together existing knowledge and scientific research, as well as spreading knowledge in an organised manner and making it available to the whole community.[4.1]

The university's main objective is the advancement of learning and thought - not its government or any other activity. But if universities are first of all associations of human beings, diverse and variously organized, they nevertheless have significant things in common : All are basically concerned with the advancement of learning. All seek to carry on their proper work in an atmosphere of freedom : freedom to pursue truth where it leads, and to talk about it. Its true goals are not preuse targets, but high ideals, the enrichment of the minds and lives of its students, its advancement of knowledge the increase of understanding among men and the unending search for truth.

What is the service of the University? The institution is tradition and old fashioned. Its greatest service is in its commitment to reason, in its search for basic knowledge, in its mission to preserve and to give continuity to the values of mankind's many cultures. The university's role is not based upon a conception of neutrality or indifference to society's problems but an approach to the problems through the only strength which a university is entitled to assert. It is a conservative role because it values cultures and ideas, and reaffirms the basic commitment to reason. It is revolutionary because of its compulsion to discover and to know. It is modest because it recognizes that the difficulties are great and the standards demanding.

Aptly described by Amrik Singh, "knowledge skills and insight are the three basic functions which ought to be performed by any university"[4.2]

4.1 Dillemans, Roger : Autonomy, Responsibility and Responsiveness of Higher Education Institutions after 1992. Pages 333-334. European Journal of Education, Vol 24 No. 4 1989 (Higher Education and Europe after 1992)

4.2 Singh Amrik: University in 21st century - A third world view: (P.223) Economic and Political weekly vol. xxvii No.5 Feb 1, 1992 (A Sammeeksha Trust Publication, Bombay.

The university is undoubetedly a unique social institution, Many of the universities of today have outward appearance of the traditional model. Hence it is hard to find examples which fully reproduce the structure and function. For that reason it is appropriate to list the main feature which form the basis of the university, as revealed by the fifteenth centuries of life.

1. It is by its nature universal

2. It must be a community of scholars with internal autonomy rested in the community

3. It should offer both scholarship and professional training to its students.

4. It should attack the frontiers of knowledge

5. It should allow and be allowed academic freedom and

6. It should have certain privileges in order to carry out its mission

The university is a part of the society, yet it is an autonomous social entity by itself. Features such as autonomy, accountability and academic freedom give it a unique character and simultaneously help it in its discharge of obligations, to itself and to the society at large. The early universities were relatively informal, unstructured and spontaneous organizations. As stated earlier, individual teachers and students associated suit. Only gradually did these gatherings became structured and grew into formal organisations which were later on incorporated and recognized as universities. There was a buoyance and zestfulness in the early medieval university. The main impression is one of dynamic institutions exploring new fields of intellectual thought with stimulating teachers and enthusiastic students. Both students and teachers travelled back and forth to various universities, carrying with them new ideas and views that stimulated intellectual debate and nourished university growth. Ideas of austerity, chastity and religious devotion were prevalent. As the university gradually became more formalized and institutionalized some of its vitality was to diminish. But while it prevailed, the range of subjects, the intensity of study and the passion of debate were such that the true mission of the university was established in the minds of scholars for centuries thereafter as being the enthusiastic uninhabited, unfeltered search for knowledge in all forms and in every manner.

In every institutions the formative years are of great importance. It is at these times, that ideology is conceived, structure developed and customs formed that soon become institutionalized and difficult to change. For instance, once the European medieval universities were established there could be only two directions of newness in the idea of a university: one with respect to who should enter, the other with respect to what he or she should learn. It was natural that the early universities should reflect the society in which they were born. The old knowledge suddenly rediscovered the need for learned men in new professions and the expansion of wealth and leisure all stimulated the growth in advanced learning. Thus was the mission of the university formed : advanced sophisticated learning, free of external censure, meeting the interests of individual scholars yet serving the needs of medieval society.

It was inevitable also that the structure and practices of the university would be drawn from the established institutions of the day - the Church, the monastery, the guild or commune. From the church was borrowed the idea of the supranational organization, something above and beyond parochial interests : a hierarchy in the form of a chancellor, a rector, a dean, rituals such as convocation and colourful dress in the form of academic gowns. From the monastery came the idea of separat-eness - an institution insulated from the practical world, a self-governing community to make its own rules and develop its own way of life. From the guild came the concept of a community of individuals bound together by an oath of mutual support and common obedience to elected officials and with authority to select its own members. Other practices emerged spontaneously as a variety of problems were met and resolved : the lecture method (in the absence of books, the master was required to read from or talk about the only existing text): the formation of faculties: a set curriculum: examinations as a means of certifying the qualified, and the awarding of degrees (bachelor, master, and doctor). These became accepted practice in all universities.

The merging of these ideas gave the university its distinctive character and structure: a self- governing community with an elected hierarchy, separated from the world of commerce, involved in a mission to learn and to teach at an advanced level, using, mysterious rituals and dress to dramatize its uniqueness, and requiring from its members deep loyalty to and enduring support for each other and the university. This conception of university is or should be deeply rooted in academic ideology and has been stoutly defended by scholars in the centuries that have followed. What is important to recognize is that this ideology and these practices, however often they were ignored, distored or abused in medieval times or in the centuries that followed. constituted a model of what a university should be.

A university, it has often been said, is a community. It is a community which is concerned with the individual - individual scholar, the individual student. The university community funds its fulfillment only through the work of the individual scholars and the individual student, and self-concern, which is not self-indulgence, is an essential ingredient.

But the university is something more than the work of individual scholars and students. Its own dimensions can be larger or smaller than the aggregation of individuals or component parts. It all depends on what kind of a university reaches in length of time beyond the span of any man, and thus represents the collective work of many generation; in addition, the university can add or substract from individual efforts.

By the direction it sets, the tone it creates it can establish an environment which demands the best. It can establish an intellectual community in which individual efforts not otherwise possible will naturally flourish. By the pursuit of inappropriate goals it can create an atmosphere which diminishes the efforts of all. The self-governance of universities denies the validity of the claim sometimes made that the individual scholar's loyalty should be only to his discipline and not to the institution. This is perhaps a luxury available to some, but it is a stolen luxury and no man's right. The individual self-concern of the scholar or student is not enough. There must be a general concern for the direction and values of the institution as a whole.[4.3]

The university which pretends to be all good things to all people is on the road to mediocrity. The university must decide what kind of a community it wishes to be. It is not enough to say that it is an academic

4.3 LEVI Edward, Point of View - Talks on Education, - The choice for a university p.p. 33-34. The University of Chicago Press, USA 1969.

community or a community of scholars. The university is one community among many: its members are members of other communities. For e.g academics are from one point of view, part of a much larger class of intellectual men (teachers, writers professional men, and so on) from whom in the public eye they are often barely distinguishable. All such intellectuals are participants in "Culture" they keep in a state of effervescence that stocks of ideas and artistic creations with which mankind has responded to the human situation. This stock is often taken to be the product of a mental faculty called intellect while explaining the university in terms of this cultural entity. Lord Annan observes that *that* is what universities are for. Everything else is secondary. Equality of opportunity to come to the university is secondary. The need to mix classes, nationalities, and races together is secondary. The agonies and gaieties of students life are secondary. So are the rules, customs, pay and promotion of the academic staff and their debates on changing the curricula or procuring facilities for research. Even the awakening of a sense of beauty or the life giving shock of new experience or the pursuit of goodness itself all these are secondary to the cultivation, training and exercise of the intellect.

It is important to distinguish the academic from the intellectual. For the university is distant from and often hostile to much of this intellectuality, somewhat as monks to diocesan clergy. Intellectuals are unmistakenably inhabitants of the practical world. They quite legitimately embrace causes, conduct vendettas, suppress inconvenient evidence, strike moral postures, succumb to intellectual fashions, scheme feud and sign petitions. In some countries they constitute an entire social class having great influence on the government. In their case for intellectual matters, the class of intellectuals is a naturally of universities, but in its practical involvement this alliance can become much more dangerous than open enmity. For it is through this dense protective medium that the blinding enthusiasms of the practical world may try to pass themselves off as ultimate truths which it is the university's duty to diffuse. And it is clear that if the class of intellectual could ever agree on some set of truths, they would not hesitate to impose it upon universities. Intellectuals are the source of those ideas which periodically seize the imagination of the masses, sometimes even capturing governments and their demand to be declaimed from the lecture rostrum as final truths. The only thing that universities ought to do is the only thing they can do sustain the academic world. It is not the wonders with which they have been associated and which constitute the splendour of universities that splendour rather from many things which feature little in the public imagination.

It becomes clear that academics are the cultivators of a secret. It does not mean that they deliberately traffic in secret; indeed the great strength of universities has been their steadfast refusal to turn understanding into a kind of vulgar esoterism. On the contrary, they have always insisted that the body of knowledge they cultivate is in principle open to anyone who is prepared to give the time and the wits to it.

Regarding the third feature of the university offering scholar-ship and professional training to its students, the social commitment of the university as an institution of higher education is well revealed. Compared to other institutions in society, higher education has a much bigger share as a fountainhead of change. Being at the higher level of the educational pyramid and thus able to influence other levels of education, and having wider access to all available knowledge and therefore, creatively integrate it, it can undoubtedly operate as a powerful instrument to help the process of social change in the society. All change implies moving from one position to another. Social change indicates changes in social attitudes, behaviour, customs, habits, manners, relations and values of individual groups of people and institutions. Social change is meant to connote fundamental structural and functional changes in society. It could be in different spheres of human life - social, economic, political cultural and so on. In a country like ours even inculcation of the true values of democracy in the minds of the young and through them in the larger community, could by itself be an action for social change.

Higher education is at the apex of the educational hierarchy with the crucial and paramount responsibility of generating and acquiring new knowledge and disseminating it. It nurtures the competency of future leadership in the students who hold the potential to develop the society. It prepares them to successfully carry out different responsibilities for social change and development.

Society is an organised entity and education must prepare individuals to fit into a variety of jobs and responsibilities; society must itself be protected against minor conflicts between its various sections, sectors or classes and society must generate resources to supply all the goods, service and education itself.

Kenneth R. Minogue points out that if the modern university sees its task as supplying the country with civil servants, administrators and technologists, the medieval university existed to train churchmen, canonists, monks and friars, schoolmen and schoolmasters. From this we can understand that the universities represented the training schools for the established order and that their studies were closely correlated to the national needs of the then society. Regardless of the society, we can understand that the university, as a social institution, is a place for teaching the young and preparing them for their social roles. "Just as Yacht Clubs were established by people who just liked messing about with boats who had no further end. So universities were established and sustained by people who liked inquiry and scholarly cultivation. Now governments may well regard Yacht clubs with approval because they are excellent sources of recruitment for the navy but it would be absurd to regard this as their function. Similarly universities have many beneficial side effects which have sometimes led states to embrace them enthusiastically. But to take any of these side - effects as the functions of university would be a distortion of their character[4.4]

The fourth feature that the university should attack frontiers of knowledge is the throbbing feature of higher education in general. Higher education is higher because it is at the frontiers of knowledge trying to expand these frontiers. This is research function of higher education. The dissemination of this knowledge involves the teaching function.

In the most ideal situation these two functions are completely fused together. Here the teacher and the student work together on a theme of common quest and in the process the student, as a junior associate also gets initiated into the secrets of this process. Even at the levels lower than this highest level, teaching can carry an authenticity of its own if it is inspired by the research orientation and experience of the teacher. At lower levels he/she may have the opportunity of dealing with smaller themes but the research attitude is the same and that is the main thing. Besides certain other functions, like administrative work and advice to and consultation with students on different aspects, higher education all over the world is taking on the third function of directly going to the community in order to study its problems or in their awareness of all

4.4 Minogue, R. Kenneth. The Concept of a University (pp 4-5) Willmen Brothers Ltd. Birken head, weiden field and Nicolson London 1973

kinds of issues. This approach is all the more urgent in developing countries like India, but it is also being emphasized in the industrialized countries as a need to move beyond the ivory tower, and accepting social responsibilities on the part of university and college teachers. The universities themselves undertake research and provide the trained manpower for research and development both in public and private sectors of various enterprises. Universities are all what the great German philosopher Karl Jaspers so aptly describes as the "corporate realization of man's basic determination to know"

Knowledge is in many respects, a living thing - it grows, it changes, and various parts of it are replaced as they become obsolete. But this dynamic nature of knowledge is traceable to this interplay and tension connected with its acquisition, transmi-ssion and application. It is this interaction that creates needs for new knowledge, that brings in accurate teaching to account, that shows, the world what could be rather than what is. Taken separately the three aspects of knowledge lead nowhere; together they can and have produced in explosion that has changed the world. The proof of knowledge and utility of knowledge are very important with regard to the application of knowledge. Proof without concern for the application of proof leads straight to the barren discussions and medieval scholasticism while proof, based on utility alone makes generalization impossible and thus leads to the destruction of knowledge itself. The two ideas of proof and utility are different but dependent, and their interaction lies at the very centre of enlightenment and progress of mankind. "This intimate union of theory and practice aids both" says Whitehead. We cannot understand the modern university unless we understand these three aspects of knowledge viz acquisition, transmission and application. This is so because the three aspects of knowledge have their institutional reflections in the three missions of the university: 1. The acquisition of knowledge is the mission of research (2) The transmission of knowledge is the mission of research (3) the application of knowledge is the mission of public service. It could be expected to follow that the three missions of the university are as organically related as are the three aspects of knowledge[4.5]

But the three aspects of knowledge have not always been given equal emphasis. On the contrary, one aspect or another has customarily

4.5 PERKINS, A James: The University in Transition. (pp 9-10) PRINCETON UNIVERSITY PRESS, 1966.

been emphasized throughout history at the expense of the other two. And the emphasis has largely been determined, at any given time, by the level of intellectual sophistication and the nature of the social environment that prevailed. Traditional societies were and are, naturally enough, bound to be preoccupied with the traditional knowledge, and that kind of knowledge is a weak elixir for the rejuvenation of that kind of society. For such a society, the idea of university- based research is almost meaningless and irrelevant. Thus the concern for knowledge was for centuries restricted to a concern for what was rather than what could be to a transmission of old knowledge rather than a search for the new. And at centre of the wheel of history was the fact that the rulers of traditional societies, both clerical and civil were not hospitable to the idea that truth could be discovered without the intervention of those specially trained in the mysteries. The authoritarian structure of the Middle Ages had to be dissolved by the Renaissance, the Reformation, the rise of the middle classes, and the revolution of scientific technology before change could become a desirable goal rather than a danger to be avoided. When the traditional crust was broken and man's curiosity and aspirations could assert themselves, the search for new knowledge was on. The universities became ready to produce it and society prepared itself to receive it and use it. Thus the promotion of basic research became the true mission of the university.

Promotion of basic research lies in the academic freedom of the members of the academic community. Academic freedom is the very essence of the universities and hence forms the foremost feature of a university. If the society or government interfere with the natural academic freedom of the university, they deprive themselves of what good the university could have done to them. It has become a cardinal principle in all enlightened societies to respect the academic freedom of university life, in particular freedom of speech and expression, freedom in framing curricula, establishing teaching methods and choosing problems for research. Thus, freedom is, undoubtedly, required for higher education institutions to discharge their true function in society. But no freedom is absolute, for example, courses cannot be irrelevant from employment point of view, freedom of expression and speech has to be within the framework of reason and responsibility. Irrational, emotional or intolerant thoughts would destroy the very enlightenment in a society providing freedom of speech. Freedom is to be enjoyed with necessary constraints and restraints. University's freedom to exercise its power to achieve its various goals set by the society or to influence change in society itself is called its autonomy.

Freedom of expression in all its forms can be justified on two fundamental grounds. For the individual, the right to speak and write as one chooses is a form of liberty that contributes in important ways to a rich and stimulating life. To be deprived of such liberty is to lose the change to participate fully in an intellectual exchange that helps to develop one's values to make one's meaning of the world to exercise those qualities of mind and imagination that are most distinctively human.

While university autonomy relates to the freedom of the university as an institution with certain functions to fulfil, academic freedom is nothing more nor less than the professional freedom of the teacher as a member of the university or college where he or she teaches. Academic freedom is generally defined as a freedom of members of the academic community, assembled in colleges and universities, which underlies the effective perfor-mance of their functions of teaching, learning, practice of the arts and research. Further elaborated, this means that it would be regarded as an infringement of academic freedom for a university to impose any censorship on the utterance of any member of its staff on any subject, whether or not it relates to the field of his expert knowledge and whether or not it deals with religion or politics or it is made in the classroom. It means freedom from freedom to. In other words, it means freedom from the fear of any constraining agency and also conducive conditions for free pursuit. Emphasizing on the importance and the sphere where academic freedom is exercised, the Education Commission (1964-66) states: we would like to emphasize the freedom of teachers to hold and express their views, however, radical, within the classroom (and outside), provided they are careful to present the different aspects of a problem without confusing teaching with propaganda in favour of their own particular views". In concrete terms it may mean: (1) that a teacher cannot be forced to teach something which goes against his/her conscience or his/her concept of truth: (2) freedom to hold and express views, however radical provided teaching is not converted to propaganda: (3) freedom to speak and write about and participate in debates on significant national/international issues: and (4) facilities and encouragement in his/her work of teaching and research and research even when his/her views are in opposition to those of his/her authority.

Academic freedom is not to be seen as merely a reflection of society's commitment to free speech; it is a safeguard essential to the aims of the university and to the welfare of those who work within it. Teachers and scholars have a vital stake in continuing to enjoy the liberty to speak and write as they choose, because their lives are entirely devoted to developing and expounding ideas. Universities, in turn, have a critical interest in preserving free expression, for without that freedom they will be hampered in appointing the most creative scientists and scholars and will suffer from forms of censorship that will jeopardize the search for knowledge and new discovery that represents their most distinctive contribution.

Obviously, the extent and kinds of academic freedom, enjoyed by teachers depends to some extent on social and political realities, and to some extent on how teachers use these freedom. Natural consolidation may be a goal or a task identified by a society for its coherence and progress and therefore any teacher tending to go against it may have to be constrained. Teachers neglecting their duties to teach, learn and research, or those misevaluating their students by reasons of prejudices. Favouritism or sheer neglect or engaged in disrupting the system by overempahsizing privileges and benefits and underplaying responsibility and duty, may be inviting outside inter ference in the affairs of educational institutions. If there is self-discipline, then no rules of discipline would be in evidence but if there is no such internal constraint then authority and enforcement of discipline become necessary for universities to play their characteristic role in society, but they call for an immense sense of responsibility on the part of institutions and individuals.

Sixthly we can state that universities should have certain privileges in order to carry out its mission. The university is undoubtedly a unique social institution. In fact, it is a part of the social entity but at the sametime, it is not a passive part. It can play a role in changing society by changing the thinking of young people, by creating new knowledge which may call for new products, services and even new modes of management. This intricate relationship requires the higher educational system to be a living and dynamic entity. If it turns passive and only carries out the orders of those who at anything are at the help of affairs in society it fails in providing positive impulses for changing the society for the better. In fact, the sixth feature of the university connotes the autonomy and accountability to the society.

When we speak of university autonomy we mean its right to govern its own affairs and particularly its rights to carry out its legitimate activities of teaching and research without interference from any outside authority. Autonomy implies university's four essential freedom - to determine for itself on academic grounds who may teach what may be taught, how it should be taught, and who may be admitted to study. In other words, autonomy means the university or college's power of decision making with regard to academic programmes and activities within financial, bounds laid down by government or by raising found from interested sources. Only an autonomous institution, free from regimentation of ideas, pressure, or power politics can pursue society. There are many spheres of activities in which universities need autonomy. Some of these are selection of students, appointment and promotion of teachers, determination of curric-ulum, methods of teaching, research activities, contents of courses, student evaluation, other administrative and financial matters and staff appraisal. Autonomy has to be seen as operating at two levels viz. external and internal. By external autonomy, we mean the existence of a university as a corporate entity and its independence in its activities in relation to other institutions in society. Internal autonomy, on the other hand signifies the autonomy of individual teachers/groups within the university, with their accountability to the academic community at large.

Now-a-days, universities growing dependence on public funds has made them increasingly open to scrutiny by the state. It is also interesting to note here that universities tend to face interference from the government in those times and places where their activities are perceived to be of national importance. In a sense when universities have been least central and important, their autonomy has been safest. Institutions that are purely "Ivory Towers" are of little relevence to the society and external authorities are often content to leave them alone.

The autonomous status for higher education institutions, thus in essence, aims at giving opportunity to the teachers and students to make innovations, utilise their creative talent, improve the standards of teaching, examination and research and quickly respond to social needs.

The tradition of the autonomy of universities is one of the oldest of all the traditions of universities; nevertheless, it has never been complete. Universities have been dependent for practically all of their history on external financial support and this has affected the degree of their autonomy. They have had to concern themselves with the external demand for the services of their graduates, and for the requirements of the professions for which their students have had to be trained.

They have also intermittently been forced to submit themselves to the powers of the rulers of their societies and they have had to adapt themselves to the demands of external opinion. Despite these constraints, the universities have managed through most of their history to enjoy a considerable measure of autonomy.

If there is self-discipline, then no rules of discipline would be in evidence, but if there is no such internal constraint then "authority" and "enforcement of discipline" become necessary for universities to play their characteristic role in society, but they call for an immense sense of responsibility on the part of institutions and individuals. Applied to higher education, this means that higher education should give an account of its performance in terms of the extent of fulfilment of its social expectations and accept responsibility for its failures. It would also mean that society can intervene in the affairs of higher education when the latter falls to discharge its obligations.

University accountability is interpreted in terms of external accountability and internal accountability. External accountability is the university's accountability or responsibility to the community or the society. Internal accountability implies the internal efficiency of the system. External accountability relates to the university with regard to the contents of the courses, extra and co-curricular activities and their linkage with societal needs, knowledge, skills and values, performance of students, students employment, teachers contribution to extension of knowledge etc. Internal accountability is the university's responsibility to the programmes and activities planned and implemented, teaching aids used, professional development of the teachers, utilization of infrastructural facilities, library facilities etc. In brevity, autonomy and accountability are the two sides of the same coin. These are complementary to each other. Autonomy without accountability may lead to anarchy. Accountability without autonomy may turn into regimentation. A balance or a "trade off" between the two is necessary. This balance may depend on prevailing social climate and has to evolve through experience.

To sum up, the university is a part of the society; yet it is an autonomous social entity by itself. Features such as autonomy accountability and academic freedom give it a unique character and simultaneously, help it in its discharge of obligations, to itself and to the society at large.

4.5 VIEWS ABOUT A UNIVERSITY BY JOHN HENRY NEWMAN AND KARL JASPERS

To substantiate the aforesaid functions and features of the university in general, the scholar has sought the views about the idea of a university expressed by Newman and Karl Jaspers. Most of the universities of to-day have apparently displayed the appearance of traditional model. Instead of relying on the apparent model of the Modern Universities and their features, it is better to seek the views and opinions of the Scholars about the university, which are nearer to the Medieval Universities of Europe. The very term university does not seem to have appeared until the beginning of the thirteenth century.

Etymologically the word university means "whole" In the Middle Ages it was used to mean every trade guild of mechanics or artisans or every corporation of men associated together in a common enterprise.

The universities could be seen as organisations, as institutions or as communion. The study of universities as organisation would imply that they exist to achieve concrete ends, which, on the whole, are capable of rational analysis. Studying them as institutions, that is, as the embodiment of certain values would involve a behavioural examination of how their internal processes contribute to the maintenance of their external value. If the study of universities as communities is given primary emphasis, the study would be more concerned with their effects upon the development of groups and individuals. These three views may be abstract but co-exist in an uneasy balance in each individual university.

New man, with his Protestant Oxford University background gives us an image of the mother university which formed the basis of many universities in the world. Being under the hegemony of the British, India has had the imprint of the Oxford model in her university system. While Taxila, Nalanda, Vikramasila and Vallabhi in India cannot be said to be the founders of the modern universities of India, it can hardly be denied that they provided a receptive cultural health into which the "heritage" of redbrick British Universities should.

John Henry Newman's idea of a university reflects the quintessence of the tradition of the English universities. The university itself was planned on the principle that all things are parts of a whole and must be done on an idea. In this case the idea was that of a Catholic university modelled on the Belgian Catholic university of Louvain, which was to be for all English speaking Catholics and which, was to teach all knowledge by teaching all branches of knowledge as an initiator. Newman had the inestimable quality of possessing a clear vision and a definite purpose. Not only was he sure what kind of an education a university should provide, but he was also quite clear in his own mind about the necessary methods and means for realising these ends. Because of his Rectorship of the Catholic University of Ireland, Dublin, he was able to discuss the nature of a university, including general discussions of 'influence' and discipline, professorial and tutorial teaching, colleges and universities. In brevity, Newman's idea of a university epitomises the salient features of a university, which are universally applicable to all over the world. The religious character of the university is rationalised on the ground that the youth of the country may enjoy all the benefits of the highest education without any detriment to their faith or morals. Further Newman is an advocate of mixed education; he deplored the separation of secular learning from religion and called for the intellectual layman to religious, and the devout ecclessiatic to be intellectual. This is well evident from the fact that Newman required his students (young bishops) to follow a course of liberal studies, involving compulsory Latin and two other subjects from a variety of options including mathematics and physical science.

The scholar views Karl Jarpers as the representative of German universities. Karl Jaspers' The idea of the University was written at the end of Hitler's dictatorship and the defeat of Germany in World War II, after the worst outward and inner catastrophies had befallen the German universities: Despite a decline in the standard of critical thinking and pursuit of knowledge, a minority of German students and teachers held firm to their commitments to honesty and independent thought. Karl Jaspers was one of these people. He offered a philosopher's search for the deepest roots and the innermost care of those strange human enterprises that we call universities in the tradition of the Western World. In doing so he showed in a brief sample the continuing vitality and greatness of the German philosophic tradition. We must understand the essentials of higher education and the quintessence of a university as institution. Hence we have the reason to listen to a philosophers' advice as to what these essentials are. As a student of philosophy, the scholar seeks the advice of Jaspers and searches for his ideas of a university, which exhibit universal validity.

Jaspers believes that in any true university three things academic teaching, scientific and scholarly research, and creative cultural life, are indissolubly linked to each other; and that each of these activities will wither and decline in the long run if separated from the others. Thus to Jaspers, an increase in the numbers of full-time research men and full-time teachers at a university would bring forebadings of intellectual decline; and he insists that no man who is not himself carrying on research can truly teach and educate students at a university. Due to firsthand experience of twelve years under totalitarian tyranny, Jaspers believes that a university must remain committed to such free intellectual communication that into its community it should even admit people who show proof of intellectual achievement and works in a scholarly way.

Because of the general ruin and turpitude under the military regimentation of Hitler in Germany, the pent-up feelings of Karl Jaspers about the higher education find vigorous expressions in the form of idea of a university. Professor Jaspers, a leading exponent of Existentialism, gives us a timely reminder that teaching divorced from research deprives the University of its basic impetus. Teaching vitally needs the substance which only research can give it; it is indeed the combination of the two that provides the spirit of university education. Although special research institutions have their part to play, one may fear that undue separation of investigation from teaching will not only imporerish the universities but ultimately lower the standards of research itself. Newman's 'The idea of a University' was published almost one hundred years ago (1852-1853). Newman appears to be a spokesman of 'gentlemanship' as the goal of university educations because of his penchant for Liberal Education. Inspite of the fact that Professor Jaspers has been constrained to write his book by considerations very different from those that animated Newman, these two books have very much more in common than virtual identity of title. They mirror the quintessence of university as an institution. To Newman, a university is not a birth-place of poets or of immortal authors, of founders of schools, leaders of colonies or conquerors of nation; but a seat of all learning. To Jaspers, the university is a community of scholars and students engaged in the task of seeking truth.

The views expressed by these two great personalities are applicable to all the countries of the world and hence they claim universal validity. It is also true that most of the Western countries like the Great Britain, France, Portugal and Spain wherein the university system of education emerged, paved the way for the western style of education in their colonial nations and these colonial nations, the developing countries of the todays world, have still got the important in their educational build up. India is not an exception as it had been under the British hegemony for nearly a century and her higher education is distinctly tinged with the British model of higher education. Hence the views of Newman and Jaspers about university are considered relevant for the study.

5.5.1 THE IDEA OF A UNIVERSITY BY NEWMAN

For Newman the single, almost visual, image that governs The idea of a University is that "all knowledge forms one whole" or "circle" from which the various branches of learning abstract this or that segment. Liberal knowledge or what he calls "Philosophy" which is the end of "idea" of a university, consists in that awareness of the bearing of each on the others by which alone the "whole" can be perceived.

The idea of a university (1853) began as deliberative rhetoric. Newman was too well acquainted with Aristotle, whose Rhetoric was a basic text at Oxford. His was an irenic approach well suited to establish his own sincerity and common sense, to keep his Protestant hearers attentive, to allay nationalist suspicion of an English intruder and to appeal to the influential element in his Catholic audience; Newman's's arguments in Discourses II-IV derive largely from those current in England following the utilitarian proposal in 1825 for the erection of a nonsectarian and nonresidential university for the middle classes i.e. the future London University. In these Discourses, by 'science' Newman means simply an organized body of knowledge and by "theology" the truths we know about God put into a system" that is, the truths derived from Revelation as well as from nature. Newman argues syllogistically that if we have such truths at all, no university can omit teaching them and yet be what it claims to be a home of all sciences; He argues that the circle of knowledge is maimed by their absence because theology, like all sciences, has some bearing on other sciences, and where it is absent, other sciences will try to fill up the gap by theologising in its place.

As an administrator, Newman strove to promote science as well as arts, to encourage professional education, to provide for research as well as good teaching, and to broaden the curriculum by including more modern subjects than Oxford had previously offered. Although Newman's conce-ption of a university was far too narrow to be acceptable to-day, his practical experience as an administrator enlarged Newman's view of a university; he always maintained that its primary function was the cultivation of the intellect and that some how it ought to be "an Alma Mater". knowing her children one by one, not a foundry or a mint or a treadmill.

The Preface begins with the uncompromising assertion that a university is primarily a place of teaching universal. But if its aim is the diffusion and extension of knowledge, this does not mean that knowledge for its own sake is the justification of a university; Its real purpose is to produce more intelligent members of society by fostering 'cultivation of mind', formation of the intellect. With his Protestant Oxford background, Newman discusses university education. It was there that he learnt the great principle of liberal education for Oxford had been at the centre of two great controversies, one concerning its remoteness from the occupations and duties of life, the other concerning its connection with a particular form of belief. Newman turns to consider the latter in the second Discourse, Theology a Branch of Knowledge. He argues simply that if theology claims to be a branch of knowledge, if religion is viewed on absolutely and objectively true, then it must be included in a university which must teach 'universal knowledge'.

The Church fears no knowledge for all branches of knowledge are connected together, because the subject matter of knowledge is intimately united in itself, as being the acts and the work of the Creator. It is, therefore, ultimately a religious conviction that supports Newman's supremely confi-dent vision of the wholeness of intellectual knowledge and truth. Underlying his belief in man's 'imperial intellect' is his belief in God's existence. Religion and knowledge, are not opposed to each other and not because they are irrelevant to one another but because they are indivisibly connected, or rather because religion forms part of the subject matter of knowledge. This is Newman's claim and it is crucial to his whole argument. If the Catholic Faith is true, a university cannot teach universal knowledge if it does not teach Catholic theology. What gives the Discourses their peculiar rhetoric is not an unresolved and unresolvable conflict between knowledge and religion but the tension between the genuinely unconditional insistence on the absolute value of knowledge in itself and the equally firm conviction that knowledge is emphatically not the highest good. Newman insists that it is better to have a simple réligious faith than a cultivated intellect which lacks or neglects religious truth. There is no question of any necessary incompatibility for Newman's but he recognizes the fact that religious belief and education, faith and reason, are not always found together. Newman was keenly aware of the perennial potential conflict.

Now it is important to clarify what Newman means by this 'special' Philosophy', this Liberal or philosophical Knowledge which he calls the end of university education and which he defines as a comprehensive view of truth in all its branches of the relations of science to science, of their mutual bearings, and their respective values. Essentially, he means nothing more than what he defines as real cultivation of mind in the preface. That form of universal knowledge which is the 'perfection' of the individual intellect is not knowing all branches of knowledge but simply is the power of viewing many things at once as one whole, of referring them severely to their true place in the universal system, of understanding their respective values, and determining their mutual dependence.

Newman's initial definition of a university as a place for teaching all branches of knowledge, has been criticized. First of the two aspects of this central criticism is that there is the change that Newman excludes from his ideal university the teaching of practical secular knowledge, useful or "utilitarian" training of any sort. The assumption is that because the end of the university is liberal knowledge, only the so called liberal arts are to be taught. In principle, as Newman makes clear in Christianity and Letters, the studies pursued in the faculty of arts are almost the direct subject matter and the staple of the mental exercise proper to a university. It is not that Newman was unaware of the special historical connection of University institutions with the Sciences of Theology, Law, and Medicine, but insists and shows from the history of European civilization how universities came to be formally based and 'live in' the faculty of arts, which in the Middle Ages comprised the seven liberal arts, namely grammar (i.e. literature) rhetoric. Logic and mathematics (divided into geometry, arithmetic, astronomy and music). But because the liberal arts formed for Newman the centres and nucleus of university studies, this did not mean that other subjects were excluded. To take Newman's own example, the study of theology ceases to be a liberal study only when it becomes an art or a business making use of theology for the specific practical purposes of the catechetical college in this kind of way, it is not a theological training. For the primary object is not that they should learn to apply certain given theological information and techniques to meet certain concrete demands and situations. And so while it is true that Newman did not include either theology or engineering among the central disciplines of a university, this did not preclude either from providing a liberal education if cultivated as a contemplation or exercised as `simple knowledge'. Although Newman naturally regarded an education in the traditional liberal arts as the best, in the sense of the most liberal education, this did not prevent him from acknowledging science as one main constituent portion of the subject matter of Liberal Education. The other was Literature which he regarded as the central study of the faculty of arts.

The second charge is that Newman lays a disproportionate emphasis on the study of theology in a university. In the Discourse V it is stated categorically that although theology is one branch of knowledge, and Secular Science as another branches, nevertheless theology is the highest indeed, and widest. Newman employs two different images to describe the structure of knowledge, that of the circle of the sciences and that he makes no attempt to reconcile the two. The former, which is of classical origin implies that theology occupies one segment of a circle which is presided over by the science of science, but the latter, which is of medieval origin, implies that she is the queen of the Sciences and herself has the ruling of all the rest. Newman makes no secret of the fact that certain key branches of knowledge like ethics and theology, whose importance is commensurate with the precariousness of then status, impinge upon (not rule over) a great number of other branches of knowledge. The image of the circle is intended to imply interdependence and not equality. Thus there is no reason why one science should not be the chief of the sciences, in the sense of first among equals rather than sovereign over the others.

There can be no question that for Newman theology is far more 'important' branch of knowledge than literature, but that does not prevent him from holding that literature is more important study for a liberal education. We think that Newman was quite wrong about the intellectual fruits of the study of science, but we should be very careful to distinguish the objection from the much more damanging objections that Newman is mistaken about the true purpose of universities and university education and that he is against science. The fact which has escaped many of Newman's critics is that he is against science, is exactly the same sense that he is against the theology if there had to be a choice between bodily and spiritual health on the one hand and mental cultivation on the other; there is no doubt that Newman would have choosen hospitals and seminaries as more useful than universities. The scholar is bound to city Lockean phrase sound mind exists in sound body to highlight the preference of Newman for bodily and spiritual health.

Regarding the twin idea of Church and University, Newman holds that the Church is the representative of the religious principle and university is the representative of the intellect. The University is an intellectual power just as the Church is religious power. The church is imperial that is one and Catholic whole the university is an empire in the sphere of philosophy and research. The Church is the guardian of the circle of dogmatic truths, the university the high protecting power of the whole circle of knowledge.

Both the church and the university are linked to political organism where the many individuals are brought into unity not uniformity and where the conflict of the various parts ensures and enhances their own vitality. Both paradoxically bring peace and harmony out of the very rivalry which they encourage, by fostering private judgement in the one case and the different branches of knowledge in the other. Both preserve and promote freedom of thought not in spite of but by virtue of the authority which each exercises in defence of the whole circle of truth against individual aberrations and excesses. Those critics of Newman who complain that ultimately he sacrifices intellectual culture to religion should note in this great passage the idea or the fact that he feels it necessary to make at one point the reservation that the university is ancillary certainly and of necessity to the Catholic Church.

After glancing though Newman's the Idea of a University couched in this Discourses and Lectures and Essays, the scholar summarizes briefly the salient features underlying the concept of a university.

i) A university is a place for learned and scientific man, a learned body, a large corporation, with professors of art and science with faculties in theology, law and medicine, with logical disputations, with examinations in intellec-tual proficiency, with degrees in token of that proficiency attained. In the minds of the generality of men, a university is pronounced as a seat of science and letters or that its end is knowledge. In this aspect the university of the nature of a university is affirmed. Newman himself reiterates that a university, by its very nature professes to teach universal knowledge.

ii) The end of the university education is the attainment of wholistic knowledge. Newman says that a university is considered with reference either to its students or to its studies and the principle that all knowledge is a whole and the separate sciences parts of one, is equally important when we direct our attention to its students. Newman says that all branches of knowledge are connected together because the subject matter of knowledge is intimately united in itself, as being the acts and the work of the Creator. Hence it is that the Science, into which our knowledge may be said to cast, have multiplied bearings one on another and an internal sympathy, and admit or rather demand, comparison and adjustment. They complete, correct, balance each other. Thus consideration, if well-founded, must be taken into account, not only as regards the attainment of truth, which is the common end, but as regards the influence which they exercise upon those whose education consists in the study of them It is a great point then to enlarge the range of studies which a university professes, even for the sake of the students and though they cannot pursue every subject which is open to them, they will be the gainers by living among those and under those who represent the whole circle. This is the advantage of a seat of universal bearing, considered as a place of education. A assemblage of learned men, zealous for their own sciences, and revival of each other, are brought by familiar intercourse and for the sake of intellectual peace, to adjust together the claims and relations of their respective, subjects of investigation. They learn to respect, to consult, to aid each other. Thus is created a pure and clear atmosphere of thought, which the student also breathes, though in his own case he only pursues a few sciences out of the multitude. He profits by an intellectual tradition, which is independent of particular teachers, which guide him in his choice of subjects and duly interprets for him those which he chooses. He apprehends the great outlines of knowledge, the principles on which it rests, the scale of its parts, its lights and its shades, its great points and its little as he otherwise cannot apprehend them. Hence it is that his education is called Liberal. A habit of mind is formed which lasts through life, of which the attributes are freedom, equitableness, calmness, moderation and wisdom. This is the special fruit of the education, furnished at a university as contrasted with other place of teaching or modes of teaching. This is the main purpose of a university in its treatement of its students.

What is the end of university Education and of the Liberal or Philosophical knowledge? Knowledge is capable of being its own end. Such is the constitution of the human mind, that any kind of knowledge, if it be really such, is its own reward. It is common to speak of liberal knowledge of the liberal arts and studies and of a liberal education as the special characterstic or property of a university and of a gentleman, what is really meant by the word? Liberal education and liberal pursuits are exercises of mind, of reason of reflection. Knowledge is a state or condition of mind: and cultivation of mind is surely worth seeking for its own sake; knowledge is called by the name of science or philosophy, when it is acted upon, informed or impregnated by Reason. In one case it is called useful knowledge, in other Liberal. What is knowledge? By knowledge, Newman means something intellectual, something which grasps what it perceives through this sense: something which takes a view a things which sees more than the senses convey, which reasons upon what it sees and while it sees: which invests it with an idea. It expresses itself, not a mere enunciation, but by an enthymeme: it is of the nature of science from the first and in this consists its dignity. The principle of real dignity in knowledge, its desirableness, considered irrespectively of its results, is the germ within it of a scientific or a philosophical process. This is how it comes to be an end in itself: this is why it admits of being called Liberal. Truth is the object of knowledge of whatever kind: and Truth means facts and their relations, which stand towards each other as subjects and predicates in logic. All that exists as contemplated by the human mind forms one large system are complex fact and this resolves itself into an indefinite numbers of particular facts, which have countless relations of every kind, one towards another. Knowledge is the apprehension of these facts, whether in themselves or in their mutual positions and bearings.

Liberal Education makes the gentleman. It is well to be a gentleman: it is well to have a cultivated intellect, a delicate taste, a candid, equitable, dispassionate mind, a noble and courteous bearing in the conduct of life: these are the conatural qualities of a large knowledge: they are the objects of a university.

iii) The university offers scholarships and professional training to its students.

Newman says that education is the preparation for knowledge and it is the imparting the knowledge in proportion to that preparation. We require intellectual eves to know withal, as bodily eyes for sight. The bodily eye, the organ for apprehending material objects, is provided by nature: the eyes of the mind, of which the object is a work of discipline and habit. This process of training, by which intellect, instead of being formed or sacrificed to some particular or accidental purpose some specific trade or profession, or study or science is disciplined for its own sake for the perception of its own proper object, and for its own highest culture, is called Liberal education. To set up a right standard and to train according to it, and to help forward all students towards it according to their various capacities, is a very business of a university. A university is, according to the usual designation an Alma Matar, knowing her children one by one not a foundry or a mint or a treadmill.[4.6]. There is a duty we owe to society as such, to the state to which we belong, to the sphere which we move, to individuals towards whom we are variously related and whom we successively encounter in life: and that philosophical or liberal education is a proper function of a university. Liberal education consists in the culture of the intellectual. If the human intellect is so excellent a portion of us, and its cultivation so excellent, it is not only beautiful, perfect, admirable, and noble in itself, but in a true and high sense it must be useful to the possesor and to all around him. Again, as health ought to precede labour of the body, and as a man in health the properties are strength, energy, agility, graceful carriage and action, manual dexterity and endurance of fatigue so in like manner general culture of mind is the best aid to professional and scientific study, and educated man can do what illiterate cannot; In this sense, mental culture is emphatically useful. Society itself requires some other contribution from each individual, besides the particular duties of his profession. Without directly qualifying a man for any of the employments of life Liberal knowledge enriches and enables all. Without teaching him the peculiar business of any one office or calling, it enables him to act his part in each of them with better grace and more elevated carriage. The main ingredients of that ability are requisite knowledge and cultivated

---

4.6 KER. I.I,(editor) John Henry New Man's The Idea of a University, Defined and Illustrated, Page (129), Oxford University Press, London

faculties: but of the two, the later is by far the chief. A man of well improved faculties has the command of another's A main without them, has not the command of his own.

IV) The university should allow and should be allowed academic freedom. Newman says that great minds need elbow-room, not indeed in the domain of faith, but of thought. And so indeed do lesser minds, and all minds. There are many persons in the world who are called, geniuses. They had been gifted by nature with some particular faculty or capacity: and, while vehemently excited and imperiously ruled by it; they are blind to everthing else. They are enthusiasts in their own line, and are simply dead to the beauty of any line except their own. Accordingly, they think their own line the only line the whole world worth pursuing, and they feel a sort of contempt for such studies as move or another line. This is the case of men of genius. On the contrary, master minds, gifted with a broad philosophical view of things, and a creative power, and a versatility capable of accommodating itself to various provinces of thought, take up some ideas and are intent upon it; some deep, prolific, eventful idea which grows upon them, till they develop it into a great system, Now, if any such thinker starts from radically unsound principles or aims at directly false conclusions, then, there is an end of the whole matter. He is seen as an opponent of Revealed Truth. Newman ventured to recommend to theologians that when their attention is drawn to the subject of scientific investigations, there is a great and firm belief in the sovereignty of Truth. Error may flourish for a time but truth will prevail in the end. The only effect of error ultimately is to promote truth; theories, speculations, hypotheses, are started: perhaps they are to die, still not before they have suggested ideas better than themselves. Their ideas are taken up in turn by other men, and, if they do not yet lead to truth, nevertheless they lead to what is still nearer to truth then themselves, and thus knowledge on the whole progress. The errors of some minds in scientific investigation are more fruitful than the truths of others unless the scientific speculator or inquiries is at liberty to investigate on the basis, and according to the peculiarities, of his, science, he cannot investigate at all. It is the very law of the human mind in its inquiry after and acquisition of truth to make its advances by a process which consists of many stages, and is circuitous. There are no short cuts to knowledge. Moreover, it is not often the fortune of any man to live through an investigation: the process is one of not only many stages, but of many minds. What one begins another finishes and a true conclusion is at length worked out by the cooperation of independent schools and the preservance of successive generations. Here, we can understand the advocacy of Newman for academic freedom of the scientific speculators and scholars and the practice of laissez-faire on the part of the authority.

However, Newman's The Idea of a university is tinged with religious fervour and staunch Catholic Faith. If is well evident from his argument that knowledge and Reason are sure ministers to Faith. The church fears no knowledge for all branches of knowledge are connected together, because the subject-matter of knowledge is intimately united in itself as being the acts and the work of the Creator: It is therefore ultimately a religious conviction that supports Newman's supremely confident vision of the wholeness of intellectual knowledge and truth. Underlying his belief in man's imperial intellect is his belief in God's existence. Religion and knowledge then are not opposed to each other and not because they are irrelevant to one another but because they indivisibly connected or rather because religion forms part of the subject matter of knowledge. This is Newman's chain and it is crucial to his whole argument but it is not illogical for Newman to declare If the Catholic Faith is true University cannot exist externally to the Catholic pale, for it cannot teach universal knowledge if it does not teach Catholic theology. In Newman Discourses, one can discerns the tension between the genuinely unconditional insistence on the absolute value of knowledge in itself and the equally firm conviction that knowledge in itself is emphatically not the highest good. However, he insists that it is better to have a simple religious faith than a cultivated intellect which lacks or neglects religious truth. There is no question of any necessary incompatibility for Newman, but he recognises the fact that religous belief and education, faith and reason are not always found together. If there has to be a choice between this kind of reason and simple faith, Newman leaves us in no doubt as to his preference.

4.5.2 THE IDEA OF A UNIVERSITY BY KARL JASPERS

Newman's The Idea of a University was published almost exactly one hundred years ago (1856). In spite of the fact that professor Jaspers has been constrained to write his book The Idea of the University by consideration very different from those that animated Newman; these two books have very much more in common than virtual identity of title. Professor Karl Jaspers has been regarded as a leading exponent of 20th century Existentialism. Karl Jaspers' The Idea of the University makes no demand on philosophical sophistication and be read by anyone with a general interest in our universities. Its aim is quite simply to reaffirm the basic purpose of the university as an institution devoted to the quest for knowledge and to stress that all worthwhile education demands the active stimulus of original inquiry. The university as envisaged by Professor Jaspers is by no means an Ivory Tower dedicated to the higher realm of academic scholarship. He is, for example, extremely well aware of the challenge of technology and pleads eloquently for its fuller assimilation into the universities. Recent years witnessed tremendous growth of research as an activity virtually independent of teaching. Professor Jaspers gives us a timely reminder that teaching divorced from research robs the university of its basic impetus. Teaching vitally needs the substance which only research can give it; it is indeed the combination of the two that provides the spirit of university education.

According to Karl Jaspers, the University addresses itself outwardly to all, but intrinsically only to the best. Yet "the best" cannot be defined in terms of a single type, whether of intellect or character and cannot be selected in any truly reliable way. In spite of his broad outlook, Professor Jaspers views are inevitably coloured by his long experience of continental- in particular German- Universities. To Karl Jaspers the university is an institution characterized simply by the idea of truth, no matter how awkward its intellectual or social consequences. He was bound to uphold this reality, as he lived through a regime (Hitlers Nazism) in which the interests of learning were sacrificed consciously and methodically, to the supposed interests of the state.

He offered a philosophers search for the deepest roots and the innermost core of those strange human enterprises that we call universities in the tradition of the western world. In so doing, he showed in a brief sample the continuing vitality and greatness of the German philosophic tradition.

Karl Jaspers believes that in any true university three things- academic teaching, scientific and scholarly research and creative cultural life - are indissolubly linked to each other; and that each of these activities will wither and decline in the long run if separated from others. He insists that no man who is not himself carrying on research can truly teach and educate students at a university.

i) The University as an Institution

"The university fulfils its tasks - research, instruction, training, communication - within an institutional framework. It requires building materials, books and institutes and then orderly adminis-tration. Privileges and duties must be distributed among its members. The university represents an independent corporate whole with its constitution. The university exists only the extent that it is institutionalized. The idea becomes concrete in the institution. The extent to which it does this, determines the quality of the university; stripped of its ideal the university loses all value. Yet "institution" necessarily implies compromises. The idea is never perfectly realized. Because of this a permanent state of tension exists at the university between the idea and the short comings of the institutional and corporate reality.[4.7]

The scholar opnes that Karl Jaspers has given four-faceted functional structure to the university. In fact, the edifice of the university stands on the four columns of research, instruction, training and communication. If anyone column tumbles down, the stately equilibrium of the university will be tilted. If this is so, even the best institutions at the university are apt to deteriorate and to become distorted.

Without an institution the life and work of the individual scholar are in danger of being wasted. Life and work should become part of a tradition safequarded along institutional lines so that later generations can profit by them. Scientific achievements in particular, are dependent on material means which the individual seldom has at his disposal. They are also dependent on the sort of cooperation possible only at a permanent institution. It assures us that a community of scholars can exist. There is special satisfaction in belonging to such an institution, if only for honour's sake. It hurts not to be admitted to it or to be expelled by it. J.Grimn observes, that universities are like gardens where wild growths are only reluctantly tolerated. In many cases what is creative comes into being outside the university, is at first rejected by the university, then adopted and so on until it comes into its own; Examples are Marxist sociology, hypnotism, long since accepted as a recognized field, graphology, just

---

4.7 DEUTSH, KARL (Editor) Karl Jaspers the Idea of the University, Peter Owen Ltd, London, SW7. 1965 of at the university, and introspective psychology as developed by Kirkagaard and Nietzsche.

beginning to be taken note of the university and introspective psychology as development by Kierkgaard and Niettzsche.

Still, once a new intellectual direction has been developed, the university will take possession of its sooner or later, promote further development by new discoveries and application and preserve it as part of its body of teachable materials. Yet it can only teach a subject in which it does independent research. This is exactly what happened at the university again and again. In several notable instances, however, the universities have pioneered notable instances, however, the universities have pioneered new directions of thinking. Foremost among these are the Kantian philosophy andthe philosophy of German idealism which followed in its wake. Moreover, throughout the nineteenth century almost all new discoveries in history and the natural services originated at the university.

The ultimate problem posed by the institutional structure of the university is the place of human beings in it, for its vitality, the university depends on persons, not institutions which are no more than a physical prerequisite. The university is judged by its ability to attract the best people and provide them with the most favourable conditions for research, communication and teaching. Tensions between the living personality of the research scholar and institutional forms are unavoidable. No idea can be realised without being modified.

II) SEARCH FOR KNOWLEDGE AS A COMMON GOAL

Various sciences emerged from practical experiences of day-to-day life and allied activities. The unity of science is a philosophical ideal. In practice the philosophical idea of unity became the search for a single organic body of knowledge. So began the cooperation of all branches of learning toward a common goal. Scientific instruction in accordance with the ideal of the university seeks to guide us to the foundations of all knowledge by the light of the idea of unity.

Since the idea of knowledge as a Cosmos does not stem from practical application but from philosophy, the vitality is tied to the diffusion of philosophical awareness throughout the university. From the very start, the ideal of knowledge as a unity has given rise to different system of classifying the various fields of knowledge: knowledge is usually classified according to some pair of opposites. Thus there are

i) Theoretical and practical studies

ii) Empirical Sciences and purely rational sciences

iii) Natural Sciences and Cultural Sciences

iv) Sciences concerned with general laws and historical sciences, the former seeking the universal, the latter, the particular and historical unique

v) Basis sciences and auxiliary sciences.

Basic sciences seek to learn by reference to the whole of knowledge; hence become representative of the whole and therefore universal in character. The unity of all knowledge is an ideal. Every classification is a provisional attempt to translate this ideal into reality from a particular point of views and in terms of a particular intellectual and historical situation. No single principle governs the organization of disciplines at a university.

Departmentalization still in use to-day dates back to the medieval period. The three upper faculties were theology, jurisprudence and medicine. A fourth or lower faculty were added - the liberal arts today's philosophical faculty. To-day, there are usually five because the old philosophical faculty has been broken up into two faculties, one of mathematics and natural sciences and one of liberal arts. These faculties claim to mirror faithfully the cosmos of sciences. They represent the whole of human knowledge. They arose from the practical needs of intellectual work, not from theoretical schemes of classifying the sciences. The continuing validity of these faculties today- after centuries of radical change in our environment, our knowledge and our research, attests to the truth of their original conception. Theology, jurisprudence and medicine cover permanent areas of inquiry understanding religious revelation, of state law, both private and public of the nature of man. The study of these subjects is to maintain ministers, judges, administrators and physicians in practical careers. They all need at least logic and philosophy as a common foundation.

The philosophical faculty enjoys a unique position. Originally, it did not prepare for a specified profession but prepared solely for the higher faculties (theology, jurisprudence and medicine). Today the function of the philosophical faculty has changed from a preparatory to a fundamanetal one. The philosophical faculty embraces all other branches of knowledge.

The three reamining faculties derive their intellectual substance from contact with the basic disciplines comprised in the philosophical faculty (the faculty of arts and sciences) Thus from the view point of research and theory alone, any classification of knowledge which includes everythings contained in the philosophical faculty is complete.

III) THE UNIVERSITY MUST OFFER SCHOLARSHIP AND PROFESSIONAL TRAINING TO ITS STUDENTS:

Karl Jaspers says that the student comes to the university in order to study the arts and sciences and to prepare himself for a profession. Overwhelmed by the sheer mass of what can be learned he wants to know what is of chief importance. Orientation lectures, practice sessions, and syllabi only partially help to overcome his difficulties. In the last analysis he must find his own way in the world of lectures, latoratories and seminars. But the student expects even more from the university. To be sure, he studies a special field and has in mind a definite profession. Still, the university with its aura of tradition represents to him the unity of all branches of learning. He respects this unity and expects to experience it, and through it to arrive at a well- founded Weltanschaung. He wants to arrive at truth, wants to gain a clear view of the world and of people. He wants to encounter wholeness, an infinite cosmic order. Science and learning are essentially of the spirit they seek relations to the totality of all there is to be known. The aspiring scholar will reflect on the broader questions of direction, order and aims of his work. For the will to know implies the will to understand clearly what one is doing. These things are required at a university : Professional training, education of the whole man and research. For the university is simultaneously a professional school, a cultural centre and a research institute. In the idea of the university, these three are indissolubly united. One cannot be cut off from the others without destroying the intellectual substance of the university, and without at the same time crippling itself. All these are factors of a living whole. By isolating them, the spirit of the university perishes.

Within the life of the university, teachers and students are driven by a single motive, man's basic quest for knowledge. For every advance in knowledge,however stubborn, indefatigable work is necessary. It is the responsibility of the university to promote intellectual work.

The idea of the university derives its educational force from the primary human will to know. It gives the educated man both sureness of purpose and at the same time great humility. Insight alone cannot decide the purpose or ultimate goal of existence. One clear and ultimate purpose is this at any rate: the world wants to be understood. Research belongs to the university not only because it is the basis of training for the professions, but because the university itself exists for research, fulfils its meaning through research.

IV. THE UNIVERSITY IS A COMMUNITY OF SCHOLARS WITH INTERNAL AUTONOMY RESTED IN THE COMMUNITY.

The University is a community of scholars and students engaged in the task of seeking truth. It is a body which administers its own affairs, despite its financial dependence on endowments ancient property rights or the state. In every case its independent existence reflects the express wish or continuing toleration on the part of the founder. Like the church it derives its autonomy - respected even by the state from an imperishable idea of supranational, world wide character: academic freedom. This is what the university demands and what it is granted. Academic freedom is a privilege which entails the obligation to teach truth, in defiance of anyone outside or inside the university who wishes to curtail it.

The university unites people committed to scholarly or scientific learning and the intellectual life. The original sense of universitas - community of teachers and students - is just as important as the unity of all studies. The idea of the university requires the open mind, the readiness to relate oneself to things with the aim of getting at a picture of the whole in terms of one's special discipline. The ideal requires that there may be communication, not only on interdisciplinary but also on an interpersonal level. The university, therefore, should enable scholars to enter in direct discussion and exchange with fellow scholars and students type, posing questions so that men may achieve clarity about themselves and about each other. An atmosphere of communication based on a community of thinking creates the proper conditions for scholarly and scientific work, although such work is ultimately always solitary.

The university is the place where truth is sought unconditionally in all its forms. All forms of research must serve truth. All the university recognizes in responsibility to truth. This struggle for truth must not be confused with a struggle for economic existence. The effectiveness of intellectual formulations and ideas is grounded in truth. Communication is itself a function of the search for truth. It tests truth by testing its effects. Intellectual exchange makes the university the place where people meet who have committed their lives to the search for truth. For the university must not be confused with the sort of school where intellectual spontaneity is rigidly channelled along curricular and pedagogical lines. For this reason the manner in which communication takes place at a university is the intellectual responsibility of all of its members. The intellectual life at a university declines when its members shut themselves cautiously off from one another, when communication changes into mere sociability; when substantial relationships become obscured by convention, conscious reflection upon the nature of communi-cation can make such communication possible. In the sphere of scholarship communication is maintained through discussion.

Every scholarly or scientific accomplishment is ultimately an individual accomplishment. It is personal achievement. It can be increased through the co-operation of many. Co-operation grows out of communication. When both of these factors are present, motivations, clarity, incentive, reach their highest point: one person's ideas awaken those of another: The continuity of intellectual tradtition is represented by "schools of thought". There are two ways in which schools of thought arise. One way is to imitate a master whose work we carry on by extension, adaptation, and analogous achievement, the other way involves an unbroken intellectual tradition, within which the student may be quite as independent as his teacher, since the tradition, within which the student may be quite as independent as his teacher, since the tradition usually does not centre around a single personality but a group. Here we have a schcol, an intellectual movement which may last through several generations. Schools of thought grow spontaneously; they cannot be induced or deliberately thought up. If one tries to do so, an artificial, sterile activity results. New ideas usually originate in very small circles. A few people, two, three or four, perhaps in an institute or clinic, are inspired by the exchange of a common group of ideas which foster new common insights and achievements. Such a spirit grows secretly among friends, proves its value through objective accomplishment; and finally becomes a fully-fledged intellectual movement. The university as a whole can never be united by such a spirit. That spirit belongs to smaller groups. The university is most alive when such groups communicate with one another.

The university is also the meeting place of different disciplines and world outlooks. At the university all disciplines unite. Their students meet. They are united and inspired by the presence of so many forms of knowledge. Their mutual stimulation leads towards the unity of studies. Left to themselves, the sciences tend to fall apart into a loose aggregate of unrelated units. Their joint presence at the university reawakens a sense of their connection and inspires efforts on behalf of their overall unity. The will to communicate turns upon everthing strange and distant, also upon people who would like to shut themselves up in a world of private beliefs. Those who want to communicate of their own accord run the risk of being put to question because only when they are questioned to the utmost does it become clear whether they are heading in the right direction. This urge to communicate has fundamental consequences for the place of intellectual movements at the university. To be permeated by the idea of the university is part of a way of life. It is the will to search and seek without limitation, to allow reasons to develop unrestrictedly, to have an open mind, to leave nothing unquestioned, to maintain truth unconditionally.

The university does not investigate the Weltanschaunung of a potential member. Rather it investigates his professional attainment and intellectual standing. The university keeps itself distinct from sects, churches, and fanatical groups which seek to impose their own outlook upon others. The university does this because it wants to thrive in feedom only and would perish rather than carefully shelter itself from unfamiliar ideas and withdraw from intellectual conflict where fundamentals are involved. Professional and intellectual standing, mastery of their tools and integrity are few traits expected by the university from its members. The university wants to live dynamically, not statically. In its will to communicate it seeks to associate even with those who resist communication. It would be contrary to the idea of the university to deny admission to a man of intellectual rank who shows proof of intellectual achievement and works in a scholarly way - even if his scholarship ultimately serves an alien interest.

V. ACADEMIC FREEDOM IS THE VERY ESSENCE OF THE DYNAMIC CONCEPT OF A UNIVERSITY

University education is a formative process aiming at meaning-ful freedom. It takes place through participation in the university's intellectual life. The idea of the university derives its educational force from the primary human will to know. It gives the educated man both sureness of purpose and at the same time great humility. One clear and ultimate purpose is this at any rate: the world wants to be understood. Research belongs to the university not only because it is the basis of training for the professions, but because the university itself exists for research, fulfils its meaning through research. The university requires absolute freedom of teaching. The state guarantees the university the right to carry on research and teaching uncontrolled by party politics or by any compulsion through political, philosophical or religious ideologies. Academic freedom extends not only to research and thought but also to teaching. For thought and research need the challenge and the communication which teaching affords and which in turn depends on the freedom of scholars and scientists the world over to speak and write as they please.

All men are potentially capable of meditation and reflection. But only a very few have the calling for intellectual work in all its complexity i.e. very few belong to the intellectual aristocracy. This aristocracy has a freedom that is self-achieved and includes men of noble birth, workers, the rich and the poor. But it is always rare and confined to a few, a minority. This minority includes members of all professions requiring univer-sity study. It is the only group which can respond intelligently and critically to the advancement of learning.

Academic freedom means the freedom of student and teacher to do research in their own way and teach as they see fit. As for actual subject matter, that the state leaves to each individual. This defines the very freedom which it guarantees against all interference, including its own. Academic freedom resemble religious freedom to the extent that each of these freedom is guaranteed not only against state interference but is so guaranteed by the state itself. Academic freedom can survive only if the scholars invoking it remain aware of its meaning. It does not mean the right to say what one pleases. It exists only where scholarly ends and a commitment to truth are involved. Practical objectives, educational bias or political propaganda have no right to invoke academic freedom. Academic freedom does not entitle them to special privilege over other citizens. It means the professional freedom from all obligations other than intellectual thoroughness, method and system.

The university owes its existence to society, which desires that somewhere within its confines pure independent, unbiased research be carried on. Society wants the university because it feels that the pure service of truth somewhere within its orbit serves its own interests. Having exempted the university from interference by its own power, the state respects the university and protects it against all other forms of interference. The university is meant to function as the intellectual conscience of an era. Society provides the university with legal and material support so that it may function as a centre carrying on basic research for the benefit of all and affording people studying for the professions an intellectual climate as well as practical training. Thus, the university is continuously serving the needs of state and society, and bound to change as society and the professions change.

As a corporation with official character, the university runs itself, yet is simultaneously responsible to the state that charters and protects it. For without the state the university is helpless. Hence, all conflict must confine itself to the intellectual plans. The initiative must come from the mind and spirit manifested by the university which must compel the public mind to clarify its thinking and discern its proper objectives. The outcome of this intellecutal conflict will, then be the cooperationof state and university, always assuming that the state does want to help realize the idea of the university. The state merely functions as the ubiquitous overseer of the university's corporate independ-ence. The university, in turn, freely acknowledges this function, neither secretly rejecting the underwriter of its independence as a necessary evil nor obediently bowing to every whim of the state. It confidently accepts state supervision so long as this does not conflict with the cause of truth. Loss of this confidence spells disaster. For state supervision may at times protect the university against acts harmful to the true deal of the university itself. And if the state should make improper demands upon the university, the university has the duty to speak up and clearly state the intellecual principles on which it bases its objections. For it is this formulation of its ideal on the part of the university which enables the state to come to know, its own mind and act accordingly. The university, in turn, achieves self-knowledge only as it achieves objectivity.

The purpose of state supervision is precisely to prevent those corruptions to which a completely independent university would be exposed. Any state interference with teaching cannot help violating the idea of the university. This danger remain even when the state must interfere to take disciplinary action against university members abusing their position for overt political ends. The state has a direct stake in education since it wants civil servants, doctors, ministers, engineers, chemists and the like. But it must be left to the university to decide how this training is to be accomplished to get the best possible results. The state must confine itself to a purely supervisory capacity.

In brief, regarding the views of Karl Jasper's about the Idea of a University, it is stated that the university is a community of scholars and students engaged in the task of seeking truth. Acacemic freedom is a privilege which entails the obligation to teach truth, in defiance of anyone outside or inside the university who wishes to curtail it. The university is a school of very special sort. It is intended not merely as a place for instruction: rather, the student is to participate actively in research and from this experience he is to acquire the truth throughtout his life. Ideally, the student thinks independa-ently, listens critically and is responsible to himself. He has the freedom to learn.

The university is the corporate realization of man's basic determination to know. Its most immediate aim is to discover what there is to be known and what becomes of us through knowledge. This eagerness to know expresses itself through observation, through methodical thought, and through self-criticism as a training for objectivity. It is active even where we confront the very limits of all knowledge and the special risks and tensions inherent in any intellectual quest. Oneness and wholeness are of the very essence of man's will to know. In practice, this oneness and wholeness is realized only in specialized fields. Integration of the various disciplines joins them into a cosmos which culminates in the vision of the unified science, in theology, and in philosophy.

The university, then, is an institution uniting people profess-ionally dedicated to the quest and transmission of truth in scientific terms. Because truth is accessible to systematic search, research is the foremost concern of the university. Because the scope of truth is far greater than that of science, the scientist must dedicate himself to truth as a human being, not just as a specialist. Hence, the pursuit of wholeman. The university second concern is teaching because truth must also be transmitted.

Understandng presupposes the intellectual maturity, not just of the mind but of the whole man. It therefore follows that instruction and research must aim for more than the tramission of bare facts and skills. They must aim for formation of the wholeman, for education in the broadest sense of the term. While delineating the idea of a university, Karl Jaspers speaks about the intellectual life as the quintessence of the university. If the university serves science and scholarship and science and scholarship are meaningful only in so far as they are part of a comprehensive intellectual life, then this intellecual life is the very life blood of the university. In tellectual life can take many forms apart from the university. At the university it is characterized by an institutionalized and orderly collaboration of scholars. Thus in order to understand the idea of the university and its institutional forms we must lay something about the intellectual life in general and about the nature of science and scholarship in particular. Science and scholarship represent a kind of knowledge which is methodical, cogent and universally valid.

Spirit, human existence, and responsive reason make up the all inclusive context of our lives. Spirit is the potentiality and power of ideas. Human existence in its fullest sense signifies our serious and unconditional commitment to the search for trans-cendence. Responsive reason is the mind open to the intrinsic meaning of things. Spirit lives and moves wherever our striving for clarity is a striving for fullness of insight. Without ideas there is no such insight. Ideas impel us from within and at the same time beckon to us as the goal we can never reach. Ideas unify and systematize study and research by furnishing us with hypothetical constructs, themselves only approximations to the ideas themselves. Spirit is the power of creative intuition; without imagination science remains sterile. Such imagination enables us to see what is essential and real, to understand from within, that which lies below the surface, and to make this available to scientific study. Spirit, human existence and reason are the foundation of the scientific outlook. They are the philosophical elements within science even though they never are explicitly acknowledged. Their presence is felt at the frontiers of science. It is these three which can make the passion for knowledge into a passion for genuine Socratic ignorance. This ignorance is not the conditional kind which recedes as knowledge advances, but it becomes apparent in its full depth precisely as knowledge advances in clarity and scope.

Philosophical igno-rance accompanies the presence of philosophy in all the sciences. Because the scientific attitude guarantees truthfulness, philosophy becomes the champion of science against anti-science. Philosophy considers the preservation of a scientific mode of thought indispensable to the preservation of human dignity.

The university is dedicated to the pursuit of science and scholarship. Research and teaching seek to contribute to intellectual culture as a way in which truth becomes meaningful and manifest. The task of the university may therefore be distinguished into the three functions of research, the transmission of learning, education, and culture. Each of these when considered in isolation is clearly inseparable from the other two. In order to do the work of the university successfully, there must be communication of thinking men. Scholars must communicate with one another, teachers with their students and the students among themselves. Communication of all with all is necessary, each according to his intellectual level. The university achieves its objective within the framework of an institution. This framework is the basic to its very existence and is reflected in its procedural and administrative practice. The institution is simultaneously indis-pensable and a standing threat to the idea of the university. By definition knowledge aims at unification. Isolated disciplines may come' and go. Within the cosmos of learning they nonetheless seek one another. The university is articulated in such a way as to represent the unity of knowlege.

CONCLUSION:

This chapter is exclusively devoted to explaining and interpr-eting the functions and features of a university. Besides these explanation and interpretation, specific views, expressed by New-man and Jaspers have been perused as the views of these two great personalities are of universal validity and worth mentioning. The pursuit of learning is an activity having value as an end in itself. But because its objects are distinguished from other's by their universality, they can be sought only in a certain kind of environment. There is no doubt that universities often provide the environment necessary to the pursuit of learning. A university must essentially be a centre of learning. They help people to acquire useful arts which later enables them to increase productivity and perform other devised economic functions: they help people turn into better citizens. Nowel Smith speaks about the skills required for living and in his opinion, the requisite skills are creative imagination, practical wisdom and logical thought. These general skills are not simply valuable by products but developing them is the essential function of the university.

To explore the concept of a university requires that we should present a more or less philosophical argument which must straddle, rather uneasily, the field of education and of social and political theory. Modern universities are extraordinarily miscellaneous institutions in which a very large number of activities are conducted. They thus supply in some degree evidence that any number of activties might be taken as central. This is the reason why it is plausible to take the view that universities are vital centes of civilization, intellectual powerhouses, areas of social criticism and all the rest. Any attempt to characterize universities in terms of a single criterion will inevitably be wrong. We must consider amongst other things, the historical circumstances of their foundations. Whatever may be inferred from their institutional arrangements and the kind of relationships that have appeared between universities on the one hand and society and culture on the other, we need in particular to be alert to what distinguishes universities from other similar institutions. For the commonest misunderstanding of academic inquiry assimilates it to intellectual uplift, the exercise of rationality or something else similarly general.

Universities are criticized for their devotion to the academic ideal. But universities can only preserve their identity if they steer by the compass of the academic: without it, their increasing involvement with society makes them the helpless pursuers of incoherent desirabilities. The choice they face is between losing themselves in an intellectual chaos, where fashion and social need are powerful unacademic forces or clinging fast to what is reliably traditional and thus dying from ossification.

5

BUDDHIST MONASTERIES : INDIGENOUS UNIVERSITIES OF ANCIENT INDIA

5.1. INTRODUCTION

Buddhism has been regarded as an off-shoot of Hinduism which arose as a revolt against the orthodox Brahmanical system of Hindu India. As it repudiates the vedic authority it is widely known as heterodox system, thus being enumerated along with other heterodox system like Jainism and Caruvaka. The doctrine of Karma and transmigration was generally accepted by thinking persons, and the question which earnest enquiries after truth sought to answer how release could be obtained from the endless round of births and rebirths. Buddism was one among many answers to the question and it has its roots deep in Hindu philosophic thought. It differed from the recognised Brahmanic philosophy, however, in several aspects and the teaching of Buddha was characterised by great earnestness and by a broad spirit of philanthrophy. Buddhism contained certain elements which were destined to bring it into hostility with the Brahmanic system - the non-recognition of the Vedas, and of the Brahman hierarchy as well as of the religious aspect of the caste system. Buddha carried on no crusade against any of these but the opposition was implicit in his system and in course of time the hostility worked itself out into a struggle for existence which ended in Buddhism ceasing to exist in India as a separate faith, though several of its ideas were incorporated into Hinduism. For over fifteen hundred years, however it was in vogue and developed a system of education which was a rival of the Brahmanic system though in many ways similar to it.

One main difference between the Brahmanic and Buddhist education was that the latter was not based on Vedic study and its teachers were not Brahmans, unless those who had become converted to Buddhism. It was open to all corners and not merely to the three twice-born castes. All castes were equally admissible to the Buddhist community, though it was welcomed and patronized by the wealthy and respectable as well as by rich merchants and powerful rulers (Emperor Ashoka, Kaniska and

Harshavardhana) to whose influence it owed a great deal for its advancement.

It was a conclusion from Buddha's views of life that for rapid progress in spiritual improvement a life of retirement from the world was necessary and this was urged upon those who wished to be earnest in their pursuit of freedom from earthly desires. A life of meditation in the solitude of a forest was considered to be the best of all, but from the first this was adopted only by the most earnest, and the majority of the monks or bhikkus lived in companies in monasteries or Viharas. These viharas formed a characteristic feature of Buddhism and for many centuries they were widely spread in India.

Buddhist Education is rightly regarded as phase of the ancient Hindu or Brahmanical system of education as Buddhism itself is rooted deeply in the pre-existing Hindu systems of thought and life. BARTH (The Religions of India p.101) calls Buddhism "a Hindu Phenomenon, a natural product, so to speak of the age and social circle that withnessed its birth" and "when we attempt to reconstruct its primitive doctrine and early history we come upon something so akin to what we meet in the most ancient upanisads and in the legends of Brahmanism that it is not always easy to determine what features belong peculiarly to it").

5.2 EMERGENCE OF VIHARAS OR MONASTERIES IN ANCIENT HINDU INDIA

The history of the Buddhist system of education is practically that of the Buddhist order or Samgha. Buddhist education and learning centred round monasteries as vedic culture centred round the sacrifice. The Buddhist world did not offer any educational opportunities apart from or independently of its monasteries. All education sacred as well as secular, was in the hands of the monks. They had the monopoly of learning and of the leisure to impart it. They were the only custodians and bearers of the Buddhist culture. Thus the rules of Buddhist education are those of the Buddhist Order. These rules are not the invention of the Buddha but modelled upon those of numerous other monastic order professing other faiths and also of Brahmanism itself, the common source from which all such sects arose.

Buddhism throve and made headway in India as a religion of the people - a religion that was bahujanna - not as the cult of a sect or a practice of monkhood. The samgha in Buddhism has an abstract aspect in which it is regarded as a spiritual entity. The SANGHA has a two fold meaning in Buddhism - an entire monk-fraternity or the bond of association among monks, referring in the former to a body of person and in the latter to the confederation which makes them one body. Bot concepts of the Sangha, concrete and abstract appear in usage. In the creed of Three Jewels (Triratna), the parity in which the Sangha is placed with the Buddha and the Dhamma is meaningful it forbids the facile half-backed notion that it represents in Buddhism only the organised missionary agency of a proselytizing faith. The sangha is differently conceived in the system. In fact a comprehension of the true concept of the creed is essential in our approach to its history. So the credal formal in the correlated concepts of the Buddha as the Teacher, the Dhamma as the sum and effect of his teachings and the Sangha as the instrument by which the Dhamma, becoming bahujanna, fulfils itself, epitomizes and rounds off the whole cycle of the faith.

The story of the growth, development and functioning of this Institution (sangha) in India has a clear beginning, a middle and an end - an integration and unity of interest. The milieu in which it was founded was the ancient community of India's wandering almsmen. It was this milieu that shaped and conditioned it- settled its ethos and basic character, the foundation upon which its own system of Vinaya (the name given to the system of Sangha life that developed in the early monk-settlement was afterwards built. Only a few compendiums of Vinaya are available. They are of different schools of Buddhism and in different language but on the whole, not different in substance. Of them, The Vinayapitaka of the Theravada Canon, is the most complete and systematic. The vinayapitaka is a collection of legends each containing a precept of the Lord that pertains either to the individual life and conduct of the Bhikku or to some institution of the collective Sangha life. Each gives a rule either positive or negative in character e.g. I allow you, Bhikkus to do this or to refrain from doing that.

Vassavasa (Rain- retreat), observed by wandering almsmen, was the starting point from which, outside the wanderers comm-unity, its evolution commenced leading it though several stages and varieties of being. The wandering sect became a settled order; the unitary Sangha became plural: with the spread of Buddhism, the monk-communities, each called a Sangha went on steadily, multiplying till they were spread wide over all parts of the country; in their life and organisation gradual changes of a transforming character came about through the action of inner and outer forces: and in the final phase of this history, we see a number of monastic establishments functioning as seats and centres of scholarship and learning and a few as far famed university. It is long and chequered history, yet not the history of a static institution but one that shows-remarkable dynamism and capacity for progress.

The monasteries from where this Institution (Sangha) func-tioned have also a long story of growth by stages. The primitive monk settlement is represented by the avasa or the arama. The former was a monks' colony staked out by the monks themselves while the latter was an enclosed site usually a donation to monks by a wealthy lay man, in or near a town looked after by the donor himself. Within its boundaries an avasa or an arama had huts for the monks dwelling and vihara was the name originally given to such a hutment. A vihara might be occupied by a single monk or by a small group of monks called a Parviena. The accommodation comprised only what is termed a senasana (bed-andsitting) and furniture of a simple kind such as a board to recline on' (apassena-phalaka), a spittoon (kela mallaka) and a seat (pitha) with jointed legs for the purpose of lowering the seat. A common storage for such articles as were allowable to monks called kappiyakuti was a necessary adjunct. The monk built avasa was after all a temporary set-up iiable to be deserted, robbed and dismantled after its evacuation by monks at the end of the vassa period. An arama was more durable and worthwhile. While in the legends we find many references by name to those aramas which became famous Sangha centres none of the avasa bear a name. The name arama denotes a pleasure-ground, usually the property within a town or city or in the suburb of a well-to-do citzen laid out as an orchard or flower-garden. When it was given to the monks by the owner not for temporary use but permanently, it was named a Sangharama. The term, meaning orginally an arama owned by the Sangha came later to shed its implication of a donated pleasure ground and meant simply a campus.

In the legends several Sangharamas i.e) aramas donated by their owners to the Sangha) are mentioned by name. The legends make them comtemporaneous with the Lord and describe them as having been sanctified by his visits or temporary residence viz.

1. Veluvanarama at Rajagaha - (said to be the first gift of an arama to the Buddha and the Sangha. It was made by king (Bimbisara)
2. Jivakarama at Rajagaha (dontated by the renowned phys-ician Jivaka, comtemporary with the Buddha).
3. Ambapali-vana at Vesali (donated by Ambapali, city-courtesan of Vesali and devotee of the Buddha).
4. Udambarikarama near Rajagaha
5. Kukkutarama, Ghositarama and Pavarikambavana
6. Jetavanarama near Savatthi
7. Badarikarama at some distance from Ghositarama
8. Nigrodharama at Kapilavatthu - etc.

Only three of these aramas have been traced by arachaeologists viz (i) Jivakarama (ii) Jetavanarama and (iii) Ghositarama. The sites of these (except for the first) were occupied by monks for many centuries and monasteries were built on them from age to age.

A typical monastery called at first a lena same into existence when the primitive sangha split up into a number of nonfraternities (Sanghas). Unlike the avasa or the arama, a lena was not a settlement of monks from all quarters, but accommodated a single fraternity. Originally there were five structural types of lena but only two types have survivied - the vihara and the Guha. Taking the vindhyan range as the Great Divide" of India, the vihara may be said to be the typical monastery to its north andthe Guha to its south. A canonical legends lists five kinds of lenas as fit for monks dwelling under the name vihara, Addhayoga, pasada, Hammiya and Guha. The transition was from the old-type settlement in an avasa or arama to a lena. A lena was not a monks colony open to all corners; it was a compact unitary establishment for a settled body of monks enabling it to function without disturbance as a corporate body - as a Sangha by itself. Etymologically lena means private abode (from sanskrit form, layana, derived from the verb li, to hide). The etymology is indicative of the nature of a lena. While the old monk-settlement had the character of a rendezvous (meeting-place), a sort of monks caravan-serai, a place of temporary shelter and rest from wandering during the rains, a lena was private-dwélling i.e. the abode of a limited and specific body of monks. Without barring outsiders, it was meant specially for a single resident sangha. Thus a lena was a Monastery proper, not a shifting and seasonal settlement of monks. Fa-hsien's descrption of the Hinayanist monasteries he visited in Udyana on India's north-western border serves to illustrate the distinction: If a strange Bhiksu arrives here, they give him full entertainment for three days: the three days being over, they bid him seek for himself a place to rest permanently.

The institution of *lenas* marks the shift of the monk-community from monk-settlements to monasteries. The break-up in the course of time of the Sangha of the Four Quarters into unitary goups necessitated a new kind of a abode, a lena for a single monk-fraternity which was thus a monastery proper different in layout and construction from the old-style monk-settlements. Of the pancalenani (five lenas) named in the ;legend three structural types had become obsolete: only the Vihara and the Guha survived. The former became the typical monastic builiding of the north and the latter of the south; complete ruin has fallen upon the Viharas and the excavated foundations are their only remains. But the Guhas in the everlasting inset in the rocks, remain: they bear evidence of the splendid wealth of art and architecture that used to be lavished on monasteries in that spacious age of art and culture known as the Gupta Age in ancient Indian history. To this day the caves of Karle, Ellora, Ajanta and Bagh attract visitiors as show-places -treasure houses of the best and finest specimens of ancient Indian art but they were built for and inhabited by monks and as such have a human apart from their purely aesthetic interest.

5.3 MONASTERIES AS CENTRES OF HIGHER LEARNING MONASTIC UNIVERSITIES AD 500 -1200)

A phenomenon increasingly evident in the decline of Budd-hism is the gradual modification of the purely coventual character of the monasteries. From being seats of monk-life and monk-culture, they grew into centres of general learning and liberal scholarship. It was the late fruition of the ancient tradition of Sangha life.

The type of monastery organisation called Mahavihara commenced during the Gupta age an aggregation of several monasteries combined in a unitary organisation. In these Mahaviharas, a re-orientation took place of the old traditional monk-culture, redounding to the loss in a large measure of its exclusively monkish preoccupation. This liberalized culture was the Indian Buddhist culture" of that age. The Mahaviharas were both its depositories and purveyors during the decline of Buddhism in India. It spread in the country from the Mahaviharas: it was there that foreign monks resorted to imbibe it.

Nissaya was an ancient rule of Vinaya dependence on a teacher for a space of years which varied with trainees ability to learn. It was part of the rule (vinaya) and but it served at the same time to create a new value in monastic life, a tradition of learning and scholarship. It continued unbroken in the monasteries and grew into an inalienable aspect of Sangha life. This traditional learning of the monasteries had been at its beginning a cloistered pursuit learning in cannonical lore for the benefit and use of monkhood. But it was progressively liberalized - extended and enlarged in its scope and contents and made available not to monks alone, but to all seekers after knowledge. It was a new development of monastic life and activity and one involved in the complex of conditions and circumstances Buddhism had passed through since the beginning of the Gupta era in its long and historic process of decline. The decline was general and continuous and this was noted by the Chinese pilgrim Hsuian-tsang who watched the process of decline at only one of its stages; he saw it objectively, on its external side - in the dwindling of the adherents of Buddhism the strengthening of rival faiths, the decline in the number of monastic establishments and their inmates, what was not apparent to him was a subtler inner side of this decline, It related to the conditions and status of Buddhism itself as it stood vis-a-vis other faiths then gaining ground. Buddhism had been born as a religion distinct and apart from current Brahmanical faiths and philosophies.

However the Gupta age, (A.D. 300-550) witnessed the emer-gence of Mahayanist Buddhism. (Lord Buddha was an incarnation of a Being who was cosmic and eternal). The Gupta kings lived in the high noon of the Brahmanical revival and professed Brahmanical faith themselves. Yet their active patronage of Buddhist monasteries andmonkhood was of a kind that went much farther than warranted by the mere spirit of toleration. This liberal outlook went on broadening till in after-centuries it reached a consummation in the acceptance of the founder of Buddhism as a deity of the Brahmanical pantheon. Set in this outlook the monasteries ceased to be regarded as organs and institutions of a faith opposed to or even isolated from currently prevailing forms of faith. In fact, since Buddhism had begun to ebb, monasteries had ceased to be propoganda - centres of the religion as in the past. They had been enlarging one aspect of monastic life that was rooted in their ancient tradition of monk-scholarship. The process is marked by a re-orientation of monastic learning, where by it outgrew its cloistered inbred character and turned into a learning that was liberal and many-sided.

In the monasteries the ancient principle of learning had been 'study of faith'. Its aim was to produce the 'perfect monk'. Within the monastic regimen, the immemorial custom of education in India, the Gurukula taking from a master who presides over a small circle of resident pupils - was reproduced. Nissaya, was its counterpart in monastic life. Nassaya refers to dependence on a teacher for a space of years which varied with the trainees ability to learn. Under the ancient Nissaya system, the monastic learning was confined to the cannon and its philosophy (Abhid-amma), it object being to turn out the perfect (bahussuta or pandita) monk. Yet the learning had to grow out of this circum-scribed and imbred character which was hardly sufficient for its own set purpose. Monasteries in fact, were not isolated from the larger life of society: the very reason for their existence was the good and happiness of the many that is, to carry the blessing and the benefit of the religious to those who were without them. It was felt at a certain stage that the mere study for faith fell short of the standard set by the Lord himself for the perfect or accomplished monk-one who, having mastered th doctrine, is able to spread it abroad and confute the doctrine of other faiths. It demanded knowledge of other faiths and also intellectual equipments to be gained from other and non-cannonical sources.

The need for a more liberal learning is suggested in a verse, ostensibly from the Sutralankara, cited among his quotations from the Sutras and Sastras by the Tibetan scholar and historio-grapher Bu-ston and made explicit in his comment. In order to vanquish and to help others as well as to obtain knowledge through knowledge of himself, he (the good monk) is earneslty applied to study : on which Buston's explicatory comment is as follows:

Accordingly the science of Logic (Hetuvidya) and of Grammar and Literature are studied in order to vanquish one's adversaries (in controversy): the science of Medicine (Cikitsavidya) and Arts

(Silakarmavidya), for administering help to others, and that of Metaphysics (Adhyatmavidya) to acquire knowledge of himself. The enumeration is from the traditional group of Five Vidyas: (i) Sabdavidya (Grammar and Philology) (ii) Cikitsavidya (Medicine) (iii) Hetuvidya (Logic) (iv) Silpasthanavidya (Fine Arts) and (v) Adhyatma Vidya (Metaphysics). The study was calculated to provide a monk with the scholarly equipments needed by him for the discharge ofhis obligations, viz to spread the religion among laity and to strengthen its cause by victory in disputations. The Science of Logic (Hetuvidya) was developed among scholar-monks out of the older vada manuals that had been composed with the object of sharpening mental faculties for success in debate. This liberalization of learning, the shift from the ancient study for faith to study for knowledge was a matter of natural evolution in the culture of the monasteries.

It brought monastic learning into a larger framework; Confined no longer to the nine parts (Navanga) of the canon). The nine Angas are the nine forms of composition of which the canon is made up viz sutta, Geyya, Veyyakarana, Gatha, Udana, Itivuttaha, Jataka, Abbhutadhamma, Vedalla.), it came into the general plan and pattern of Indian learning. Since its remote beginnings in the vedic schools, this learning had grown and expanded from century to century branching off, with the growth of specialization and expertise, into different Sastras and Vidyas.

The categories of Sastras and Vidyas expanded but the group of five mentioned by Buston (14th century) had been traditonally current in the seventh century A.D. for it is mentioned as such by both Hsuan-tsang and I- tsang. The five vidyas were taken up in the scheme of monastic learning and large contributions to their development were made in course of time by Buddhist monk-scholars - the largest being to Hetuvidya (Logic).

5.4 NATURE OF HIGHER EDUCATION IN VIHARAS

The history of the Buddhist system of Education is practically that of the Buddhist Order or Sangha. Buddhist education and learning centred round monasteries as vedic culture round the sacrifice. The Buddhist world did not offer any educational opportunities apart from or independently of its monasteries. All education, sacred as well as secular, was in the hands of the monks. They had the monopoly of learning of the leisure to impart it. They were the only custodians and bearers of the Buddhist culture.

A Bhikku means an almsman. He is differentiated from an ordinary beggar by the sacramental character of his begging. His beggary is not just a means of subsistence, but on outward token that he was renounced the world and all its goods and thrown himself for bare living on the chances of public charity. A community of men of this type is not found in comparable ancient civilizations, but since remote antiquity they have been a feature of the Indian scene. When the Buddha himself, renouncing the world, became an almsman, the almsmen's community already existed in India. The Legend of the Four Signs, from which the story of his Great Renunciation derives, states that the prompting came to him from one of this community. The four sings (Nimitta) are conceived in the legend as four beacons guiding him to the path of the Buddhahood, and the first three are said to have been an old man, a sick man and a dead man, seen on three successive occasions for the time by Prince Siddhartha on his pleasure drives in a chariot. The fourth was something different: it was a wandering almsman, a Bhikkhu.

Men of the community are recognised by others by the token of their Begging Bowls. The Begging Bowl (patra = patta in pali) has to them a certain sanctity as the visible symbol and token of the almsman's calling. People are aware of their difference in standing from vagabonds and beggars and recognise that their wandering is not wilful vagabondage, but a quest controlled by a purpose and direction : it is Brahmacariya, a spiritual quest. Being a professed man of religion he is supposed to wander about in search of a Dhamma most congenial to his own mind and spiritual aptitude : and it is the hallmark whereby he is distinguished and known.

The Bhikkhu sangha took shape, not comformably the ideal cherished by the Founder, but to the type and configuration of a sect in the wanderers community. It looked up to the Buddha as the sattha: its bond was the Dhamma given to it by the founder and the cement of its cohesion common allegiance to the sattha. From the other sects, it was distinguished by its Dhamma; the sect rested on the basis of its cult, and there were as usual defections from as well as accrection to it. Those who were wanderers by their calling had to reckon with the monsoon conditions which made inevitable an annual break in their wanderings. So it became customary for all sects of the wanderers community to suspend wandering and seek shelter for the season, and the custom was already very old - it had even gained from antiquity the character of a ceremonial observance in the community when prince Gotama forsook the world and joined it.

The rule that a wanderer must suspend wandering and remain in retreat during the season of rain occurs among the canonical regulations of different sects: the Buddhists call it vassa, Jainas Pajjusana, and the Bráhmanical Sannyasins are enjoined to be at fixed residence (Dhrivasila) during the time. This rain-retreat had been a universal customary observance among wanderers of all sects. The first step in the individuation of the other sects in the community was taken when the general custom was specialized by the Buddhists. The Jaina and Brahmanical wanderers had no regulations prescribing living together during rain- retreat. The Buddhist idea of rain-retreat was not to live anywhere or alone and companionless or in promiscuous company, but to settle in a congregation of fellow-monks. For that purpose, the settlement needed sequestration within its own boundaries. The demarcation and fixing of boundaries (sima), therefore became a matter of some importance in order to allow a body of Bhikkhus to live together by themselves. This was the character of the Buddhist vassavasa (rain-retreat) and no other sect practised this.

The ancient ideal of a free wandering life was never given up by the Bhikkhus. But they ceased to be wanderers like almsmen of other sects. There are indications of the growth of a custom among them of returning to and occupying same avasas and aramas, on the termination of the wandering period: that they had left after the last rain-retreat so that those who habitually lived together for the vassa in one avasa (samana samvasaka) were distinguished from those who habitually lived together in another Nana-samvasaka). The co-dwellers were distinguished from others in the matter of allotment of accommodation (senasava) and in the exercise of the rights of sangha life. As this custom of resorting to the same avasa for rain-retreat became more and more the use and went among the Buddhists, the Bhikkhus came to be distinguished from wanderers and they themselves recognized and accepted the distinction. The idea of continuing congregation in spite of its annual regulation break-up after the vassa, was responsible for the development of those features of collective life viz parimokka recital, the pavarana and the kathina.

The founders idea had been that the sangha should be one entire body and a unitary organisation of monks hailing from all quarters irrespective of regional provenance - a Ctuddisa (four quarters) Bhikkhu -Sangha.

This process of transition from wandering to the settled life was a slow and gradual one, but undoubetely accomplished early in sangha - history as early as the 4th century B.C. Its consequence was two-fold, first the sangha became an organisation independent of the wanderers community: the Buddhist Bhikkhus were by themselves as well as by others distinguished from wanderers secondly it marked the beginning of cenobium among them. In the Vinayapittaka the Bhikkhus sangha appears not as a body of wanderers, but as a settled cenobitical society.

Thus a new unit came to be recognized a company of monks belonging to an avasa (avasika). It is not a fortutous group of monks out of the Brotherhood of four quarters, but a body limited by its habitual occupation of the same avasa. The avasikas dwellers at an avasa, constituting a unit called themselves collectively a sangha. It was not "The sangha of the four quarters" but a single non-fraternity. Thus there was a shift from wandering to settled life in the growth and development of the concept of sangha and the leisure time of the settled life was devoted to the pursuit of scriptural studies. This traditional learning of the monasteries had been at its beginning a cloistered pursuit-learning in canonical lore for the benefit and use of monkhood. But it was progressively liberalized- extended and enlarged in its scope and contents and made available not to monks alone, but to all seekers after knowledge. It was a new development of monastic life and activity and one involved in the complex of conditions and circumstances. Buddhism had passed through since the beginning of the Gupta era in its long and historic process of decline. Monasteries were not isolated from the larger life of society; the very reason for their existence was the good and happiness of the many that is, to carry the blessing and the benefit of the religion to those who were without them. It must have been felt at a certain stage that the mere study for faith fell short of the standard set by the Lord himself for the perfect or accomplished monk- one who having mastered the doctrine, is able also to spread it abroad and confute the doctrines of other faiths. It demanded knowledge of other faiths and also intellectual equipments to be gained from other and non-canonical sources. In fact, since Buddhism had begun to ebb, monasteries had ceased to be propo-ganda centres of the religion as in the past. They had been enlarging one aspect of monastic life that was rooted in their ancient tradition of monk-scholarship. The process is marked by a re-orientation of monastic learning whereby it outgrew its cloistered inbred character and turned into a learning that was liberal and many-sided.

In the monasteries the ancient principle of learning had been study for faith. Its aim was to produce the perfect monk within the monastic regimen the immemorial custom of education in India, the Gurukula-taking lessons from a master who presides over a small circle of resident pupils- was reproduced. Under the ancient Nissaya system, the monastic learning was confined to the canon and its philosophy (Abhidhamma) its object being to turn out the perfect (bahussuta orpandita) monk. Yet the learning had grown out of this ciucumscribed and imbred character which was hardly sufficient for its own set purpose. The need for a more liberal learning was felt. this liberalization of learning, the shift from the ancient study for faith to study for knowledge was a matter of natural evolution in the culture of the monasteries. It brought monastic learning into a larger frame-work. Confined no larger to the nine parts (navanga) of the canon, it came into the general plan and pattern of Indian learning. Since its remote beginnings in the Vedic schools, this learning had grown and expanded from century to century branching off, with the growth of specilization and expertise, into different sastras and vidyas. The categories of sastras and vidyas expanded but the group of five had been traditionally current in the seventh century A.D for it is mentioned as such by both Hsuan-tsang and I-tsing. The Five-vidyas (Sabdavidya, Chikitsavidya, Hetuvidya, Silpasthana vidya, and Adhyatma vidya) were taken up in the scheme of monastic learning and large contributions to their development were made in course of time by the Buddhist monk-scholars- the largest being to Hetuvidya.

5.4.1 AIMS OF BUDDHIST EDUCATION IN GENERAL

Due to certain lapses of Brahmanism, Buddhism came into being. The existing religion was reshaped into meaningless forms. The ennobling study of the Upanisads and Sutras fell out of use. Ancient social and moral values were disfigured by the unhealthy distinctions, of castes and as a result sutras were deprived of religious instructions. The lower classes of society had to go without any education worth the name. Buddhism started as monastic movement in the 5th century B.C. Buddhist society was monk-ridden and viewed religion as the basic element of developing personality. In ancient India for a long time education was given by individual teachers on their own initiative and responsibility. Buddhism played a vital role in re-organising the educational structure of the period. The history of the Buddhist system of education is particularly that of the Buddhist monasteries and education, either secular or sacred was absolutely in the hands of monks. Learning centred about monasteries and monks were the true custodians of that culture. Buddhist Sanghas (monasteries) were based upon common democratic principles. The monks had right to receive religious and general education.

In the beginning Buddhist education was open for those who entered or intended to enter the monastic order. This was but natural, for worldly life was neglected for them and Buddhist workers believed that present world was full of sorrow and salvation could be possible by renouncing it. No interest was shown in the education of those who intended to follow secular life and pursuit. But later on in due course of time, it was, however realized that it was essential to win public sympathy and support for its complete flourishing. Since this religion was contemporary to the prevalent predominating old religion, Brahmanism, it helped the cause of education as done by the Brahman priest. Buddhist monks realized that the spread of religion was possible in better way, if they enabled to influence the minds of the younger section of the society. This idea won a massive support and helped also in the recruitment of right types of persons. Altekar writes:

Buddism therefore threw itself heart and soul into the cause of the general education of the whole community from about the beginning of the Christian era. Therefore education was open to all and was not limited to only monasteries. There was no caste discrimination in education like Brahmanism. The lower classes of society had now to undergo religous instructions and achieve real education. The aim of all education, professional or non-professional was the freedom of the soul from the sufferings of life and discipline was the effective means to accomplish it.

The Buddhist philosophy played an important role in the Buddhist scheme of education but adequate importance was also given to the study of religion and philosophy of different sects in Hinduism and Jainism. Education was not only continued to theology, philosophy and logic but the ascetics had to engage themselves in various kinds of practical and secular works instead of being exclusively occupied in religous or spiritual deeds. The ideal synthesis between the theorotical as well as practical knowledge was one of the unique feature of the Buddhist education. The Buddhist education was not merely for the develop-ment of mental, intellectual and spiritual powers for the sake of culture but it was primarily given for the purpose of training every member to meet the callings of society. In this connections it is also mentioned here that the ideal of serving the society in best way was satisfied by opening the doors of learning to women also.

The Buddhist society was of simple humans, of ascetics and monks. The ideal society according to the Buddhist scheme adopted the attainment of Nirvana, as the chief aim of education. This aim of education was to be fulfilled by abiding the rules and regulations of Buddhism. Buddha was of the view that the knowledge and learning can only completely abolish the burden of sorrow and ignorance. According to Buddhism it was possible in the existing life of humans. Nirvana was treated to be another form of Mukti. The ascetics and monks after achieving Nirvana divested themselves of the complex and complicated earthly bondage and attained finally Mukti, the supreme end of life. Education based upon the Buddhist scheme was responsible for enabling monks to attain this aim. The Bhikshu was prohibited from having sexual life and to live by mendicancy was a must for him. Education which monks received in monastery by a regular scheme was responsible for infusing the idea of religious spirit, and piety among them. The aim of life was to achieve the supreme end of life and in support of this utmost need of society, educational institutions were established.

5.4.2 THE BUDDHIST SYSTEM OF ADMISSION

The history of the Buddhist system of education is practically that of the Buddhist Order of Sangha. Buddhist education and learning centred round monsteries as Vedic culture centred round the sacrifice. The Buddhist world did not offer any educational opportunities apart from or independently of its monasteries. All education sacred as well as secular, was in the hands of the monks. They had the monopoly of learning and of the leisure to impart it. They were the only custodians and bearers of the Buddhist culture.

When the Buddhists first settled down to coenobitical life in the monasteries (4th century B.C) the question arose of training the neophyte who had been ordained and had joined a monastery. The system was known as Nissaya, meaning literally dependence on a teacher. The Nissaya period was one of learning and novitiate which preceded the attainment of the full status of a monk and it is sometimes called by the same term bramacharya as is used in Brahmanical books for the student period of a man's life. It was a system which reproduced within the communal monastic life the pre-Buddhistic Brahmanical small school or teacher and a union of the master and his disciples after the Brahmanical model. The finding of a teacher was a condition of Ordination as laid down in the text (vinaya). "Let no one, O Bhikkhus, who has no upajjhaya receive the Upasamapada ordination" The teacher must be an individual person and not a fictitious one like the sangha as a corporate body. The text does not permit such a fraud on the system. "Let no one receive the Upasamapada ordination with the Sangha as Upajjhyaya" The idea of the individual responsibility of the teacher for his pupils training and conduct was thus rightly emphasized.

The first step in Buddhist initiation is called Pabbajja or "going forth". It means that a person presents himself for admission into the order by "going out" of his previous state whether it be that a layman or householder or a wandering ascetic or monk belonging to a different sect. The admission to the order was thrown open to all the casetes. The candidate for admission must take leave of all the visible marks of the life he has left, the marks of caste as of clothes. But though in theory the order might be recruited from all castes, in practice the admission to it was sought by a few that small and select class of persons who were spiritually advanced enought to adopt the life of asceticsm renouncing the life of pleasures and out going activities.

During the two centuries and odd between Fa-hsien (5th c.A.D) and Hsuian tsang (7th c.A.D the studium- generale character of a number of monasteries were so developed that their strictly conventional outlook had to be somewhat modified. Though they remained monastic establishments, run and administered by the monks and functioning under monk-made regulations, therc were besides the monks many lay students, interested in studying either Buddhist literaure or purely secular subjects, who had come to reside there just for the sake of learning. These laymen in a monastery are divided by I-tsing into two categories, Manavas and Brahmacarins, between whom the monk authorities used to make some distinction. Those white-robed (i.e laymen) who come to the residence of a priest and read chiefly Buddhist scriptures with the intention that they may one day become tonsured and black-robed are called children Manava. Those who (coming to a priest) want to learn secular literature only, without having any intention to quit the world are called "students". Brahmacarin. Those two groups of persons (though residing in a monastery) have to subsist at their own expense. As noted by I-tsing (7th c A.D.) in the monasteries of India there are many "students" who are the Bhikshus and instructed by them in secular literature.

Between these two classes of resident lay students - the Manavas who studied the scripture intending to qualify for monkhood and the Brahmacarins who only studied secular subjects - the former were treated more liberally. The latter used to render personal services to the teacher as was the immemorial custom of India; but the cost of their maintenance was not defrayed out of the monastery funds, "The students (i.e the Brahmacarins) says I- tsing, must not be fed from the permanent property of the Sangha for this is prohibited in the teaching of Buddha: but if they have done some laborious work for the Sangha they are to be fed by the monastery, according to their merit. Food made for ordinary purposes or presented by a giver to be used by the "students" (Brahmacarins) can be given to them without wrong doing. It has been inferred from this that learning at a monastery by a layman was not a costly proposition: there is no mention of fees in I- tsing's account and the cost of living could be met by serving the sangha. I-tsing speaks of many students being instructed in secular subjects by monk-teachers in Indian monasteries, but it is not known what proportion the lay students bore to the number of monk inmates. In any case it could not have been negligible, as these monasteries attracted general students presumably by their superior efficiency of instruction . Some of the monasteries which had grown into seminaries of learning between (5th century and the seventh century B.C.) developed as an organization entitling them to be classed as Universities.

It may also be noted that the Pabbajja this going out" of home into the order, is akin to the Brahmanical system of studentship under which the young disciple has to go out of his own home the care and company of his parents and relations to live with his chosen preceptor as an antevasi in his hermitage or Asrama in a new home and environment under rigorous conditions of discipline and training under the Buddhist system, too the layman admitted to the order is placed under discipline of a preceptor who is to control his conduct. As in the Brahmanical system, a minimum age limit was fixed for initiation, viz eight years, and children below that age were not accepted by the Order. Against the minimum period of studentship in the Brahmanical system was twelve years: the same is the period of Buddhist novitiate. Corresponding to the epithet Brahmachari conferred upon a youth after his upanayana is the Buddhist epithet samanera applied to the youth who is a pabbajita i.e. has become a homeless one on his performing the ceremony of initial or preliminary ordination (pabbajja).

5.4.2 (I) RULES OF FIRST ORDINATION (PABBAJJA)

In the case of a layman under the twenty years of age seeking admission to the Order, he approaches tonsured the vihara or monastery of his choice with a suit of the yellow robes of the monk in his hands and presents himself before an elder of the monastery for initiation. The elder then invests him with the yellow robe and calls upon him to take the following oath of Three Refuges (saranattaya) three times. "I take refuge with the Order". Next the following ten commandments are administered to him (the dasasikkhapadani) viz. abstinence from i) taking life (2) taking what is not given (3) impure practices (4) telling a lie (5) intoxicating drinks arrack etc 6) eating out of time (7) dancing singing and seeing shows (8) using garlands, scents, ingments, ornaments and fingery (9) use of a high or large couch or seat, and (10) receiving gold and silver. Most of these interdicts figure in the code of regulations governing the life of a Brahmaehari too. Then the ceremony is over and the novice is committed to the care of his elder or preceptor who brings him up till he is fit for the higher ordination.

5.4.2 (II) RESTRICTIONS TO ADMISSION

After the completion of the ceremony the monk was comm-itted to the care of his preceptor. Buddhist literature clearly revealed that there were certain imposition upon the admission seekers. Admission was not given tothe seekers without the consent of their parents. This restriction presented the most appreciable instance of Buddhist system of education showing due respect for the discipline of family life without which family as well as society would have disintegrated. Physical defects such as serious sickness, contageous disease leprosy, boils and itches were the hurdles for their admission. The government servants and soldiers were devoid of benefit of admission to the order because of their inviolably useful service to the country. The author finds that these regulations governing the life of viharas had much concern for the spiritual as well as physical health of its members. The Bhikkus were expected to join the order with an untarnished record. The pabbajja did not permit the "going out of" or a self-willed, cowardly, fraudulent, or dishonest escape from one's obligations to the family, the state, and the society. Prof. R.K. Mukerjee in this connection clearly states:

The sacredness and inviolability of these moral, political social and economic obligations were thus very properly emphasized recognized by the Order which did not countenance the violent and revolutionary methods of accomplishing spiritual evolution.

In addition to the chief limitations of admission to the Order the texts lay down a few minor ones. Persons who were found to be "shameless" and not duly "modes" were not to be admitted. This was to be ascertained by the regulation of keeping the proposed pupils under observation for the first four or five days until it was seen how they behaved to the other Bhikkus of the order. Again, persons who "furtively" attached themselves to the Order were also to be kept out.

5.4.2 (III) FINAL ORDINATION OF UPASAMPADA

The preliminary ordination of the Pabbajja inaugurates of the upsampada, the arrival at the full status of monkhood or a Bhikshu a full fledged member of the order. The period between the two ordinations was twelve years at its maximum and was not continued beyond the twentieth year of the postulant. The period of novitiate was, however, reduced to four months in the case of the postulant being previously a member of another monastic order.

The higher ordination of the Upsampada by which a Samanera completes his course of probation and enters upon the full membership of the sangha for which he is determined and has been prepared since his Pabbajja ordination marks an important point of distinction between the Brahmanical and Buddhist systems of education. Under the former system, the Brahmacharin, on completion of his studentship and coming of age returns to his home and family as a Snataka and presently marries and becomes a Frihastha or householder. His "going out of home" or pravrajya was for a temporary period. In the case of the Buddhist, the "outgoing from home into homelessness" (agarasma anagariyam prabbajja) is final. The Brahmanical system, however, provided for exceptions. Brahmacharis were given the option to remain as such through life at his teachers and after his death with his family according to his choice the special desgination of Naishthika being applied to them as a mark of distinction. But the exceptions became the rule in the Buddhist system. While the Pabbajja is a one-sided transaction with which the Order as a whole has nothing to do the Upasampada consisted of a ceremony which has to be completed before the order and by their participation.

The ordination can be conferred only by a Chapter of at least ten elders who should all be learned, competent, and of not less than ten years standing. One of them must introduce the novice to the president of the chapter in a formal resolution, natti. Then he or any other member is appointed by the Chapter to give to candidate preliminary instructions. The instructions are to be given aside. They comprise a series of questions to the candidate to ascertain his ability under the specifed conditions (regarding his being free from certain disceases, debts obligations of royal service, his age, the consent of his parents). He was also asked his name, the name of the Upajjhaya he had chosen and whether he had his alms bowl and robes in due state. He was also instructed as to the manner of answering these questions before the Chapter when they would formally put them to him. On completion of these instruction, the instructor takes permission of the Chapter to present the candidate. The candidate is to present himself in a proper respectful manner specified. He should "adjust his upper robe so as to cover one shoulder, salute the feet of the /bhikkus with his head, sit down squatting raise his joined hands" and entreat the order three times to confer intitation on home " out of compassion"Then a member of the chapter other than the instructor formally moves the Resolution for initiation of the candidate and with the permission of the Assembly, asks him about the Disqualifications" and other requirements and on the answers being satisfactory, the Resolution is repeated three times and then declared as carried the members expressing their assent by silence. At the conclusion of the ceremonies, the hour, date and season of ordination, together with the details of the assembly (Sangiti) are recorded and communicated to the newly ordained monk so that he may also know his spiritual age. Then he is carefully taught the form Requisities (nissaya) the four Inderdicts (akaraniyani) of the monastic life. The four requisites are (1) eating of the food collected in the alms-bowl only (pindiyalopabhojana) (2) wearing robes made of rags collected (pamsukulachivara): (3) lodging at the foot of a tree (rukkamulasenasana) and (4) using cow's urine as medicine (putimuttabhesajja). The monk was however, permitted to accept better things as gifts from laymen. The four Interdicts comprised (1) sexual inter course (2) theft (3) taking life (4) boasting of superhuman powers.

Thus the ordination of the Upasampada was performed in a most rational and business like way without the use of any mystical symbols and methods indicative of the special solemnity and significance of the occasion to the person taking orders or of his spiritual transformation and re-birth. But if the admission to the order was so simple in its process the withdrawal from it was also not more difficult.

5.4.2 (IV) RULES FOR RENUNCIATION OF MONKHOOD:

Infringement of any of the prohibitions is punished by explusion from the order, while an ordained monk might seek separation from the order if he feels the promptings of the flesh "if his father, mother, wife or the daughter and the jest, the pleasantry of the old days are still in his thoughts". Only he has to declare his weakness before a witness (who need not be a monk) who must hear and understand him to say that he renounces the Buddha the Doctrine, and the Order. Thus the order did not try artifical methods to keep themselves together in the interests of their real spiritual growth, which was not a matter to be forced. Two fundamental principles viz chastity and poverty mark out the monastic life from ordinary layman's life in marriage and property. To become a monk meant the dissolution of the marriage tie. "As a man whose head is cut off cannot live any longer with his trunk alone, thus a Bhikku who practises sexual intercourse is no samana. The texts (mahavakkaya) make a monk address his forsaken wife as his quondam partner and as sister. Monkhood meant, indeed a dissolution of all blood relationships. The relations of the monk do not, however necessarily disown him. From their standpoint the relationship continues and is open to the monk for resumption whenver he wants it. But Buddhism is indifferent to such backslidings of monks. A monk was also allowed, even when he has entered upon Vassa or residence during the rainy season, to visit his sick relations such as his parents, brother or sister, if they desired it. He was also allowed to give robes to his father and mother if he so desired. Next to the vow of chastity is that of poverty as an essential mark of monastic life. A monk must live by mendicancy and not by his property the letter which binds man to the world. Hence he is called a Bhikshin beggar. The vow of poverty · so rigorously enjoined upon the individual monk was not at all meant for the sangha which the Buddha himself permitted to grow rich by permitting it to receive the benefactions of its lay well-wishers which the Buddha himself permitted to grow rich by permitting to receive the benefactions of its lay well-wishers which flowed in an abundant stream under the Buddhas direct encouragement. A monk who digs the earth or causes it to be dug, is liable to punishment" but the Mahavagga has a passage alluding to the cultivation or sowing of the land belonging to the Arama of the order. While the sangha was thus allowed to receive property of various kinds and grown steadily rich, there was no reaxation permitted in the vow of poverty imposed upon the individual monk who could not as his exclusive possessions more than the following eight articles. viz the three robes (the full complement of the Bhikkus dress comprised three parts and hence was called Ticivara. The three parts were known as Antaravasaka, uttarasanga and sanghati), a girdle for the loins, as alms-bowl, a razor, a needle and a water- strainer not only to remove the impurities of his drinks but also to intercept destruction of life. These are all objects for individual and exclusive and not for collective and common possession and enjoyment. This self-imposed poverty of monks was proclaimed daily by his begging rounds.

5.4.3 TEACHER PUPIL RELATIONSHIP

The Buddhist concept of Teacher Pupil relationship indicates the arrangement for educating the monks. Even the higher ordination of upasampada does not give the ordained monk liberty of conduct or independent status. He was placed in charge of two superiors qulified by learning, character and standing who were called the Acharya and upadhyaya.It is difficult to distinguish their functions from the texts. They are described in Mahavagga. The distinction seems to be that the upadhyaya was the higher authority entrusted with the duty of instructing the young Bhikku in the sacred texts and doctrines, while the Acharya assumed responsibility for his conduct and was thus called also karmacharya in reference not merelyto his part in the ecclesiastical act but also to his tutorial responsibility as regards discipline. According to Buddhaghosha (commentator on Mahavagga) the Upadhyaya is to be of ten years and the Acharya of six years seniority. But, of course mere seniority is no qualification unless the monk was also learned and competent. In the Brahmanical education, however, the Acharya ranks higher than the Upadhyaya. Thus an upsampanna bhikshu has to live under the control of two teachers for his mental and moral training. This period of training or dependence (nissaya) is for at least ten years but the period is reduced to five years for a "learned andcompetent Bhikkhu" and extended to all his life for an unlearned one" after which he was allowed to give a nissaya to others i.e. receive pupils as an Acharya. For it is the Acharya who is called the nissaya-da (giver of protection) while his protege was called nissaya- antevasika (pupil in dependence. The relation between the two are also indicated. The Achariya Bhikkhus, ought to consider the Antevasika (ie. disiple living with his teacher) as a son; the Antevasika ought to consider the Acharya as a father. Thus these two united by mutual reverence, confidence and communion of life, will progress advance and reach a high stage in this doctrine and discipline. Corresponding to the Achariya and his Antevasika are the Upajjhaya and his saddhiviharika with similar relations (nissaya) between them. The higher rank of the upajjahaya is evident from the fact that a nissaya or the relationship between the Acharya and Antevasika will be in abeyance in the presence of the upajjhaya whom the pupil will be bound to follow for the time being.

The Bhikshu has to make a formal application to his proposed preceptor, upajjhaya, for accepting him as his pupil in the following manner : Let him who is going to choose an upajjhaya adjust his upper robe so as to cover one shoulder, salute his feet, sit down squatting, raise his joined hands and say Venerable sir, be my uppajjhaya three times" The upajjhaya will then indicate by nodding or words his acceptence of the applicant as his pupil.

5.4.3. (I) MUTUAL OBLIGATIONS BETWEEN TEACHER AND PUPILS

The Buddha's concept of the obligations of both teachers and pupils is enunciated well in the Siglovada Sutta which enumerates the duties of teachers and pupils :

The teacher should

1) give the Bhikshu under his charge all possible intellectual and spiritual help and guidance "by teaching, by puting questions to him, by exhortation and by instructions,

2) train him in virtue and good manners

3) carefully instruct him, impart upto him a knowledge of the science and wisdom of the ancients :

4) supply the articles such as an alm-bowl or a robe out of his own belongings to his disciple in case he lacked his necessary articles.

5) nurse the pupil in sickness as long as his life lasts and wait until he has recovered. During this period of illness, the teacher is to minister to his pupil in the same way as the pupil serves him in health, down to even rising from bed early to give his pupil "the teeth cleanser and water to rinse his mouth with". getting water for the washing of his feet etc.

6) speak well of him to friends and relations and

7) guard him from danger

The pupil should

1) minister to his teacher

2) rise up in his presence and wait upon him:

3) listen to all he says with respectful attention

4) perform the duties necessary for his personal comfort: and

5) carefully attend to his instructions- The teaching would be in the form of answering questions or delivering a discourse.

Thus the pupil has to serve his teacher, and him alone, for he is not to render such service to or accept it from, anybody else. Nor is he to give or receive anything without his teacher's permission. He is not to enter the village or go to a cemetery or go abroad on journeys without his teacher's permission. The permission might be granted if he would travel with a learned Bhikkhu in his company to control him.

6) Lastly if his teacher is sick, he must nurse him as long as his life lasts and wait until he has recovered.

These were meant to be obligations between the teachers and pupils in a secular setting because the same sutta lays down a similar set of duties between religious teachers and their lay disciples. Here the ethical content of what is taught is emphasized and interestingly accessible to their teachers. In both cases of secular religious education, the obligation cast on the pupil or disciple as regards learning is very important. The pupil is expected to listen to everything the teacher says with respectful attention. The lay disciple is similarly asked to minister to his teachers with respectful attenion in his words, deeds and thcughts.

5.4.3 (II) PUPIL HELPING TEACHER.

The relations between the teacher and pupil were expected to be so intimate that the latter even tried to minister to his teacher's mental troubles. To remove his teachers "discontent" or " indecision the pupil would first try his own means and beguile him by religious conversation or get the help of others. The pupil was also to combat by discussion any false doctrines which the teacher might take to or get to do it.

The relations of the pupil toward his teachers did not however, transcend those toward the Order as a whole to which they bowed a common allegiance as members. Where the teacher offended gravely the Order, the pupil was to get him duly punished by the Order, and when the penal discipline is duly undergone, to get the Order' to rehabilitate his teacher. In the case of the Order passing any unduly severe sentence, the pupil is to do what he can to get it modified, or nullified by arguing with the order on the one hand, and seeing that the teacher "may behave himself properly, live modestly, and aspire to get clear of his penance that the Order may revoke its sentence.

5.4.3 (III) EXPULSION AND TERMINATION OF STUDENTSHIP

There were also rules for the expulsion of a pupil by his teacher." In five cases a Saddhiviharika ought to be turned away, when he does not feel great affection for his upajjahaya nor great inclination towards him, nor much shame great reverence, nor great devotion.

There are again enumerated five cases of cessation of a nissaya between the upajjahaya and Saddhiviharika or the Achariya and Antevasika, viz when teacher " is gone away or has returned to the world, or has died or is gone over to a schismatic faction or when he gives order to the pupil to separate under rules of expulsion stated above

5.4.3 (IV) THE QUALIFICATIONS OF A TEACHER

The duties of the teacher point to the qualifications required of him. Without these a monk was not entitled "to give a nissaya" or "ordain a novice." These are exhaustively enmerated in Mahavagga. He must be well up in what belongs to moral practices self-contradiction, wisdom, emanicipation and the know-ledge and insight thereto", must be able to help others to full perfection in these: must be believing (not guilty of heresy) modest fearful of sinning, strenouous, of ready memory, not guilty of transgressions in morals or conduct, not uneducated or foolish and must be able to train a pupil in the precepts of proper conduct, to educate him in the elements of morality to instruct him in what pertains to the Dhamma, to instruct him in what pertrains to the Vinaya, to discuss or to make another discuss according to the Dhamma a false docrine that might arise and so forth.

Regarding the number of pupils a teacher could entertain, we have the following direction. I" allow, O Bhikkhus, a learned competent Bhikkhu to ordain two novices or ordain as many novices as he is able to administer exhortation and instruction to".

The unit of the Buddhist educational system was thus the group of a youngh Bhikkus or monks living under the guardianship of a common teacher, the Upajjahaya or Achariya who was individuallly responsible for their health and studies manners and morals, their spiritual progress. The groups or schools into which a knot of teacher and his pupils was organised were not always existing as isolated and independent units or institutions in the Buddhist world as they did so largely in the Brahmanical world of culture. They federated themselves into a larger unit called the Vihara or monastery. Thus we have to view them as parts of that larger organization and in their relations to its general, collective life which developed its own code of discipline and regulations building upon all. While Brahmanical culture depended upon the system of individual schools and ideal successions of teachers and disciples, the Buddhist culture was the product of confederations of such schools in larger monastic institutions comprising numbers of teachers and students (sometimes as many as 10.000 as at Nalanda) promoting partaking of a wider, collective, academic life with its own advantages as an educational and educative agency and factor.

Since the Monastery was a federation of individual educational groups or schools, the efficiency of its organization was dependent upon the federal principles of administration which aimed at three distinct objects viz (a) the independence and efficiency of each constituent groups of pupils bound to an individual teacher (b) the adjustment of relations between the different constitutent groups, and (c) the framing of laws governing the establishment as a whole and building upon all its members, the teachers and the taught alike.

5.4.3 (V) TRAINING OF MONKS

It was, however, chiefly for puposes of their religious education and spiritual culture that the monks were brought together in the monasteries. We have already seen how the monastery was a kind of federation of groups of teachers and pupils of junior monks living in dependence upon the seniors. Every Bhikku is expected to accept a pupil, to provide himself with a samanera to give a Nissaya and to confer the Upasampada ordination.

The Vinaya texts distinguish four principal kinds of probation for the Bhikkus. The first of these applied when the follower of another of the reforming sects was received into the Buddhist order. Upon such a person was imposed a Parivasa (a probation -time) of four months. The probationer is required to submit to a strict courses of discipline. He must not enter the village to early nor come back to the Vihara too late. He must not frequent the society of objectionable persons such as harlots, widows, adult girls, eunuches or Bhikkhunis. The probation is to be condemned when he does not show himself skilled in the various things his fellow Bhikkhus have to do, is not diligent, not able to consider how things are to done, not able to do things himself and not able to give directions to others. He is also to be condemned when he does not show keen zeal when the doctrine is preached to him or when questione are put on the same. He is also expected to be pleased when the Buddha is praised and not to be pleased when the sect he has deserted is criticized. A probationary Bhikkhu, further is not entitled to the full privileges belonging to a regular Bhikku. His shall be the worst seat, the worst sleeping place and the worst room in the hostel. He must live on alms personally received. He is not fit for a forest life (for he always needs control and guidance). "He must always live with a regular Bhikkhu. But he must not live with Bhikkhus of communities different from him own. And while living with a regular Bhikkhu he is to observe various forms of showing honour to him.

5.4.4. CURRICULUM IN THE BUDDHIST SYSTEM OF EDUCATION

From the discipline of the monks under training we now pass on to their studies. The ordinary instruction of a pupil-monks comprised the giving of recitation, holding examination, making exhortation and explaining Dhamma. The Bhikkhus as students were assigned to different classes according to their progress in studies. The lowest class was made up of students who were repeaters of the suttantas. The method recommended for this rote-learning was to chant over the suttantas to one another. The next higher class was of those students who were in charge of the Vinaya which they would master by discussing it with one another. To a yet higher class belonged those Bhikkhus who were training themselves up as teachers of the Dhamma. And as part of this training they were required to talk over the Dhamma with one another before they should preach it to others. There were, lastly Bhikkhus of the highest classes who were given to meditation i.e. the practice of the four Jhanas or meditations. Besides these classes of students, some Bhikkhus were distinguished and classed Epicurians, being "wise in worldly lore and abounding in bodily vigour. All these different classes of students were separately lodged in the hostel lest their mixing up should cause disturbance to their different studies.

Thus a community of Bhikkhus was like a school made up of different forms or classes representing different grades of talent, maturity and progress in studies. But the Bhikkhus also differed from one another in other respects. Hailing from different parts of the country, they differed in their dialects, besides differeing in name lineage, birth and family. We are told of two Bhikkhu brothers who were Brahmans by birth, excelling in speech, excelling in pronounciation, trying to reduce this confusion of tongues among Bhikkhus by a proposal to adopt Sanskrit as their common language. But the Buddha did not approve of the proposal because it would not conduce to coversions but rather hinder them. Sanskrit would repel the ordinary people or masses who were to be reached through their own vernaculars. The religion of the Buddha meant for the classes as well as masses thus cultivated and was preached through the popular speech as distinguished from the difficult and refined language, Sanskrit especially in its earlier form Chhandas or veda-dialect for which the two Brahman brothers pleaded. The Buddha with perfect wisdom ruled: I allow you, O Bhikkhus, to learn the world of the Buddhas each in his own dialect. Thus Buddhism gave an impulse and impetus to the study of vernacular dialects of the country which so much facilitated its spread to distant and different countries by men of missionaries as organized under the great Emperor Asoka for instance. The aforesaid episode indicates that Sanskrit was supplanted and superseded as a medium of instruction in the Buddhist schools by the vernacular dialects.

Along with Sanskrit were tabooed several subjects of study viz. the Lokayata system together with low arts of divination, spells, omens, astrology sacrifices to gods, witchcraft and quackery. Hence it is clear that curriculum of the monks included what are terms Suttanta, Dhamma and Vinaya together with Suttas and suttavibhaga. (In the treasure-house of Buddhist literature, the Pali Tripitaka represents the earliest available and most complete collection of Buddhist sacred literature. It is preserved in three systematic collections: (1) the Vinaya-pitaka or the Book of Discipline (2) the Sutta-pitaka, the popular book or discourses and (3) the Abhidhamma-pitaka, the collection of books on abstruse philosophy based on psychological ethics). The main classification of the three pitakas is given below:

TRIPTAKA

VINAYA-PITAKA (5 Books)	SUTTA-PITAKA (5 Collections)	Abhidhamma-pitaka (7 books)
	Digha - nikaya	Dhamma - Sangani
	Majjhima - nikaya	Vibhanga
Sutta khan - Parivara	Samyutta- nikaya	Dhatu - katha
Vibhata dhaka	Anguttara- nikaya	Puggala- Pannatti
	Khuddaka- nikaya	katha- Vatthu
		Yamaka
		Paatthana

Mahavagga Chullavagga

Maha-vibhanga Bhikkuni-Vibhanga

5.4.4. (I) RELIGIONAND HUMANITIES:

The invariable mention of the three vedas shows that the study of the Atharva Veda was not included in the curriculum for general education at the time of the Jatakas. The vedas were of course to be learnt by heart. We are told of a teacher at Takkusita from whose lips 500 Brahman pupils learnt the vedas. The Bodhisatta is frequently referred to as having learned the three vedas by heart. Instead of the three vedas we sometimes find mention of sacred texts holy books or the law', Some of these terms may indicate the sacred literature of the Buddhist. We find even the direct mention of a Vinaya scholar and a Sutra scholar.

5.4.4. (II) SCIENCE, ARTS AND CRAFTS

The subjects under the Sciences and Arts are not individual mentioned. Their number alone is frequently mentioned, For example the Milinda Panha speaks of the individual names of the nineteen sippas then current and Jataka makes individual mention of some subjects under scientific and technical education which would come under the eighteen sippas. We have the mention of the following arts being taught in some of the colleges of Takkasila. viz (1) Elephant Lore Hathi Sutta) (2) Magic Charms (3) spell for bringing back the dead to life (4) Hunting (5) spell for understanding all animals cries (6) Archery (Issatthasippa) (7) The ART of Prognostication (8) charm for commanding all things of sense (9) Divining from sings of the body and (10) Medicine.

It is to be noted that students are mentioned as taking up for their study only one of these subjects in which they wanted to specialize and make themselves experts.

The study of these Sciences and Arts seems to have had a theoretical and practical course. Knowledge of the literature of a subject had to be followed by its practical applications. In regard to some subjects like Medicine for instance, the practical course had to be gone through under the direction of the teacher. The practical course in Medicine at Takkasila included a first hand study of the plants to find out the medicinal ones, as shown in the story of Jivakas education

5.4.4 (III) EDUCATION IN MEDICINE AND SURGERY

Buddhist literature from the Vinaya texts downwards conveys a continuous volume of striking evidence regarding the progress achieved in ancient India in medicine and surgery. The most distinguished medical expert of the age was Jivaka Komarabhachha, of whose life and career the Vinaya gives several concrete and interesting details (Mahavagga). He was the son of the courtesan Salavati of Rajagriha, who was thrown away on a dust heap from which prince Abhaya rescued him alive. He also brought him up till Jivaka thought : In these royal families it is not easy to find one's livelihood without knowing an art." Thus thinking he went to Takkasila to study medicine under a world renowned physician who lived there. He learnt much and learnt easily, understood well, and did not forget what he had learnt, After studying this for seven years he asked his teacher when his studies might be regarded as completed whereupon his teacher prescribed to him the following test : Take this spade and seek round about Takkasila a yojana on every side and whatever plant you see which is not medicinal bring it to me. "Jivaka examined all the plants of the area specified and reported that he had not come across any plant that had no medicinal properties. The teacher satisfied with his answer, said you have done your learning, my good Jivaka, and gave him a little money for his passage home. The money was sufficient for his journey only up to Saketa where he was therefore forced to earn by his art. At that time fortunately a Sethis' wife had been suffering for seven years from a disease in the head whom many great and world- renowned physicians had failed to cure, though much gold was spent on them as their fees. But young Jivaka would not either be given a call until he proposed that his fees might be paid only if the patient were cured. Jivaka had one pasata (handful of ghee boiled up with various drugs and administered the medicine to the patient through her nose. By one dose she was cured and gave the doctor in all 16000 kahapanas together with a coach, horses and two servants. These fees and presents Jivaka tended on his return to Rajagraha to the prime who brought him up for the expenses incurred for it. Next Jivaka cured the Emperor Bimbisara of his fistula by one anointing and was then appointed as the royal physican and the physican of the Buddha and his Sangha.

In other subjects, the practical course was left to be completed by the students themselves when they left their colleges after fininshing their instruction. Thus we read of a Brahman student "of a market town in the north country" who specialized in the science of Archery at Takkasila and after finishing his studies went as far as the Andhra pradesh in prosecution of the practical application of his art. There is mention of the prince of Magadha who, having mastered all the arts of Takkasila, wandered through towns, villages and all the land to acquire all practical usages and understand country observances. A practical turn was indeed given to all instruction as a pedagogic principle. We have already referred to the first hand observation of plant-life as a compulsory part of medical education. The point of some of the examples cited above is that they demonstrate how the students of these days after their graduation undertook an extensive foreign travel to give a practical turn to their theoretical studies at the colleges and qualify themselves for the life in the world by broadening the range of their experience and deepening their insight into human affairs by a first hand study of the diverse manners and customs prevailing in the different parts of the country. Besides its direct educational value, his post-graduate travelling as giving a finishing touch to a student training was encouraged and even insisted upon for another very substantial reason especially in the cases of the students of the well-to-do classes who were brought up in luxury.

5.4.4 (IV) STUDIES OF MONKS

After the ordination begins the regular course of monastic education and discipline the upadhyaya imparts to his pupil the contents of the pratimoksha as the first lesson, explaining to him the character of the offences and how to recite the precepts. These having been learnt, the candidate begins to read the larger Vinaya-pitaka: he reads it day after day, and is examined every morning, for if he does not keep to it constantly he will lose intellectual power. When he has read the Vinaya-pitaka he begins to learn th sutras and sastras. Such is the way in which a teacher instructs in India. I- tsing also refers to the Vinaya practice of requiring for each priest under training two teachers called the upadhyaya and the karmacharya, the former being the teacher of personal instruction (adhyaya literally "teaching to read and upa "near) and the latter "the teacher in discipline who teaches pupils rules and ceremonies.

To the ordinary and traditonal curriculum of specialized priestly studies in the monasteries which included the Vinaya works, the sutras and the sastras some new works had been added in course of time. Among these, I-tsing mentions the two hymns of 150 and 400 verses attributed to Matricheta (the former of which was translated by I-tsing during his stay at Nalanda). I-tsing says that throughout India everyone who become a monk is taught Matrichetas two hymns as soon as he can recite the five and ten precepts. This course is adapted by both the

Mahayana and Hinayana schools. After one is able to recite them, one proceeds to learn other sutras. These two hymns were valued not merely for their contents but also for their language showing how to compose verses. Next to them, I-tsing mentions the Buddhach-aritakavya of Asvaghosha which is widely read or sung throughout the five divisions of India and the countries of the southern sea as well as the two other works viz Nagarjuna's Suhrillekha and the Jatakamala. Advanced studies and specialization were also carried on in a few other subjects on which considerable literature had been developed as described by I-tsing. Thus some Bhikshus might elect to study the yoga system for which the curriculum included, as the first book of study the yogacharya sastra to be followed by Asanga's Eight sastras, which are named. If a priest wanted to distinguish himself on the study of Logic he was to master Jina's Eight Sastras which are also named. Similarly six padas or treatises are mentioned in connection with the study of the Abhidharma or Metaphysics and four nikayas or classes of works in connection with the Agamas. The mastery of the Abhidharma and Agama works was regarded as essential for any Bhikshu who wanted to successfully combat heretics and disputants.

5.4.5 METHODOLOGY OF FORMAL LEARNING IN BUDDHIST SYSTEM

The formal system of the Buddhist Education shows three aspects of learning process 1. The first aspect refers to the importance attached to memorization. In the Buddhist system, without exception, memorization of large volumes of textual and commentarial material is resorted to primarily as a means of training and exercising the mind. The second aspect is the stress laid on calligraphy. In the monastic system, good hand-writing is regarded as the very sign of scholarship. As such, a student spends a major part of his time perfecting his script.In Tibetan monasteries, that is about the main activity because memory training accompanies writing and a student produces volumes and volumes of copy books as proof of studying. The third aspect is the special attention given to clear and faultless diction articulation. Oral communication has been of primary importance in Buddhist circles. Therefore, the student has to acquire the ability to read clearly and correctly articulating each syllable. It is a training needed for group chanting of scriptures (both as a daily monastic ritual and as a service to the laity) and for the delivery of sermans.

Thus a good memory legible and well-rounded hand-writing and clear speech were associated with learning. The disciplined drill which is required to achieve them over years of applications is still regarded worthwhile and strongly upheld by some scholars to be the very essence of learning.

5.4.5 (I) TEACHING MAINLY ORAL

Education in the age of the earlier Buddhist texts (Patimokkha, Suttas, Mahavagga and Chullavagga, suttavibhanga) was not yet depending upon written literature. This however, does not mean that the art of writing was not developed them. It is referred to as a source of livelihood or an occupation in the Mahavagga. The Mahavagga states that the Bhikkhus of a certain place not knowing the Patimokkha, one of them is commissioned to learn it from a neighbouoring fraternity and import the knowledge. Similarly we read of a lay-devotee or a Upasaka inviting a fraternity of Bhikkhus to hear him recite an important suttanta so that they might learn it and preserve it from oblivion. These passage show that the Buddhist was as of Brahmanical education, though the causes of its adoption might be different in the two cases. Rhys Davids and Oldenberg (scholars of the Buddhist studies) state that there was very limited use of writing in those days for purpose of education and the use of writing was not for the purpose of preserving and transmitting an extensive sacred literature. The disuse of writing was due to the scarcity of any convenient practical material on which the known characters might be inscribed.

Listening to religious discourses as a means of instruction is also instanced in another passage (chullavagga) which describes how Devadatta instructed and aroused and gladdened the Bhikkhus far into the night with religous discourse and yet the Aseembly was still alert and sleepless, whereupon he requested Sariputta to continue the religous discourse. The Sariputta discoursed on the manuals of preaching, followed by Moggllana who discoursed on the marvels of Iddhi (chullavagga). One of the ideal sanghas whose seat was at the Eastern Bamboo park made it a rule that every five days they should spend a whole night sitting together in religious discourse (Mahavagga)

5.4.4 (II) DISCUSSION AS A METHOD OF EDUCATION

The Buddhist system of education, like the Brahmanical lays equal stress upon the efficacy of the method of debate and discussion in Education. In fact, Buddhism being more proselytizing than vedism or Brahmanism was more interested in the cultivation by its leaders and votaries of the powers of debate by which it could spread and win converts from other religions. The Buddha's whole career of forty five years of ministry was practically continuous round of debates and discussions with the exponents of other Schools of Thought or answering of questions put to him at the Assemblies of his own disciples. The cannonical Buddhist texts are full of references to the conversions of the Buddha, following his delivery of discourse. Indian religion had already then, split up into any number of schools and sects whose followers, organized into ascetic brotherhoods like the Buddhists, were constantly meeting at Assemblies for discussion of their different doctrines.

The *Sutta* Nipata characterizes these Brahmana ascetics, Parivrajakas, as Vadasila, disputations Vitandas and Lokayatas, sophists, casuists and materialists. There are many instances recorded in Buddhist Texts of the leaders of Brahmanical ascetic sects meeting the Buddha at discussions. Similarly, Jainism also had to take its part in the religious disputations of the day. The places of such important discussions which marked cultural and religous life in those days were public halls which are called in Pali texts Santhagaras or Samayappavadaka salas. They also mention some places where such discussions actually took place; the Hall in Queen Mallikas's park at Sravasti for "discussion of different systems of opinion". The cabled pavilion erected by the Lichchavis in the Mahavana outside Vaisali: the sweet smelling Champaka grove on the lake of Queen Gaggara at Champa or the Moranivapa (where peacocks were fed) at Rajagriha, a privrajaka centre under Sakuladayi (Hindu civilization by R.K. Mookherji)

Buddhist literature throws considerable light on the rules for the conduct of such discussions and proceedings of the sangha. The earliest work describing the methods of disputation is the Kathavatthu of Asoka's time. The Chullavagga gives an elaborate account of the working of Sanghas as democratic parliamentary assemblies. We may only refer here to a special treatise on the subject of debate A.D. 400, which was translated into Chinese in A.D. 646 and was known to the great Asanga at Ayodhaya. The fifteenth volume of this important work is a treatise on the art of debate in seven chapters. The first chapter defines the subject of debate which must be a useful one. It rules out useless subjects. The second chapter defines the place of debate which should be an assembly of scholars, the palace of a king or the office of a Minister or the Parishad. The third chapter points out the means of Debate. The thesis to be proved (sandhya) depends on eight kinds of proof viz (1) Siddhanta, conclusion (2) Hetu, reason: (3) Udaharana, example: (4) Sadharmya, affirmative example: (5) Vaidharmya, negative example: (6) Pratyaksha perception (7) Anumana, inference: and (8) Agama, scripture. The fourth chapter lays down the qualification of the debaters. They must be acquainted with each others scriptures: should be able to speak in harmony, sometimes soft and sometimes loud to please their audience. The fifth chapter mentions the points of defeat (nigrahasthana), viz (1) opposing a proposition and their speaking in agreement with it: (2) leaving the subject started and introducing another: (3) talking irrelevantly (atila-vakya). The next chapter discusses the fitness of the debate by its subject, place or audience. The seventh chapter recommends self-confidence in the debater.

5.4.5 (III) LEARNED MEETINGS:

Another agency of education, especially moral education, furnished by monastic life, was the institution of the periodical gatherings of the monks from different monasteries in religious congreagations for the purposes of confession of sins twice in the month at full moon and at new moon. These meetings helped the monks to transcend the limitations of life in individual monasteries in a larger public life and brotherhood. It was ordained that the monks of a district must assemble. The meeting was to be convened by the seniors among the monks. The complete fraternity must be present at the meeting. The completeness was in relation to the diocese which was defined as extending so far as one residence, the landmarks of which were determined by mountain, tree, rock, wood, path and hill, a sheet of water and a river, but not up to its opposite bank, unless there was provision for regular communication by a ferry boat or a dyke. The place or the hall of the confessional gathering had also to be fixed and proclaimed before hand. The sangha as a body by a Resolution must fix the place of meeting, which must be duly announcd, so that members might cognizant of it. In the meeting, the Theras must assemble first. They must get the young Bhikkhus who are residents of that place to sweep it before hand, prepare seats, light lamps and provide for drink and food. The meeting must be attended by every member of the fraternity. If a member is sick, he must send a declaration of his innocence before the assembled chapter through another Bhikku. Otherwise he must be carried on his bed or chair to the Assembly or if he is too ill, the Assembly must go to him and hold their meeting so as to secure his attendance. The exemption from attendance was granted only to a member who had turned mad. The confession was not common or collective but individual. The common offence of the whole Sangha was to be confessed before the guiltess Bhikkhu of another diocese.

Next to these fornightly confessional meetings was the yearly recurring ceremony Pavarana or Invitation to be initiated with the following words : "I invite the Sangha to charge me with any offence they think me guilty of, which they have seen or heard of or which they suspect during the period of Vassa (Mahavagga).

5.4.6. *A BRIEF ACCOUNT OF THE BUDDHIST EDUCATION BY THE CHINESE PILIGRIMS*

The very fact of the pilgrimage of Chinese scholars like Fa-Hien (5th century A.D) (A.D 399-414 - duration of his travel in India) or Hiuen Tsang (7th century A.D) to India testifies to the tribute paid by China to the soverignty of Indian thought and culture. India was in those days the holy land of China and other countries, teeming with centres of Buddhist faith and learning to which the devout youth of the foreign countries were flocking for their instruction, to return home later as fully equipped and trained missionaries Fa-Hien or for the matter of that, Hiuen- Tsang or I-Tsing were but individual members of nobel bands of missionaries who during the period of well high ten centuries (from kanishka to Dharmapala) came to India on religious and literary pilgrimage to drink at the very fountains of the culature they professed.

Fa-Hien's evidence thus brings us into touch with Buddhist India, the chief centres of its learning the actual working of its institutions, their internal conditions, rules, and regulations. Buddhist India in Fa-Hien's time embraced a large area, extending from Udyana on the north-western frontiers to Tamalipti on the east, and was noted for the abundance of its monastereies the strongholds and distributing centres of Buddhist culture which enable it to maintain its hold upon the country, and helped to spread it eventualy among the diferent parts thereof. Fa-Hien does not mention any monasteries in Takkasila which figures so largely in the

Buddhist Literature as a Centre of learning. One of the most prominent centres of Buddhist leaning Fa- Hien's time was Pataliputra where he saw two monasteries, one Mahayana and another Hinayana, together containing six or seven hundred monks. Shamanas of the highest virtue from all quarters, and students, inquirers wishing to find out truth and the grounds of it, all resort to these monasteries. This shows that besides offering elementary instruction to the younger monks and novices, these monasteries served as centries of advanced instruction for the maturerd monks. This was due to their having as their residents several farfamed teachers.

Even in Fa-Hien's time, the time-honoured Brahmanical system of oral tradition was still obtaining as method of instruction even among Buddhists. In the various kingdoms of north India he had found one master transmitting orally the rules to another but no written copies which he could transcribe. This was a great disappointment to the traveller who had set out on his travel with the object of finding copies of the Vinayas. Out of the numerous monasteries he had visited, it was only in two that his object was realized. Manuscripts of sacred texts which he could copy were found in the Mahayana monastery at Pataliputra and in the monasteries in Tamalipti. Thus oral instruction was the only educational method followed in the north while the rule was relaxed in the east where the aid of written literature to education was recognized.

It is interesting to note that the study of Sanskrit was continued in these Buddhist monasteries. At the Pataliputra monastery, Fa-Hien stayed for three years, "learning Sanskrit books and the Sanskrit speech and writing out the Vinaya rules."

Life in these monasteries was governed by regulations which followed the lines laid down in the Vinaya. The regular business of the monks is to perform acts of meritorious virtue, to recite their Sutras, and sit wrapt in meditation. Besides the individual study and meditation, the monks and always to meet together in the common room or hall of the monastery for purposes of religious discussions, "All the monks come together in a great assembly and preach the law" observed Fa-Hien.)

5.4.6. (I) HIEUN-TSANG'S ACCOUNT OF BUDDHIST EDUCATION IN THE 7TH A.D

These monsteries were in charge of the higher education of the country, which was led up to by a well developed system of elementary education. The monasteries were like colleges to which students were admitted on completion of their preliminary education, of which a separate account is given by Hieun-Tsang. A child is first introduced to a Siddham or a prime of twelve chapters giving the Sanskrit alphabet and at the combinations between vowels and consonauts. After his mastery of the Siddham, he was introduced at the age of seven to the "great Sastras of the Five Sciences" viz Vyakarana (grammar), Silpasthanavidya (the science of Arts and Crafts), Chikitsavidya (Science of Medicine), Hetu-vidya (Nyaya, logic, Science of Reasoning), the metaphysical and argumentative treatises of the great doctors of Abhidharma. It is thus clear that the elements of both secular and religions knowledge, of philosophical and practical subjects, entered into the composition of this elementary course of education meant for the sons of Buddhist parents, so that it provided the necesary basis of a good general culture upon which specialization could be successfully attempted in the monasteries. Thus the Buddhist qualification for the religious teacher or leader demanded a knwledge of the practical arts and crafts necessary in serving humanity, such as a knowledge of medicine. We read, for instance, of the Great Buddhist leader Kumarajiva who studied the Sastras of the Five Sciences (grammar, science of Arts and Crafts, Medicine, Logic and Metaphysics) and of the famous scholar Gunabhadra that he, too, had learnt in his youth the Sastras of those Five Sciences together with Astronomy, Arithmatic, Medicine and Exorcisms.

Seventh century India has been described by another Chinese traveller who set foot on Indian soil in A.D. 672 within a few years after Hiuen Tsang had left it (A.D 645). I-tsing was a great admirer of both in seeking to stake his thirst for knowledge at its very fountains in India. Like Fa-Hieun, I-Tsang object was to study and gather the genuine texts of the Vinaya rules to correct their misrepresentations in China, and to combat to erroneous views held by the Vinayadharas there in those days.

5.4.6 (II) I-TSING ACCOUNT OF EDUCATION IN THE SEVE-NTH CENTURY A.D

Like Hiuen Tsang, I-tsing gives an account of the general and elementary education of the time prior to specialization and higher education in the monasteries. The course of elementary and general education comprised the study of the five subjects or vidyas viz (1) sabdavidya (grammar and lexicography) (2) silpasthanavidya (arts) (3) chikisatsavidya "medicine": (4) Hetuvidya "logic" and (5) Adhyatmavidya: science of the universal soul" philosophy. The competion of the study of the five vidyas completes the course of elementary and general education. Then follows bifurcation of studies of specialization.

There is a course of specialized and advanced studies in Vyakarana which was " the name for the general secular literature. The following textbooks were prescribed: (1) the Churni which is the name of Patanjalis famous commentary on Panini's sutras usually called Mahabhashya, containing 24,000 slokas. It cites the sutras, explains the obscure points, analyses the principles involved and clears up many difficulities. Advanced scholars learn this in three years (2) The Bhartrihari Sastra which was a commentary in 25,000 slokas on the former work by the great scholar Bhartrihari who was very famous throughout the five parts of India and who became seven times a priest and seven times returned to the laity. He died in A.D. 651-2. (3) The Vakyapadiya, another work of Bhartrihari, with 700 slokas and a commentary portion in 7000 slokas. It is a "treatise on the inference supported by the authority of the sacred teaching and on Inductive arguments (4) The pei-na (probably Sanskrit Beda or veda), a grammatical work of 3000 slokas composed by Bhartrihari, with a commentary portion in 14,000 slokas attributed to his contemporary Dharmapala. It treats of the secrets of heaven and earth and of the philosophy of man. Students completing this advanced study were regarded as masters of grammatical science and earned the title of Bahusruta (much heard or "knowing much of sruti"), This course of specialization in Grammar was open to both priests and laymen.

There were again courses of specialization in religious or priestly studies which were organized and offered by the monasteries. The most famous of such seats of higher learning in the time of I-tsing's visit to India were "the Nalanda monastery in Central India and that in the country of Valabhi in Western India.

I-tsing gives an account of rules govening the education and organization of the monasteries, as laid down in the Vinaya texts regarding admission to monasteries to priesthood or ordination.

5.5 THE BUDDHIST MONASTERIES -INDIGENOUS UNIVERSITIES OF ANCIENT HINDU INDIA - AN ANALYTICAL EXPOSITION

Without a centre, a radius and a circumference a circle cannot exist. Of the circle of Buddhism, the Buddha is the radiant centre, the Dharma, as the shortest distance from potential to actual enlightenment the radius and the sangha the perfect unbroken circumference. Each of these terms in multidimensional possessing sphere within sphere of spiritual significance which no one religion can exhaust. The Buddha is, simultaneously a unique historical figure, the supreme object of the religious consciousness, and Reality itself:His Dharma is the sum total of conceptual formulations of the Teaching as well as the spititual principle which both transcends all formulations and, running at the same time through everyone of them communicates to them vitality and meaning. Even so does the Sangh (assembly) meet not at one level of existence only but at several. The term stands, according to context, for a spiritual elite an ecclesiastical corporation, and the whole community of the faithful monk and lay as well as covering various intermediate shades of significance. Of the three principal meanings that of the spititual elite is the primary one: all the rest are secondary. Whether one is in spiritual relation with the Buddha, through the Dharma and therefore whether one is truly a segment of the circumference of the circle is determined not by the assumption of external differentiate nor by verbal professions, but by whether one acutally practises the Dharma or not.

In a well-known episode the Buddha declares that he who walked step by step behind the Master, holding fast to the him of His robe, but who did not follow His instructions, was far from Him. But one who, on the contrary through living a thousand miles away yet realised the import of the Teaching, dwelt in His very presence. The true criterion of the relation between the Buddha and his followers is not physical, not spatio-temporal, but spiritual whether now or in what we call from the historical point of view, his own times or whether in the future ven, we are nearest to him when we must perfectly follow his example. The sangha is primarily the community of those who by virtue of their immediate or remote approximation to Enlightenment, stand in spiritual relation to the Buddha and dwell spiritually in his presence. It is the community of those who their relationship with him, are also all spiritually related to one another. The Sangha is the Buddhas' spititual family. In the Nikayas heis indeed represented as telling his disciplies : Ye are mine own true sons, born of my mouth: of the Dharma not of worldly things Centuries later the same theme finds beautiful expression as a trinity consisting of the Buddha as Father, the Dharma as Mother and the Sangha as Son.

As the spititual elite the Sangha is known as the ary sangha or Assembly of the Elect, the word arya here connoting an aristocracy not of race but of transcendental attainment. As an ecclesiastical corporation is known as the bhiksu- sangha or Assembly of Monks and as the whole community of the faithful as the maha-sangha or Great Assembly and the Caturvanga or "Four classes.

This sangha as a community of men and women was treading the path and striving to realise the Goal of Nirvana. This Buddhism as an institutional religion comprises both a large body of lay followers known as upasaka (fem. upasikas), whose practice of the Dharma is occasional and partial and a very much smaller body of bhiksus (fem. bhisunis) who dedicate to its realisation their whole life and the sum total of their energies. The latter form of the bhiksu sangha, the Order of Monks was the Monastic Order which the primary ecclesiastical sense in which the word Sangha is now used. This order did not come into existence all at once. Like other living things, whether organism expires or survives, it has in the course of its history passed through various stages of development.

With a few months of the commencement of his mission, the Buddha recognized that the spread of a message such as his, needed an organisation and some procedures. With the coverts who could join him in the state of homelessness, he formed the sangha -a very informal organisation to begin with. The procedure he adopted was to send the first batch of sixty members inall directions announcing the advent of the new doctrine. This very early missionary exercise paved the way for the rise of the Buddhist educational system in which every monk was potentially a teacher, converting new recruits to the angha or winning lay supporters. The content of their teaching came from the Buddha and so were the methods, in that the monks initiated the Buddha. The Buddha himself explained occasionally his methods as well as his concept of learning and teaching. As the numbers grew larger and the peripheral units had their contacts with the Buddha only at intervals a system of institutionalized training and updating of knowledge and experience became necessary.

The words of the Buddha were carefully committed to memory, arranged and classified according to literary form in a very early classification called "nine elements" (navangasatthusana). Withing three months of the Buddha:s demise, the disciples could embark on a general rehearsal of all teachings and a codification under quite a systematic classification. The Tripataka in its present form was also completed within the first two centuries. Commentaties on some of the teachings had already begun to appear. Menemonical summaries had been developed to facilitiate the recall of narratives. A system of indexing was also established. Monks and nuns prepared and delivered their own sermons and even composed poetic appreciations of their way of life and the Buddha's guidance. They produced a massive scholastic literature in which they submitted the Buddha's teachings to a thorough and systematic analysis. All these could not have been possible over a brief period of the first two centuries unless the education function of the Buddhist sangha was firmly established with almost the beginning of the Buddha's missionary activity. This would mean that even before the monastic establishments came into existence, the Sangha was an itinerant educational institution. The fact that in such a system some had to specialize is borne out by designations given to certain monks as specialists of the doctrine (i.e. Dhammadhara and Vinayadhara).In due course, the tendency to specialise extended further and further.

Thus through a gradual process, the Buddhist monastery became an educational institution a tradition preserved up to-date in that even the humblest Buddhist temple in the remotest corner of a Buddhist country is essentially a centre of learning. In the growth of this monastic system of education, a number of significant principles appear to have operated and details of such principles have already explained earlier in this chapter. The monks and nuns were expected to have mastered a minimum quantum of the Buddha's teaching. Even today in the Buddhist tradition of Sri Lanka a monk is tested for his knowledge of basic text of the Canon before ordination is granted. The senior monks and nuns were required to engage themselves regularly in scholarly discussions to deepen their knowledge and understanding and to guide their practice while at the same time, educating new recruits and novices. The monastery was to be a centre for the formal as well as informal educaton of the laity living in the vicinity.

The expectations meant that the monstery should organize itself into an educational institution in a variety of ways. First it had to provide for the initial and continuing education of the monks and nuns themselves. In the initial stages, this menat that a monastery should have at least the periodical services of specialist reciter of texts. The travelling specialist was quite a phenomenon in the early stages. Second, it had to organize the education of the laity. It was possibly restricted to regular or occasional sermons on religious themes at the early stages. But with laity who either sought deeper knowledge as a preparation to join the Sangha or were engaging themselves in studies for their own edification, this service had to assume wider propotions. It was not very long before the teaching of the young became a social responsibility of the monks.

As per the present study, the Buddhist monasteries have been exposed to have already displayed the essential features of a university, as evolved by the universities of medieval Europe during the 11th and 12th centuries A.D. It would be thought that the idea of a university was alien to India. Hence it might be asked "how could it be applied to an institution which was purely Indian? Before we use it with reference to the Buddhist Monasteries, let us recall the salient features, enumerated and explained in the Chapter IV.

First the word 'University' originally means a number or aggregate of persons. In this sense, it was applied to a scholastic body of teachers or scholars, but never to a place, where such a body was established, or even to its collective schools. In course of time it was used with reference to an institution which embraced all the arts and sciences. whereas Newman described a University as a place which attracted students of every kind. The word 'University' then has a definite meaning and conntation. It stands, first, for a place which imparts knowledge in all the arts and sciences and secondly, for a place which attracted students of every kind from all over the world. To Karl Jaspers, the university exists only to the extent that it is institutionalized. The idea becomes concrete in the institution, training, communication - within an institutional framework. In considering the idea of the university we must consider certain realities which are simultaneously prerequisites and restrictions of that idea. First, there are the human beings who come together at the univeristy, then attitudes and abilities and second, there is the power of state and society whose will and needs sustain the university.

In the light of the aforesaid idea of a university, the Buddhist monasteries are regarded as centres of higher learning where the monk scholars and pupil monks assembled for instructional purpose. In fact the seeds of the monastic education were sown by the Buddha himself. Every founder of a religious system was a teacher. In Indian religious tradition, there had been many who, by popular consensus, were so designated. The Buddha himself figures as a teacher of men and gods (Sattha devamanussanam). How effective a teacher was he? What innovations in teaching procedures can we attribute to him? What was his concept of learning? What impact did his ideas of teaching and learning have on the later educational efforts of the Buddhist Order?

The Buddha believed strongly in the power of the spoken word to convince people to change their way, adopt new values and seek new goals. At a time when rival religious teachers resorted to magical and miraculous deeds to win disciples for themselves, the Buddha upheld only one type of miracle: The Miracle of Instruction". Clarity and logical presentation marked his longer sermons which he had delivered on his own accord. In these he addressed small or large group and sought to taken them step by step to a point of view he sought to establish. The Buddha used similes and analogies freely and frequently and drew them usually from the day to day life of the people e.g. the work of the butcher, the florist, the boatman, the soldiers, the royal officials. The discourse led the audience gradually to a conclusion which usually was strong plea for the pursuit of the path of deliverance he advocated.

Whether in sermons and expositions or in dialogues and debates,. the Buddha resorted to a series of standard educational practice. He aimed at the intellectual level of the "Pull". He had expounded the same idea in so many different ways according to the nature and compostiton of the audience. He started with the known and insisted on it as a fundamental principle in all his teachings. He eschewed speculation as a waste of time. He urged that one should endeavour to "Know it as it really is"- the emphasis being on both knowing and reality. The Buddha assigned little value, however, to knowledge per se. Knowledge was valid only up to the point it was applied. A little knowledge but duly applied in life was rated far superior to vast stores of knowledge with no effort to practise what was learnt.

He encouraged his pupils to discuss and debate and he was often only an arbitrator. He arranged prominent pupils to become teachers for others. He evaluated their teaching ability and ranked them according to their specialization and instructional methodologies. The Buddha organized the Sangha to be a learning society in which the members spent their life-time learning practising what they learnt teaching others, engaging in debates and discussions to clarify concepts memorizing sermons and utternaces of the Buddha and transmitting them by word of mouth for preservation, developing commentaries and winning more and more members who would similarly continue a life long learning process. We could say that monk- scholarship was encouraged by the Buddha, the founder of the religion himself.

In the beginning the Buddhist monasteries functioned as centres of religious gathering. They were represented by a body of learned monks, assembled for the puprsuit of Truth and service to the society i.e humanity. All education sacred as well as secular was in the hands of the monks. They had the monopoly of learning and of the leisure to impart it. They were the only custodians and bearers of the Buddhist culture. The Buddhist among all religious groups of India, were the first to recognize the importance of literacy. As far back as 84 B.C the Buddhist canon was reduced to writing and the earlier reliance on oral tradition was relaxed. The art of writing travelled to many countries with Buddhism. The monks were the promoters of literacy and the reading habit among their followers.

In the monastic system a class being taught collectively by a teacher is relatively late development. A teacher, ordinarily, met each student individually to ensure whether the assigned tasks were correctly accomplished and to set new tasks. Teaching in the sense of lecturing or explaining a lesson to a group of students was race and was strictly confined to matters which students had either misunderstood or failed to comprehend. The actual learning process was personal and the student spent almost all his time in self-learning. The literacy material for that purpose was available in plenty. Commentaries, sub-commentaries, glossaries, indexes and lexicons facilitated self-learning. The method of evaluating learning outcomes was two fold : the student was required either to show his capacity to draw from the self-learning materials and present his own commentary or explanation of a given text or to enter into a debate with his teachers and peers and defend a particular point of view. An original composition by the student usually marked the culmination of linguistic studies.

Under the monastic system, a group of pupil monks were placed under the guardianship of a common teacher, the Upajjhaya or Acharya who was individually responsible for their health and studies manners and morals and their spiritual progress. These groups federated themselves into a larger unit called the Vihara or monastery. Thus we have to view them as parts of that larger organisation and their relations to its general collective life which developed its own code of discipline and regulations binding upon all.

The role of the Sangha as a band of self-sustaining and self-renewing change agents had been a significant feature of the Buddhist educational system. In constitution as decentralized democratic organization of the peers, it enabled to evolve according to the genius and needs of different peoples of different places and times.

Secondly, the Buddhist monasteries, encouraged monk-scholarship. The main purpose of the Buddhist system of education was to produce perfect monks for the monasteries in order to propagate the teachings of Lord Buddha. The senior monks and nuns were required to engage themselves regularly in scholarly discussions to deepen their knowledge and understanding and to guide their practice while, at the same time educating new recruits and novices. The monastery was to be a centre for the formal as well as informal educaion of the laity living in the vicinity. The search for knowledge took Buddhist monks and nuns on incredible missions accorss the world of the entire Asian continent. Either they went on their own in search of teachers and books like the famous Chinese travellers or were invited by distant lands to come as teachers, Others travelled as self-appointed missionaries, motivated solely by their keen desire to spread the message of Buddhism.

The monasteries became repositories of valuable manuscripts and documents. Every Buddhist temple has its modest library and the older institutions had turned out to be veritable treasure houses of literature. Libraries of the Maha Vihara of Anuradhapura and and Nalanda were described as vast collections of books on many subjects amassed over several centuries. The educational activity which was originally restricted to religious knowledge extended in due course to cover all known knowledge. Starting with linguistic and literary studies, the monasteries, extended their fields of study to include medicine astronomy and mathematics. Centrally located monasteries developed into the stature of Universities (Nalanda being a singularly important example) and attracted scholars from all over the then known world. Besides the scriptures, science, Arts and Crafts were taught. The study of Sciences and Arts had theoretical and practical course, knowledge of literature of a subject had to be followed by its practical applications. In regard to some subjects like Medicine, the practical course had to be gone through under the direction of the teacher. For instance the practical course in Medicne at Taxila included a first hand study of the plants to find out the medicinial ones as shown in the story of Jivaka's education, the renouned physician of the Magadha kingdom.

The monasteries perfected sculputure and painting as effective visual aids to the teaching of Buddhist stories and doctrines. The use of art for both aesthetic beauty and educational reinforcement is a significant Buddhist innovation. It even overcomes the earlier reluctance to depict the Buddha in human form and resorted to a set of symbolic representations. The Vinaya texts refer to industrial education also. The Bhikkus were allowed facilities in their very monasteries for training and practice in the handicrafts such as spinning and weaving, tailoring etc. The Vinaya texts refer to a few other occuptions pursued by the laity and the general public as sources of livelihood e.g. writing or the occupation of the clerk or scribe, Accountancy and Drawing.

As stated earlier, monk-scholarship was encouraged very well by the Buddhist monasteries. Provision for higher and specialized study stands to prove this. Advanced studies were regarded as masters of grammatical science and awarded the title of Bahusruta. There were again courses of specilaization in religious or priestly studies which were organised and offered by the monasteries. For instance, we hear in inscriptions of Asoka of the monks who were specialists in particular texts of the Buddhist Canon (i.e. Dighabhanaka, Majjhimabhanaka etc.)

A very important task assigned to the teacher under the Buddhist system is to find out the individual difference among the pupils and to design each one's course of training to suit his particular traits. Particularly, in mental exercising, the subject of meditation have to be handpicked according to each student's innate and potential capacities. In this concept, learning is not an end by itself: it is a process leading to self-realization, which is equated in Buddhism to deliverance or liberation-the ultimate aim of the religious life.

While recognizing the importance of scholastic achievement and rewarding scholarship with both honours and material benefits, the monastic system maintained that learning without ethical sensitivity and moral principles was comparable to a beautiful flower with no fragrance. Learning was valuable only up to the point it made the individual a better person morally and spiritually.

With reference to the academic freedom, the scholar-monks were allowed freedom of choice of studies which all castes except the Chandalas were admitted to instruction. As a great teacher, Lord Buddha himself encouraged his pupils to discuss and debate and he was often only an arbitrator. This encouragement itself is a sign of academic freedom, given to the Bhikkus of the Sangha. In later stages, the scholar- monks were free to partake in the intellectual tournments which promoted active intercourse between different monasteries, representing different schools of Thought. Movement of the scholar- monks from South to North and North to South was allowed by the monasteries. Here the scholar would like to bring in one of the objectives of the University, as stated by Jaspers that in order to do the work of the university successfully there must be communication of thinking men. Scholars must communicate with one another, teachers with their students and the students among themselves. Communication of all with all is necessary each according to his intellectual level. The university unites people committed to scholarly or scientific learning and the intellectual life. The original sense of universitas a community of teachers and students is just an important as the unity of all studies. The idea of the university requires the open mind, the readiness to relate oneself to things with the aim of getting at a picture of the whole in terms of one's special discipline. The ideal requires that there be communication, not only on interdisciplinary but also on an interpersonal level. Reflecting this ideal, the scholar monks and pupil monks were of different monasteries were brought together under the wider umbrella of brotherhood of letters while partaking in the intellectual tournments. In the sphere of scholarship, communication is maintained through discussion. According to the ideal, this communication must be the Socratic type, posing questions so that men may achieve clarity about themselves and about each other.

An atmosphere of communication based on a community of thinking creates the proper conditions for scholarly and scientific work, although such work is ultimately always solitary. We can quote many number of Acaryas or Sastra-masters for their rich contribution to the Buddhist literature and culture. The outstanding names are: Asvaghosa, the two brothers Asanga and Vasubandhu, Dinnaga, Nagarjuna, Kumaralabdha, Buddhapalita and Bhavaviveka (or Bhavya). ASVAGHOSA is perhaps the most venerable name among the acaryas. The legened about him (both Chinese and Tibetan) is that he played a most important part in the Council covened by Kaniska which according to Tibetan legend, was the first great gathering in Buddhist history of Bodhisattvas- the first Mohayanist council. Asvaghosa was among the assembled Bodhisattvas and his literary genius was availed of for precise and effective formulation of the doctrines arrived at by the council.

We can quote another famous Buddhist personality NAGARJUNA an idealist philosopher who was author of the Madhayamaka kaniska and as a magician and alchemist, author of Rasaratnakara. Nagarjuna Bodhisattva, according to Hsuan-tsang, was not only a great teacher and philosopher, but also a maker of the elixir of life and an alchemist who could turn stone into gold. Nagarjuna Bodhisattva was well practised in the art of compounding medicines: by taking a preparation (pill or cake) he nourished the years of life for many hundreds of years so that neither the mind nor the appearance decayed. Yet another Buddhist scholar VASU BANDHU is regarded as the putative author of a number or works - thirty six in the Chiness collection and eight in the Tibetan. His magnum opus is Abhidharma-kosa with an auto- commentary entitled kosabhasya.

Like the modern universities, the Buddhist monasteries enjoyed a unique position in the then society. They enjoyed royal patronage because of their missionary zeal to serve the humanity. Indeed the monasteries played a leading role in community activities. The Buddhist monks organized the population to build roads, hospitals, orphanges and such other community services. They promoted co-operative undertakings in agriculture and construction of private and public utilities. The monastery remained in Buddhist countries the main meeting place of the people to organize community development activities.The monk was invariably the convener, patron and animator. It provided thus a focal point from which new ideas and techniques could be propagated through its ceremonials and the monastery had also been the principal promoter of folk art. In addition the monasteries maintained special religious classes usually in the form of a sunday school. It is the student population of the monastic system that provides the teachers for these classes. The student monks also found opportunities to exercise leadership traits and organize community development activities. In terms of epidemics, natural calamities and special festivals, they took part in the first aid and medical help service. They mobilized public charity and often provided the bulk of the volunteers to assist reconstruction measures.

All this was considered a part of their education because they were trained for a career in which social service figures prominently. The instructured programme of studies, with no time bound requirements like examination or promotions, enabled the student monks to combine studies, work experience and social service and extend their period of student as long as circiumstances permitted.

The actual learning process was personal and the student spent almost all his time in self-learning, the ultimate objective of the Buddhist system of education and the process of mental development connected with it, was the liberation of the individual from all types of bondages. In Buddhism, unlike in most other religious system, there is no look or a set quantum of literary material to be studied or mastered. To know just enough to set one's self on the path of mental training has been the primary objective of learning. The old vedic system of memorizing and reciting voluminous vedas and their ancillary literature was considered a fruitless effort. The Buddha consistently discouraged those who wanted to be masters of the books.

The Buddhist monasteries are thus said to reflect the principal features of a university as stated and explained under chapter IV of this dissertation. These features are presumably stipulative in nature and these features are widely acknowledged as the essentials of a university. Though the Buddhist monasteries belong to the age of 5th and 6th centuries B.C,. even before the emergence of medieval European universities of the 11th and 12th centuries, the Buddhist monasteries have been found imbued with the quintessence of a university to a certain extent if not strictly in terms of modern university.

5.6 CONCLUSION

The aforesaid analysis in the terms of stipulatory features of a university is an attempt to establish that the ancient Hindu India had developed a systematic higher education (university type of education) which stands parallel to the European Medieval Univeristies of 11th and 12th centuries. The Buddhist Monasteries of the ancient Hindu India of 5th and 6th centuries B.C are found exhibiting the similar features of the modern universities to certain extent.

Though it is universally accepted that the medieval European universities like Paris, Oxford and Bologna are the mother universities of the most of the universities of the paresent-day world, India is proud of her indigeneous universities like Taxila, Nalanda and Valabhi of the Northern part and Kanchi of the South. In the course of the study, certain assumptions have been made in the light of the socio- historical and cultural background of the centres of higher learning of the world civilization in general. One of the assumptions is that religious faith, in general, forms the substratum for the quest for knowledge. The quest for knowledge propelled man to prusue incessantly to reach the Infinite. Oneness and wholeness are the very essence of man's will to know. In his pursuit however, man realises the limitation of human reasoning and yet the goal of his achievement is still set on the horizon. In his endeavour he swings like a pendulum between his faith on the infinite and the quest for knowledge. This Buddhist monasteries stand to prove this oscillation from faith to knowledge which made them grow and blossom into universities.

It is true that the developed countries like U.K. France, Spain and Portugal had established their suzerainty over the countries of third world as their colonies and put the stamp of their university system on the educaional system of these colonial countries which are now the developing nations of the world today. Unfortunately India had not been politically destined to establish her sovereignty over the world to popularise her indigeneous system of education like the Buddhist Monastic ystem. However she was fortunate enough to attract her neighbouring countries like China, Burma and Japan where we find the widespread influence of the Buddhist Culture.

6

CONCLUDING CHAPTER

6.1 INTRODUCTION:

There can be no study of the present without the study of the past. The present study about the concept of a university as reflected by the Buddhist monasteries of (ancient Hindu) India has traced the past in order to concretise its reflections. This present study speaks about the image of a university in terms of functions first and of the essences, thereby derived, second. These essences form the salient features of a university and they, in fact, form the substratum of a university. However, universal characteristic features are attributed to the concept of a university to present a wholistic image in tact. These essences are found independent, indisputable and absolute. These essences (salient features) make the appearance (university) possible.

6.2 ESSENCE AND APPEARANCE:

The knowledge of essence permits to separate the true objective content of appearance from its outward aspects, and to rid the research of distortion and subjectivism. The tasks of cognition are not confined to mere revealing essence. They call for a theoretical explanation and substantiation of the laws that laws that have been formulated earlier, the sphere of their application, their correlation with other laws and the like. This involves cognition of deeper structural levels of matter, or else the discovery of a system of more general ties and relations of which the phenomenon under consideration constitutes an element. To do this, it is necessary to cognize more general and fundamental laws of being, with the laws and processes discovered earlier as their particular manifestations. A transition is made to deeper Essence on new structural levels of matter. The dialectics of the unity and diversity reveals itself in the relations between Essence and Appearance. One and the same Essence may have many different appearance while any sufficiently complex Appearance may be determined by several Essences, related to different structural levels of matter. Essence is always more stable than concrete Appearances but in the longrun the essence of all systems and process in

the world are subject to ultimate change in accordance with the universal dialectical laws governing the development of matter."[6.1]

Essence is a sum total of latent ties, relations and internal laws determining the main features and trends in development of a material system. Appearances are individual phenomenon, properties or processes expressing outward aspects of reality, a form of manifestation and revelation of some Essence. The categories of Essence and Appearance are always inseparably linked. There is no Essence that would not make any outward appearance and lend itself to cognition, and there is no Appearance that would contain no information about Essence. However, the unity of Essence and Appearance does not mean that they are identical since Essence is always hidden behind the surface of Appearance and the deeper it lies the more difficult and lengthy is its cognition in theory.

Essence can be cognized by abstract thinking and through the creation of a theory of the process under investigation. This cognition is a qualitative leap from the empirical to the theoretical level of knowledge and implies the discovery of the determinative in objects, the laws of their change and development. This is concurrent with the transition from the description (q,v) of Appearance to their explanation (q.v) to the discovery of their causes and grounds.

The Essence may be considered as cognised if, among other things, there is the exact wording or the laws governing movement and development of the objects, if the forecasts made on the basis of these laws and the conditions of their operation are confirmed, if, in addition, we know the causes of the emergence and the sources of development of the object under consideration, if we have revealed the ways of its formation or technical reproduction, and if we have created in theory or in practice, its adequate model, the properties of which are identical with those of the original. In accordance with the aforesaid exposition, we have traced back the emergence of higher education from the ancient civilization to the blossoming of university-type education of the Medieval Europe of 11th and 12th centuries under Chapter III of this theoretical build-up. A typical model of a university has been found in the medieval universities of Bologna, Paris and Oxford which are, in fact, the mother

---

6.1 Frolov. I, (Ed.) Dictionary of Philosophy, Progressive Publishers, Moscow (USSR) 1984 (P.131) Essence and Appearance.

universities of the most of the modern universities of the world. As the society is dynamic, there occur changes in the nature of the functioning of the universities. We have come across OPEN universities and Deemed-to be universities. Universities are being pulled up to be involved in the social processes of the community.

Before grasping the essences, we come across important functions of the universities. These functions, in due course, become concretised as features which, in turn lead to the formation of mental image i.e. a concept. These features form the very essence of the universities and these essences are the keys for ushering in appearance i.e. the university. Thus, the search for the meaning or the connotation of the concept of a university is the crux of the present study. The scholar has made an attempt to show that India is proud of her indigeneous universities in the Buddhist monasteries.

During the study, the scholar was able to make few observations which are given as assumption and suggestions (i.e. prescriptions) for the future study. Due to the social changes and attitude of people towards acquirement of education concept may change, accommodating new development and thought processes. However certain basic constituent elements may persist.

The scholar has stated her observations as assumptions because these assumptions are formulated on strong beliefs that they may be proved or disproved in due course.

The first assumption is that the centres of learning especially higher learning and universities developed only after the appearance of settled civilization. This observation has become well evident while glancing through the scribal cultures of Mesopotamia and Egypt. This is the case with the Upanisadic age of (ancient HIndu) India.

Man is here recognized to be a curious animal who collects bits of knowledge, the way the squirrel collects acorns. The moment the cave dweller had a little leisure from the business of fending off mastodens and spearing supper, he traced out the path of rivers and tried to make sense of the stars. An important part of this monistic picture of human intellectual development is that knowledge and invention went hand in hand, fire and wheel stimulating men's thought as much as maps and theories transferred his power. The growth of knowledge often interrupted

as often resumed is the main evidence for the doctrine of progress. (Monism is the belief that there is a single world of facts for man to use and it may best be seen in intimate association with a set of related doctrines: the doctrine of progress, the theological doctrines that God gave the fruits of the earth to man for his compart, and the commonsense view that the point of getting to know things is to control them.) The more knowledge the more control until we may even achieve that elusive key to human evolution the knowledge that gives us the power is control ourselves.

It is argued that the centres of higher learning like universities developed only often the appearance of settled civilization. According to Basil Fletcher's the first of these institutions of higher and adult learning were the Forest Ashrama of India, the origin of which is traced back to as far as 1500 B.C. by the HIndu. In addition to the Forest Ashramas of India there were other early centres of civilization which had their own forms of higher education.

It has been observed from the exposition of vedic culture of ancient India that Nature is the great sanctum sanctorum for our ancient Hindu Indians. Forests have always been home to our saints and seers whereas to the West, Forests are uninhabited. To the Indians, in general, temples do not confine God but they try to transcend and perceive God as Omnipresent 'Religion as culture survives in the hearts of men, but religion as temple-cult depends on patronage. In the heart of the country, both in North and South India, every sect points with pride to the innumerable cave and temples images and statues, of unsurpassed splendour in religious architecture and sculpture, that bear testimony to the popular devotion to the gods, and to social and State support of religious institutions. There are huge and rich temples in South India, wonderful specimens of titanic architecture, each one of which can house and run a whole university of thousands of students. In the heyday of of their glory, the income temples went mainly to benefit people at large by way of promotion of education and help to the needy. Later such practices gradually recorded into the background mainly due to the descent of lineal succession in ownership of temples and places of religious worship.[6.2]

6.2 TEWARI,UDAI NARAIN, India: A Cultural Voyage (A Cultural Survey of the Land of Eternal Resurgence) (P.26-27) Select book Service Syndicate, New Delhi, India, 1993

From the Vedic Culture it has been seen that India has an oral culture whereas the West has a tradition of writing. not only sastras but even subjects like archery could not be confined to libraries. Institution of higher learning were not bound by limits; Only facts based subjects are confined to knowledge. The forest atmosphere provided an ideal environment for the pursuit of learning undisturbed and uninterrupted.

It has been observed that in Mesopotamia there had been institution of higher learning connected with temple and libraries where subjects such as astronomy, medicine, architecture and engineering were taught and wherein qualified youngmen were required to undergo periods of internship under a master of his chosen profession. In Egypt Helipolis had been a popular center of higher learning. It has been pointed out that excavations have unearthed a ruined building the bricks of which are stamped with the words "The House of Life" (the Egyptian term for university) along with lists of names of regency professors of that university. The Chapter III (Theoretical Build-up) gives details about the scribal culture in Mesopotamia. In the Mesopotamian Civilization, temple formed the neucleus of socio-economic life of the people. Social and Political life continued to be organised around the temple. The priests considered themselves the guardians and conservators of knowledge. Learning was in fact a process of imitation too be conferred seriously. By virtue of soverignty the king remained high priest but much authority had to be exercised through delegated offices. The minor priests and temple staff, in addition to religious task attended to the numerous social and economic functions of the temples and among their number were the scribes and teachers. In due course a high degree of secularization had occured and that the common scribe was no longer a priest because of the demand for larger number of scribes and thus scribal training became inevitable. The House of Wisdom, operated as a place of advanced instruction during the second millennium, was attended by some graduate scribes and studies proceeded there at a higher level. Though the house of Wisdom was not concerned with higher thought in the sense of speculation, advanced training in notation and reckoning were the practices in vogue.

In ancient Egypt the priest and the scribe were the two main members of the Egyptian literate. The background of the scribes training was permitted with rigorous moral conditioning. Since it is established that the scribal crafts were learned either in the home by direct apprenticeship, or in the school of books, and that the House of LIfe literature makes little reference to any teaching within its walls, it seems certain that the House of Life was not primarily a school. It provided the model for other aspects of higher learning. Such 'higher learning' was itself of craft variety.

From the details given in the chapter III (Theoretical Build-up), it has been observed that in general terms, these scribal cultures of Egypt and Mesopotamia have been viewed from two points of view, the technical and the moral. From the technical point of view, they emphasize the written word: the scribe is essentially a person who has mastered the technique of writing; socially the scribe was a civil servant: he put his knowledge of writting at the service of civil administration. In Egypt this was essentially a kingly affair; in Mesopotamia it was at first apparently, sacerdotal, but there too it soon came under the direction of the king. The training of the scribe aimed higher: it proposed to achieve a complete formation of mind and character and lead to which can only be called wisdom. The old oriental societies attached importance to education as the gateway to success. For the child education was the, means of entry into a privileged class. This high opinion of the scribes art found symbolic expression in the idea that writting was sacred activity, of divine origin and inspiration, placed under the patronage of a god, such as Thoth in Egypt, and Nabu, the son of Ea, the god of wisdom, in Mesopotamia.

Hence it is assumed and argued in the light of the evidence available about the Mesopotomian and Egyptian Scribal culture that the centres of higher learning emerged as the civilization was once settled and developed. *2. In all cultures religion forms the basis of the quest for knowledge. The seeds of intellectual inquiry are sown in the soil of religion, thus tending towards secular pursuits in due course.*

Ample evidences are shown in the chapter-III (Theoretical Build-up). It has been observed that the temple formed the centre of attention in the socio religious life of the ancient Mesopotomian and Egyption people. Initially the world of early oriental man was pantheistic, he was in blissful ignorance of the mystery of the universe. He was not aware of the rhythm of Nature and of the mystery of the gods. The gods could not be known, their workings inscrutable and man could only propitiate. The temple supplied the need and the high priest became the mediator between man and god. The Priest developed lunar calender; the calender and astronomical observations were linked with prediction and propitiation; from these activities astrology developed as a study of the influence of nature on man and it remained a significant element of Mesopotamian thought, writing and reckoning had their beginnings in this context.

Our Indian heritage speaks high of our Vedic Wisdom. The technical name for the Vedic Study is "Swadhyaya" The study includes the three fold knowledge -that of Rgyajur and Saman. Besides the three Vedas the branches of knowledge cultivated by the Hindus included not only literature both sacred and secular with its accessories, grammar, phonetics, exegetics and Matrics but also Logic, Philosophy, Itihasa, Vartha (economics) Dandaniti (science of Government), Dhanurveda (science of war), Astronomy Law, Medicine and Mechanics and Fine arts of all descriptions. Besides these we find innumerable reference to the Supreme of highest knowledge, technically called paravidya, as distinguished from all other knowledge, termed apara. By the paravidya the Mundaka understands that knowledge through which the ultimate Reality is known. All knowledge para or apara is opposed to ignorance, avidya; paravidya, however, is extolled as Sarv-vidyapratistha the foundation of all arts and sciences, as Vedant the final and the highest stages of Vedic wisdom, is verily the science of sciences wherein lies implict the knowledge of every thing.

A singular feature of ancient Hindu civilization is that it has been moulded and shaped in the courses of its history more by religious than by political or economic influence. Religion, as understood by the ancient Hindus practically dominated every sphere of their national life. The fundamental principles of social, political and economic life was welded into a comprehensive theory which is called religion in Hindu thought. Practical attitudes thus followed theoretical orientations. The total configuration of ideals, practices and conduct is called Dharma (Religion, Virtue or Duty) on this ancient tradition. Thus it is religion that gave its laws to the social organization of the ancient Hindus and regulated even their economic activities and pursuits.

The book of knowledge in those day was called "Sruti" 'what was heard'. This character of knowledge also fixed its form known as Mantra or Sutra by which the maximum of meaning was compressed within the minimum of words of which the crowning example is the letter 'OM' containing within itself a world of meaning. Another point to be noted in this connection is that Sabda or sound by itself has its own potency and value, apart from its sense, and its intrinsic attributes, its rhythm, and vibrations should be captured. Sabda is Brahma "the word is God". In short, the system of education, interpreted in the Rigveda concerns only with the acquisition of the highest knowledge and saving wisdom and not of ordinary secular knowledge or intermediate truths for purposes of worldly life. The method of attaining the knowledge of the Absolute "Parabrahma jnnane" is not the method of acquiring knowledge of the objective sciences, arts and crafts. It is the method of realisation of the highest by inhibition of the senses and the objective, the method of meditation (Dhyana) sustained by a life of austerities tapas or yoga. These highest and ultimate truth are reveled by the language of the Vedic Mantras evolved out of the popular speech by means of Tapas and yogas by learned man called vipras, Vedhasas or Kavis, Risis, Manisis and Munis who live in a state of trance and in the subtle body and are worshipped by the gods themselves.

These learned used to gather in their Assemblies Brahmana-Sanghas and discuss the hymns they had themselves individually attained as the result of their tapas and meditation. In short the epistemological inquiries are the results of the ontological pursuits. The Rgvedic Education proper being religious and literary in its charactor was for the few who were fit and eager for a dedicated life in quest of the highest truths and supreme knowledge. It was thus not meant for the many or the masses. In due course, in the age of Brahmanas, the other three later Vedic Samhitas of Sama, Yajur and Atharva ushered in a different type of literary activities exclusively for the purpose of ritual application. The fact is that in their time the old Rigvedic religion showed considerable development of ceremonial and priesthood out of their beginning in the Rigveda. Higher education now related itself to the requirements of this priesthood and ritualistic religion. The Samaveda is the song book and the Yajurveda is the prayer book. The Yajurveda has two divisions called black (Krishna) and white (sukla) also called Vajasaneya-Samhita. The white Yajurveda contains only the Mantras, the prayers and sacrificial formulas, while the black Yajurveda contains the Mantras in verse and also a portion in prose, the earliest Indian prose, presenting the sacrificial rites that go with the Mantras alongwith discussions thereon, anticipating the later Brahmana literature. Thus from the point of view of education the Yajurveda has made a material contribution to it by the creation of a prose literature which later culminated in the literacy master piece of the Upanisads. The Atharvaveda, indeed contains much new and original matter, not be found in the Rigveda. A large part of this Vedic Samhita refers to and mention appropriate herbs as remedies against diseases like fever, leprosy and jaundice and surgical ailments like fracture and wounds, like snakes and other injurious insects, and against poison in general, mania and other complaints. The Atharvaveda thus ranks as the oldest work of Indian medicine. Thus these later Vedic Samhitas, besides extending religions literature in response to the growing needs of worship, gave the start to a variety of speculations which resulted in the growth of number of secular science and arts still subscribing the ends of aforesaid interpretation of the emergence of the Vedic Samhitas that the quest for knowledge, based on religion tend to develop secular pursuits also.

Again in the chapter III of the Theoretical Build-up, it has been observed that the higher studies imparted in the Buddhist Viharas, consisted of not only studying the advanced text of religions and philosophical importance but also conducting debates and discussions on the various doctines of different creeds. The instructions in the Buddhist Vihars were based on the Buddhist scriptures. Being more proselytizing than other religions, Buddhism was keen on cultivating its leaders and votaries, of the power of debate, by which, it could spread and win converts from other rival sects. Buddhist education made diabetic skill and ability in argumentation, a most important part of the intellectual equipment essential in leadership. But there intellectual debates were practised not only by the Buddhist but also by the scholars belonging to different creeds from the days of the Upanishads.

From the aforesaid observation it is assumed that the Viharas trained the monks with religious cause in dialectic skill and ability in argumentation which entailed in the mastery of tarkasastra. Again it is argued that religion forms the basis of secular subjects.

To substantiate further the assumption that religion forms the basis of the intellectual quest, the Arabic Madrasas of medieval India.

chapter III theoretical build-up-3.4.1 (iii) Arabic Madrasa of Medieval India) speak about the Islamic Education. The maktabs and madrasas were invariably attached to the mosques; and these institutions had a strong religion. In the spiritually minded countries of the East the main aim of education has been to produce religious man. Quran prescribes the path of well-being in the present world and well-being the hereafter. Muslim education in India envisaged for people a discipline for the material as well as spiritual progress. Though education Islamic faith and beliefs were imparted to all the sectors of society. That is why, Muslim education touched not only the spiritual but simultaneously the material needs of people as well as a minimum necessity irrespective of their individual temperament. Hence it was that religion was at the root of all study. As already stated, every maktab and madrasa had a mosque attached to it, and in every mosque there were separate classes for the instruction of students in sciences other than religious so that secular education might go hand in hand with religious instruction.

Hence it is argued once again in the light of the Islamic education of madrasas that religion forms the basis of the intellectual pursuits. It is further emphasised by the observation of S.M. Jaffer Education in Muslim India (1973) that "Religion, the back bone of Indian culture and civilization, was once the root of all study.

Again in the chapter III of the Theoretical Build-up. 3.4.1. (IV) Ghatikas, Sahbas and Agraharas, Mathas and Salai as centres of higher learning in South India, it is observed that invariably religion forms the basis of the pursuits in all these centres of learning. The aim of education in South India as in North India was not only intellectual, moral, religious and spiritual but also to equip people for different persuasions and service to society. In ancient and medival South India, education was promoted mainly by institutions like the Ghatika, Matha, Agrahara, Temple Colleges and Salai. These institutions served as great residential colleges and provided facilities for the study of religious literature and secular subjects. Ghatika had been a centre of advanced studies- a centre of Vedic learning. A Ghatika at Sholingan hill of north arcot distt. of Tamilnadu promoted Sanskrit learning with religious background (Vaishnavism).

Again the Theoretical Build-up under chapter III gives us a brief but detailed sketch about the mathas in South India. The Mathas are indigenous Indian example of educational organisation by which different and distant centres of culture and religious life, religious brother hoods of different localities, are affiliated to a central and common seat of the authority at head quarters and regulated and controlled by it: These mathas were of the two great faiths of medieval HInduism in South India. Both Saiva and Vaismva ,mathas were founded by the followers of the respective creeds through out South India. There Mathas just like the monasteries of medieval Europe were important religious institutions, maintained by their wealth. The Advaita Philosopher Sankara is said to have founded a matha at Kanchi after having won the Buddhists in a controversy. For the conversion of the common mass Sankaracharya is said to have founded Vidyapithas with a great teacher presiding over each. (e.g.Kanchipuram vidyapitha). Others were at four important corners of India-Sarada (Badrika) in the North, Puri in the East, Dwaraka in the West and Sringeri in the South. In these mathas, besides Vedic and Vedantic lore, Logic and Grammar were taught. The Tamil Saiva mathas concentrated on the development of religious literature. Though these mathas appear to have been primarily seminaries for imparting religious education, they at the same time disseminated secular knowledge as well. Once again it is argued that religion forms the basis of knowledge, thus leading to the acquisition of secular knowledge too.

Similarly we can cite the example of the involvement of Church in the propagation of education in the medieval Europe. The Church understood the business of education because it found that it could not do its own proper work without giving its adherents and especially its clergy as much of the former learning as was required for the study of the sacred writing and for the performance of their religious duties (Chapter III - The Theoretical Build-up.). Initially there was no thought of instructing the young in preparation for the needs of ordinary life. In due course, it became necessary for the Church to extend the scope of its educational interests. Here and there were Churchmen who advanced their scholarship beyond the limits of what was directly valuable for religious purposes and cultivated learning for its own sake. The monks were regarded as the pioneers of education in Europe after the fall of the Roman Empire. In the monasteries men who embraced ascetic life were little likely to be interested in learning for themselves or to be desirous of imparting it to others. In the fourth century there were men like St. Jeroma who clung passionately to their books after renouncing every thing else and found satisfaction in the imparting of secular instruction as part of their religious duties. This shows the scholarly side of the monastic life. In the Irish monasteries, the monk scholars studied theology along with the classics the literature of Greece and the literature of Rome for academic pursuits and they were acclaimed to write purer and better Latin than any of their contemporaries. Irish monks maintained a lively interest in the native language and literature. The academic pursuits of the monk scholars of the monasteries of the medieval Europe also supports the presumption that religion forms the basis of the study initially and then leads to the pursuits of secular interest.

John Henry new man explicitly argues (the idea of a University) (1979) that there are different kinds or spheres of knowledge, human, devine sensible, intellectual and the like; and that a university certainly takes in all varieties of knowledge in its own line, but still that it has a line of its own. It contemplates, it occupies a certain platform, of knowledge........I cannot so construct my definition of the subject-matter of university knowledge, and so draw my boundary line around it , as to include therein the other success commonly studied at Universities, and to exclude the science of religion For instance, are we to limit own idea of University knowledge by the evidence of our senses? Then we exclude ethics; by intution? We exclude history; by testimony? We exclude metaphysics; by abstract reasoning? We exclude physics. Is not the being of a God reported to us by testimony handed down by history, inferred by an inductive process, brought home to us by metaphysical necessity, urged on us by the suggestions of our conscience? It is a truth in the natural order, as well as in the supernatural. So much for its origin; and, when obtained, what is it worth? Is it a great truth or a small one? Is it a comprehensive truth? Say that no other religious idea whatever were given but it, and you have enough to fill the mind; you have at once a whole dogmatic system. The work 'God' is a theology in itself, indivisibly one, in exhaustibly various from the vastness and simplicity of its meaning. Admit a god, and you introduce among the subjects of your knowledge, a fact incomprising, closing in upon, absorbing every part of any order of knowledge, and stop short of that which enters into every order. All true principles run over with it, all phenomena converge to it, it is truly the first and the last. In work indeed, and in idea, it is easy enough to divide knowledge into human and divine, secular and religious, and to, lay down that we will address ourselves to the one without interfering with the other; but it is impossible in fact. Granting that divine truth differs in kind from human, so do human truths differ in kind from human, so do human truths differ in kind one from another. If the knowledge of the creator is in a different order from knowledge of the creature, so, in like manner, metaphysical science is in a different order from physical, physics from history, history from ethics. You will soon break up into fragments the whole circle of secular knowledge, if you begin the mutilation with divine [6.3]

6.3 New man John Henry, the Idea of a University, Defined and illustrated, edited with introduction and notes by I.T. KER Oxford University Press, 1976 pages 37-38

Here, Newman uniquely exposes the supreme position of theology and indispensability of Religion as the basis of all knowledge. According to Newman, the Church 'fears no knowledge' for all branches of knowledge are connected together, because the subject matter or knowledge is intimately united in itself, as being the acts and the work of the creator. It is, therefore ultimately a religious conviction that supports Newmans' supremely confident vision of the wholeness of intellectual knowledge and truth. Underlying his belief in man's 'imperial intellect' is his belief in God's existence. Religion and knowledge, then, are not opposed to each other- and not because they are irrelevant to one another but because they are indivisibly connected, or rather because religion forms part of the subject-matter of knowledge. This is Newman's claim and it is crucial to his whole argument. We may deny the premises, but we should not allow our disbelief to turn into a misgining over the logic of what naturally follows from it. It may be provocative, but it is not illogical for .Newman to declare: 'If the Catholic faith is true, a University cannot exist externally to the Catholic theology.

Hence it is again argued in the light of the aforesaid convictions of Newman that Religion forms the basis of knowledge, leading to the secular pursuits.

3. During the study of the evolutionary development of higher learning it has been observed that there was a gradual shifting from FAITH to KNOWLEDGE, signifying the quest for intellectual reality.

The shifting from faith to knowledge indicates the transit of thought process from metaphysical inquiry into epistenological inquiry. In the chapter III of the Theoretical Build-up, it has been discussed in the context of the Indian heritage with reference to Vedic education, that the system of education adumbrated in the Rigveda concerns only with the acquisition of the highest knowledge and saving wisdom and not of ordinary secular knowledge or intermediate truths for purposes of worldly life. The method of attaining the knowledge of the absolute "parabrahma jnnaue" is not the method of acquiring a knowledge of the objective sciences, arts and crafts. It is method of realization of the highest and ultimate truths called Rita and Satya by inhibition of the senses and objective, the method of meditation (dhyana) sustained by a life of austerities, tapas or Yoga. Ancient Hindu education is individual centered and hence education is necessarily individual. Indeed, the main part of education was the work of student and not of the teacher leading to a mediate knowledge . For an immediate knowledge of the ultimate Truth and Reality, the pupil must depend upon himself. The knowledge of the Real cannot grow out of the knowledge of the unreal of the realm of experience, which is the realism of ignorance. The knowledge of the Atman cannot be gained by mere speculation (tanka) concerning it, but only by revelation as the result of the proper degree of self growth. Th acquisition of such knowledge which means emancipation is not a matter of study but of life. For this acquistion the pursuer must have staunch faith in his quest.

In his pursuit of the Absolute, he tended towards the acquisition of the knowledge too. The Rigveda describes the popular speech, the spoken tongue as "imperfect" and untrue because it cannot serve as the vehicle of Truth of Supreme knowledge. These highest and ultimate truths are revealed by a different language, the language of the Vedic Mantras evolved out of the popular speech by means of Tapas and Yoga by learned men called Vipras, Vedhasas or Kavis, Rishis, Manishis and Munis who live in a state of trance and in the subtle body and are worshipped of the gods themselves. We are further told that these learned men and seers developed Vedic knowledge and speech by their discussions at Assemblies or Conferences, meeting on occasions of sacrifice where this knowledge and speech are atained mastered, collected and distributed. These learned men are the members of these bodies, described as sakha i.e. those who come together by the bond of fellowship in learning meet in their assemblies where through their discussion language was refined into the language of the Vedas, like grates through a sieve. As fellow seekers of Truth, they are bound by a community of ideas in which they give expression in that language, the source of the highest good and knowledge. Thus the vedic sanskrit was hammered into shape out of spoken sanskrit of the times at learned Assemblies where it was the vehicle of philosophical discussion.

It is argued in favour of the assumption from faith to knowledge ' at the absolute faith in search of the Absolute leads the seers towards the philosophical discussions where in the Vedic Sanskrit was hammered into shape out of the spoken Sanskrit.

The Christian monasteries of the medieval Europe also reveal that ascetic scholars, in the course show in academic pursuits. A notable case of the kind is that of Cassiodorus who attempted maintenance of learning. In addition to certain commentaries on the sciptures he compiled for the benefit of his monks a treatise entitled institutions divinarum et secularum lectionum, the first part of which was devoted to sacred literature, the second to the liberal arts. The idea that knowledge was comprehended in seven arts had found expression in the treatise of martianum Capella, but the pagan atmosphere of Capella's book had prevented its general adoption. The work of Cassiodorus emphasized aftresh the seven-fold grouping of knowledge and gave it sancitity by connecting with the text that wisdom had builded her house she hath hen out her seven pillars." Hence forward the seven arts constituted a standard part of education and the work of Cassiodorus became one of the texts commonly studied. The Christian aimed at preparing monk but in due course monk-scholars emerged. Chapter V. The Buddhist Monasteries as Universities of ancient Hindu India - An exposition of conceptual Analysis discusses in great detail the emergence of the Buddhist monasteries and its organisational development. It has been observed here that as and when Buddhism began to ebb under royal patronage, the Buddhist monasteries had ceased to be propoganda centres of the religion as in the past. They had been enlarging one aspect of monastic life that was rooted in the ancient tradition of monk-scholarship. The process is marked by a re-orientation of monastic bearing whereby it outgrows its cloistered inbred character and turned into a learning that was liberal and many-sided.

In the monsteries the ancient principle of learning had been 'Study for faith'. Its aim was to produce the perfect monk within the monastic regimen the immemorial custom of education in India, the Gurukula taking lessons from a master who presides over a small circle of resident pupils- was reproduced under the Buddhist terminology Nissaya. Nissaya refers to dependence on a teacher for a space of years which varied with the trainees' ability to learn. Under the ancient Nissaya system, the monastic learning was confined to the common and its philosophy (Abhidamma) and its object was to turn out be perfect monk. Yet the learning had to grown out of this circumscribed and inbred character which was hardly sufficient for its own set purpose. Monasteries in fact, were not isolated from the larger life of society, the very reason for their existence was the 'good and happiness of the many' that is, it carry the blessing and the benefit of the religions to those who were without them. It was felt at a certain stage that the mere study for faith fell short of the standard set by the lord himself for the perfect or accomplished monk-one, having mastered the doctrine, is able to spread it abroad and confute the doctrine of other faiths. It demanded knowledge of the faiths and also the intellectual equipments to be gained from other and non-commonical sources.

The need for a more liberal learning is suggested in a verse, ostensibly from the Sutra lankara, cited among his quotation from the Sutras and Sastras by the Tibetan Scholar and historiographer. Bustom and made explicit in his comment. In order to vanguish and to help others as well as to obtain knowledge through knowledge of himself, he the (the good monk) is earnestly applied to study: on which Bustom's explicatory comments is as follows: Accordingly the science of Logic (Hetuvidya and of Grammar and Literature are studied in order to vanquish one's adversaries (in convtroversy), the science of Medicine and Arts, for administering help to others and that of Metaphysics (Adhyatmavidya) to acquire knowledge of himself. The study was calculated to provide a monk with the Scholarly equipments needed by him for the discharge os his obligations, viz to spread the religion among laity and to strength its cause by victory in disputations. The Science of logic (Hetuvidya) was developed among scholar monks out of the older veda manuals that had been composed with the object of sharpening mental faculties for success in debates. This liberlization of learning the shift from the ancient study for faith to study for knowledge was a matter of natural evolution in the culture of the monasteries. It brought monastic learning into a larger frame work.

In Chapter IV- The University - an institution of higher education. J.H. Newman's Views are specially focused. According to Newman idea, a University should teach universal knowlege. With his protestant oxford background, and his inclination towards liberal education Newman delivered his discussions about the idea of a university to the young Irish Bishops. Invariably Catholic faith is the basis of the idea of a Univerisity. To Newman, a University is primarily a place of teaching universal knowledge. But if its aim is the diffusion and extension of knowledge, this does not mean that knowledge for its own sake in the justification of a university: its real purpose is to produce more intelligent members of society by fostering cultivation of mind, formation of the intellect. Newman's idea of a University is tinged with religious fervour. This is well evident from his second discourse on theology which he claims to be a branch of knowledge. He argues simply that if theology claims to be a branch of knowledge, which it must if religion is viewed as "absolutely and objectively true" then it must be included in a University which, by definition, must teach 'Universal knowledge'. But if you begin the mutilation with divine by excluding theology, then you will soon break up into fragments the whole circle of secular knowledge. For, he argues in discourse III, Bearing of theology on other Branches of knowledge all knowledge forms are whole, because its subject matter is one: for the universe is so intimately knit together, that we cannot separate off portion and operation from operation except by a mental abstraction which results in the sciences. Consequently, the man who indentifies the world with one particular scientific view is not a teacher of liberal knowledge, but a narrow- minded bigot. In the next discourse IV, Bearing of other branches of knowledge on theology the point is reinforced that if you drop any science out of the circle of knowledge, you cannot keep its place vacant for it, that science is forgotten, the other sciences close up exceed then proper bounds, and intrude where they have no right. The danger is that one individual branch of knowledge will be made the centre of all truth.

Assuming that the narrow specialised study of only one subject is to be avoided, still the student will only be able to pursue a few sciences out of the multitide: it is a great point then to enlarge the range of studies which a University professes, even for the sake of the students, and though they cannot pursue every subject which is open to them, they will be the gainers by living among those and under those who represent the whole circle. The result of this 'liberal' education will be a philosophical habit which is 'its own end' and in acquiring which we are satisfying a direct need of our nature. Therein lies the 'use' of knowledge which is 'liberal' because it 'stands on its own pretensions, is independent of sequels, expects no complement, refuses to be informed by any end, or absorbed into any art. Knowledge is especially liberal, or sufficent for itself when and so far as it is philosophical, when it is acted upon, informed and impreganted by Reason.

Knowledge is called by the name of Science or philosophy, when it is acted upon, informed or impregnated by Reason. Reason is the principle of that intrinsic fecundity of knowledge, which, to those who possess it, is its especial value and which dispenses with the necessity of then looking abroad for any end to rest upon external to itself.

Knowledge indeed, when thus exalted into a scientific form is also power; not only is it excellent in itself, but whatever such excellence maybe, it is something more, it has a result beyond itself. Prior to its being a power, it is a good, that it is, not only an instrument, but an end. It may resolve itself into an art, a terminate in a mechanical process and in tangible fruit, but it also may fall back upon the Reason which informs it, and resolve itself into philosophy. In liberal, the same person may cultivate it in both ways at once: there are the two methods of education: the end of the one is to be philosophical, and of the other is to be mechanical: the one rises towards general ideas, the other is exhaustive upon what is particulars and external.

Newman speaks of knowledge which is intellecual- something which grasps what it perceives through the senses: something which takes a view of things, which seems more than the senses convey: which reasons upon what it sees and how it sees: which invests it with an idea. It expresses itself, not in a enunciation, but by an enthyme, it is of the nature of science from the first, and in it consists its dignity. The principle of real dignity in knowledge, its worth, its desirableness, considered irrespectively of its results, is the germ within it of a scientific or a philosophical process. This how it comes to be an end in itself, this is why it admits of being called liberal.

Moreover such knowledge is not a more extrinsic or accidental advantage which may be got up from a book and easily forgotten again: it is an acquired illumination, it is a habit, a personal possession, and an inward endowment. And this is the reason, why it is more correct as well as usual, to speak of a University as a place of education than of instruction when knowledge is concerned. We are instructed, for instance, in manual exercises, in the fine and useful arts, in trades, and in ways of business, for these are methods, which have little or no effect upon the mind itself, are contained in rules committed to memory, to tradition or to use and bear upon as an end external to themselves. But education is a high work: it implies an action upon our mental nature, and the formation of a character, it is something individual and permanent, and is commonly spoken of in connection with religion and virtue. When we speak of the communication of knowledge as being Education, we there by really imply that the knowledge is a state for condition of mind, and since cultivation of mind is surely worth seeking for this own sake, we are thus brought once more to the conclusion, which the work 'Liberal' and the work 'philosophy' have already suggested, that there is a knowledge, which is desirable, though nothing come of it, as being of itself a treasure, and a sufficient renuneration of years of labour.

There are three great subjects on which Human Reason employs itself:- God, Nature and Man. Of these, Nature and Man, when respectively subjected to Human Reason, form two books: the nature is called science, the book of Man is called literature. Literature and science, thus considered nearly constitute the subject matter of liberal Education, and while Science is made to subserve the former of the two injuries (The two injuries which Revelation is likely to sustain at the hands of the Masters of human reason unless the Church protects the sacred treasure which is in jeopardy are (1) ignoring of theological truth altogether, under the pretence of not recognising differences of religious opinion, which will only take place in countries or undergovernments which have adjured catholisim and (2) is a recognition of catholicism, but an adulteration of its spirit its exclusion, literature suliseven the latter its curruption.

Newman argues that if at all secular knowledge (art and Science) is encouraged and patronized, it is for the sake of Religion and in their relation to the interests of Revealed truth. He is of the firm conviction that truth is his real ally, as it is his profession: and that knowledge and reason are sure ministers to faith. The church fears no knowledge for 'all branches of knowlege are connected together, because the subject-matter of knowledge is intimately united in itself, as being the acts and work of the creator. It is therefore, ultimately a religious conviction that supports Newman's supremely confident vision of the wholeness of intellectual knowledge and truth under lying his belief in man's imperial intellect is his belief in God's existence. Religion and knowledge, then, are not opposed to each other and not because they are irrelevant to one another but because they are indivisibly connected, or rather because religion forms part of the subject matter of knowledge. This is Newman's claim and it is crucial to his whole argument.

In general, Newman's Discourse exposes the tension between the genuinely conditional insistence on the absolute value of knowledge in itself and the equally firm conviction that knowledge is emphatically not the highest good. Thus, while on the one hand Newman will have no party with those who wish to justify education solely on moral or religious, on the other hand, without any self-contradiction, he insists that it is better to have a simple religious faith a cultivated intellect which lacks or neglects religious truth. There is no question of any necessary incompatibility for Newman, but he recognises the fact that religious belief and education, faith and reason, are not always found together. Right Reason, that is Reason rightly exercised leads the mind to the Cathelica Faith and plants it there and teaches it in all its religious speculations to act under its guidence. But Reason, considered as a real agent in the world, and as an operative principle in man's nature is far from taking so straight and satisfactory a direction. If, there has to be a choice between this kind of reason and simple faith, New-man leads us undoubtedly to Faith.

It would be of interest to compares Newman's faith with the Kantian Faith. Immanuel Kant (1724-1804), in his famous critiques of Pure Reason, showed that knowledge a priori is possible, which means that by virtue of the forms and categories of the mind,like space, time and causality, man possesses the presuppositions for coherent and intelligible experience. To be sure, we know only appearances, colours, sounds and the like, never the things -in-itself. Kant maintained that true knowledge cannot transcend or go beyond experince. Still, for the sake of religious and morality, we need such concepts as God, freedom and immortality. To satisfy these demands of human nature, Kant wrote Critique of practical Reason, in which he acknowledges the necessity and validity of these foundation for morality by enjoining man to act in such a way that the maxim of his will may at the same time be raised into a principle of universal law.

According to Kant, human experience is itself a mode of knowledge which implies inteelligence, and intelligence has a rule of its own, which must be an a priori condition of all knowledge of objects presented to it. To this rule as expressed in a priori conceptions, all objects of experience must necessarily conform, and with it they must necessarily conform, and with it they must agree. For we are brought to the conclusions that we never can transcend the limits of possible experience, and therefore never can realize the object with which metaphysics is primarily concerned. In brief, Kant speaks of two worlds viz. noumenal and phenomenal. Through perception and understanding, man enters into the phenomenal world i.e. the world of objects and happening - the practical world. But entry into the noumenal world - the world of ideas cannot be possible by understanding human reason but by faith Man must make a leap on to the noumenal world and that leap is possible only through faith. This Kantian faith is reflected in Newman's faith which forms the basis of all knowledge. Though faith leaves man to knowledge, still faith governs all knowledge.

4. Two essentials of a university are that it is 'built of men' and that its aim is 'intellectual health'. Universities began as professional schools and later on developed as repositories of the culture of society as well as the culture of the intellect.

That university is 'built of men' is well evident from the very definition of the word 'university'. The word 'university' comes from the Latin Universitas Magistrorum et sko-lare-jm meaning 'a company of scholars who are in intellectual pursuit. The university's main objective is the advancement of learning and thought.

That university is 'built of men' stands true to the statement that Plato founded his Academy which has been acclaimed as the first university of the world. Following the suit of his master, Aristotle also founded Lyceum which was equally famous as Plato's Academy. These great Greek philosophers built up their instititions of higher academic pursuit. In Chapter III the Theoretical Build up gives a brief account of the intellectual pursuits of the Greek scholars. Glimpses at the educational history of the Medieval Europe help us undertand that inspite of a political instability and military turmoil, a collection of cathedral schools came into existence to kindle the dying embers of learning and in due course they became the soil in which the universities could grow. It is stated that in the 12thC, a collection of intellecual endeavours - editing, collecting, systematizing - culiminated in bands of scholars setting up studi generalia which were places of learning. Our Indian Haritage speaks of Parishads and Brahmana Sarighas as centres of higher lerning. Before interpreting the meaning, let us recall the several types of institutions known as Sakhas, Charanas, Parishads, Kulas, Gotras and the like. All of these were of the nature of assemblies, academies, literary or religious guilds, serving as schools of Vedic learning in which that learning was conserved, commented upon, and communicated by successive generations of teachers and pubpils gathering round a distinct tradition bequeathed to them by the particular founder of a school named after him. The term Sakhas was originally applied to the three original Samhitas of Rg,

Sama and Yajus regarded as the three branches of stems of the Vedic tree, having the same root, revelation (Sruti) and bearing the same fruit, the sacrifice (Karman). More frequently, the term 'Sakha' was used with four Vedas. Literary works did not then exist in writing and were devoid of any tangible, external form. The Vedic hymns had no outward existence except through those who heard and remembered them. Thus a book then existed merely as a body of thought handed down in schools or in families. A man who had mastered a book was himself the book. A work once composed might either wither for want of an audience or grow, like a tree, of which every new listerner who would learn it by heart would become a new branch (literally, Sakha). But, we should not fail to distinguish between the branch, as the book and the branch, as the reader, that is to say, between the trust and the trustee. The former is to be esignated Sakha and the latter as the reader of a Sakha, while we should also note in this connection that the term Charana is to be applied to those ideal successions or fellowships to which all those, reading the same Sakha, belonged. Thus Dr.R.K.Maokerji has used the analogy of a branch of a tree to convey what we have understood by an edition of a hundered copies in modern times. Literary works were handed down by oral tradition in different works or even different recensions of one and the same work, like so many Mss in later times. Further it had led to the growth of the special class of literature called the Pratisakhyas associated with what are known as the Vedic Sakha. Pratisakhya does not mean a treatise on the phoneticas rules peculiar to one of different texts in which each of the Vedas had been handed down for ages in different familes and different parts of India. The Sakha, as already explained, were not independent collections of the old hymns but different editions of one and the same original collection which, in the course of a long continued oral tradition had become modified by slight degrees. The texts of the Vedas as they existed and lived in the oral tradition of various sets of people became Sakhas differing, from other Sakhas. Along with this variety in the texts, there was also an inexhaustible variety in the methods of their pronunciation pursued by the different Sakhas or seats of Vedic learning. There thus grew a certain nunber of local varieties in accent and religiousity adhered to out of the natural respect paid by each teacher, by each family, and by each Brahamanic community guild to its own established oral tradition. Thus the Pratisakhyas, besides giving general rules for the proper pronunciation of the Vedic language as safeguard against its further corruption and were intended to record what was schools inthe absence of any criterion for determining what was the ancient and most correct way of reciting the sacred songs of the Veda. The original sense of the term Sakha takes it to be a literary work as in the expression Sakhainadhite, "he reads a particular recension of the Veda". But from its various traditions that branched off from each of the three original branches of the Veda, and in this latter sense it became synonymous with the term Charana. Dr.R.K.Mookerji has stated that the reason of this change in the use of the word seems to be that the Sakha existed in those time not as a written book but only in the traditions of the Charanas, each member of a Charana representing what, in our modern times we should call the copy of a book. Thus the two terms were used in the same way as we speak of the jews when we mean the Old Testameant or the Koran when we mean the Moslems.[6.4]

The best definition of a Charana occurs in a passage in Jagaddhara's commentary on the Malatimadhava, where the Charana is defined as "a number of men who are pledged to the reading of a certain Sakha of the Veda and who have in the manner become one body." Thus, while the Sakhas denoted the texts, their propagators or pravartakas were the Charanas. Thus the Charanas were practically the Schools for the cultivation and propagation of particular texts of the Vedas. Just as the sacred Vedas under the system to oral traditon developed a variety of texts, so also did the Brahmanas which, being not written in metre, like the Vedas, were more exposed to alteration in that process of propagation. The Brahmana was not necessarily any idependent work but merely one of the various recensions branching out of a common Brahmana. There was also a third type of institutions developed for the cultivation and propagation of learning. These institutions are known as Parishads. The term, as used in the Upnishads, means an assembly of advisers in questions of philosophy. It was a settlement of Brahmanas, a community or college to which members of any Charana might belong. Thus members of the same Charana might be Fellows of different Parishads and Fellows of the same Parishads might be members of different Charnanas. In later literature, the term 'Parishad' not only denotes an academic institution but also the assessors of a judge or the Council of ministers of a prince. To sum up, we may say that a Parishad is parallel to a university, in modern phraseology, comprising students belonging to

---

6.4 Mookerji R.K. (1951) Ancient Indian Education (Brahmanical and Buddhist) second edition, Mae Millan and Co. Ltd. St. Martin 8s st, London (page 80)

different colleges called Charanas. To Newman, a university is not a birth place of poets or of immortal authors, of founders of schools, leaders of colonies or conquerors of nations: but a seat of all learning. To Jaspers, the university is a community of scholars and students engaged in the task of seeking truth.

Karl Jaspers says that the university fulfils its task research, instruction, training, communication within an instructional framework; It requires buildings, materials, books and institutes and their orderly administration. The university exists only to the extent that it is institutionalized. The idea becomes concrete in the institution. But for its vitality the university depends on persons, not institutions, which are more than a physical pre-requisite. The university is judged by its ability to attract the best people and provide them with the most favourable conditions for research, communication and teaching.

As stated by Rashdall, universities were 'Products of that instinct of association which swept like a great wave over the towns of Europe in the course of the eleventh and twelfth centuries'. Chapter IV gives in detail the characteristics of human association leading to the blossoming of the university. The factors responsible for the birth of universities were the need for learned men for new profession and the expansion of wealth and leisure. These factors stimulated the growth in advanced learning and hence the mission of the university was the advanced sophisticated learning, free of external censure, meeting the interests of individual scholars, yet serving the needs of medieval society, the university is basically based on the concept of "Community", drawn from "guild"of the medieval Europe, of individuals bound together by an oath of mutual support and common obedience to elected officials and with authority to select its own members. The university initialy drew its structure and practice from the established institutions of the Medieval Age- the Church, the monastery and the - guild or commune. All these indicate that the universities are built of men with deliberate common goal of academic pursuit.

There seemed to be a purpose in not bindig the 'university' to buildings, external paraphernalia, so much so that even books were used very discreetly. The modern day university in its concretised form focuses more activity on administration and very little on men.

The great university historican Rashdall attributes the rapid multiplication of universities during the fourteenth and fifteenth centuries to the direct demand for highly educated lawyers and administrators. Originally the universities were vocationally oriented to create leaders for the state and clergymen for the church and practitioners in law and medicine. The history of Medieval Universities reveals that the Italian universities tended to emphasize the practical (the professions of law, medicine, theology and administration,) whereas Paris, Oxford and Cambridge were dominated by doctors of theology who taught what became known as the seven liberal arts: grammar, dialectics, rhetoric, geometry, arithmetic, astronomy and music. It is this latter form and tradition that took root in England and later spread to the United States and Canada. Newman's conception of a university is also based on the aim of training young catholic bishops that rulers for the state. This is well evident from Plato's statement as the philosophers should be the kings. All these show that universities arose as centres of *professional training.*

But at the same time we should not forget the fact that the rise of the Universities belongs to a class of cultural moments in which a generation's dissatisfaction with the state of its intellectual inheritance led to a range of new achievements. To illustrate one such moment, we can cite Socrates' dissatisfaction with moral and political notions of his contemporary Ionian Greeks standing as an image of this kind of moment. It was Socrates' pupil Plato who founded in the grove an Academic school which in some respects and for some purposes might be counted as the first university. There is another movement which has a similar celebrity; the multiplicity of intellectual events from about 1450 to 1700 to which the labels of Renaissance and Scientific Revolution are often attached. The rise of the universities was cultural moment of comparable importance but it failed to elicit the same enthusiasm from the custodians to our intellectual past.

The forest ashrams of the Upanishadic age and the Viharas of Ancient Hindu India are looked upon as treasure houses of the then prevailing culture too. Any conception of the university in terms of productivity and mere output is mistaken since it assimilates academic inquiry- a thoroughly human activity to an industrial process in which a regular input of materials which are efficiently combined, yield a reliable and homogeneous product. All human activities require time of thought and relaxation, just as human beings require sleep if they are to sutain their vitality. 'Culture is an activity of thought and receptiveness to beauty, or human feeling. Scraps of information have nothing to do with it. A merely well informed man is the most useless one on God's earth. Education is the acquisition of the utilization of knowledge.....The problem of education is to make the pupil see the wood by means of the trees.'[6.5]

The scholar repeatedly emphasizes that the universities are essentially centres of learning. They do other things too. Besides teaching which is the principal duty of the universities, they preserve and even further culture, they help people to acquire useful arts which later enable them to increase productivity and perform other desired enocomic functions. They are supposed to turn people into better citizens. The goal of gentleman and prescription of liberal arts in accordance with Newman's conception stands to this reality. To Karl Jaspers, culture is an acquired state and that man is culture who has been shaped by a given historical idea. A coherent system of associations, gestures,values, ways ofputting things and abilities have become second nature to him. Culture must become one's second nature through practice as if all were in born rather than acquired. For the German,culture is always a purely personal matter. As far as culture originates at the university, it takes theform of scholarly and scientific outlook and of the particular subject emphasized. The scholarly and scientific outlook is more than a specialized knowledge and competence. It is the ability to suspend temporarily one's own values for the sake of objective knowledge, to set aside bias and special interest for the sake of an impartial analysis of data. In doing this, we not only achieve essentially impartial knowledge, but also our personal bias is put in a new light. The scientific outlook stands for more than specific factual knowledge. It involves the transformation of our whole person in accordance with reason. The scientific method calls for objectivity for devotion to the task, for careful weighing, searching out of contrary possibilities, self-criticism. It does not permit one to think as one pleases and to forget everyting else at the whim of the moment. It is characterized by a sceptical and questioning attitude by caution when drawing general conclusions, by testing the limits and conditions of our assertions. Without the continuous exercise of reason in the science, education in accordance with a fixed ideal will prove rigid and confining.

6.5 Peters, Richard, (1959) Authority, Responsibility and Education (Revised Edition) (Page 133), George Allen and Unvin Ltd. London.

When education trains us to apply reason to every problem we achieve the flexibility of reason in our life as a whole.

5. The Universities are the instruments of society as they are concerned first of all with the needs ofsociety. While tracing the evolution of education system in the ancient civilization under the Chapter III - Theoretical Build-up for the study, it is argued that in the earliest human societies, what mattered most to the primitive man was survival. Now-a-days in the highly competitive world, only the fittest could be able to withstand the challenges of the situations and survive in all spheres of life. In such a situation education was not a separate component of human activity and it was a means of handing over racial erxperience from older to the younger generation. There evolved the transmission of knowledge as the function and responsibility of the society which aims at perpetuating the social process. Society is an organised entity; and preparing the individuals for multifarious responsinilities makes the society create an agency for producing and disseminating knowledge. Education as an agency of society must prepare individuals fit into a variety of responsibilities.

In fact, the emergence of higher education with its own aim, content and pedagogy was due to the substantial increase in the fund of knowledfge and even more to man's increasing desire and need to know more and more. Realising the utmost importance of the responsibility of producing and disseminating knowledge, the medieval ancestors of the modern universities started Universites (Corporations), communities of scholars committeed to the search for dissemination of knowledge. In the scribal culture of Mesopotamian and Egyptian civilization, training of scribes was based on the transmission of knowledge to apprentice scribe.

Realising their responsibilities towards the society, the modern universities are 'already making their irreplaceable position in preparing for the third millennium, and will have a decisive impact on the first decades of the twenty-first century. Around these two axes (research and education) they are rapidly emerging from the long tradition of the medieval universitas studiorum, having passed through the era of von Humboldt and Newman, and decades of isolation devoted to training in the few major and much sought-after liberal professions. Now, after years of direct, hard and critical confrontations with the society, some of them are finally becoming true centres of excellence in Europe, North

America and recently in Japan. At this point in their history,the universities are discovering new tasks and responsibilities towards society, and are deploying new techniques and methods of teaching that are beginning to operate alongside the traditional forms: correspondence courses, 'teleclassing'open University, etc., aimed at new groups (as in the case of continuing education) or atthe whole community.

The definition of the vocation of the university is complex as far as the objectives are concerned. Briefly, they could be described as having a vertical and a horizontal mission; pursuing deeper knowledge by bringing together existing knowledge and scientific research, as well as spreading knowledge in an organised manner and making it available to the whole community.[6.6]

The Universities Magna Carta, signed in Bologna on Sept.18, 1988, defines universities in terms of their two main tasks-research and education and above all focuses on the essential link between the two. Universities must be willing to share the research theyundertake and feed the results into the educational process. Our future way of life will depend to a large extent on the new technologies based on scientific research, and on those who invest actively in the research and development of the new advanced technologies - new materials, bio-technology, artificial intelligence but also in many other fields which still remain to be explored, and which could continue to play a role in subsequent developments. Research is becoming increasingly important for every product. If we draw up a coherent policy to protect intellectual rights and patents, we will be able to control the whole process: invention, perfection, development and application, up to production and international marketing. The same institutions will be able to continue to exert a considerable influence on applications from the ethical, social and ecological points of view-in short, in a global humanistic perspective.

In Chapter IV the salient features of a university have been discussd in detail. Here, the university's accountability towards society is interpreted in terms of external accountability and internal accountability. External accountability is the university's accountability or responsibility to the community or the society. External accountability relate to the

---

6.6 Europoean Journal of Education, Vol.24, No.4 1989. (higher Education and Europoe after 1992) I.,Roger Dillemans, Atonomy, Responsibility and Responsiveness of Higher Education Institutions after 1992. P.P.333-334.

university with regard to the contents of the courses, extra and co-curricular activities and then linkage with societal needs, knowledge,skills and values, performances of students, students' employment, teachers' contribution to extension of knowledge etc. Internal accountability is the university's responsibility to the programmes and activities, planned and implemented, teaching aids used, professional development of the teachers, utilization of infrastructural facilities, library facilities. In short, in order to carry out the responsibilities entrusted to it, the university makes itself accountability to the society as interprerted just above. Only then, they are considered as the instruments of the society.

As stated by Peterson A.D.C. (1971) in A Hundred years of Education, the historical meaning of universitas has no connection at all with universal knowledge. It meant simply a corporate body and it cannot therefore be used to suggest that, unless institutions are prepared to teach everything or admit everybody, they are not truly "universities". Even Newman, in the `idea of a University' is emphatic that a university must concern itself not merely with teaching and research, but must administer a code of conduct and furnish principles of thought and action.

6. During the conceptual analysis of a University it has been observed that prior to the emergence of the Universities the Medieval in Europe, Hindu India had been Buddhist monasteries functioning as Universities on her soil. The Buddhist Monasteries are found to imbibe the chartacteristic feature of a university as they were represented by a body of learned monks, assembled for the pursuit of Truth and service to the society i.e. humanity. Initially they were centres of religious gathering and gradually they blossomed into the cenres of higher learning thus proclaiming the Buddhist culture and rich heritage of ancient Hindu India. Under Chapter V an exposition of conceptual analysis of the Buddhist Monasteries has been dealt with. This chapter gives an account of the emergence of Viharas in ancient Hindu India and now they functioned as Centres of Higher learning attracting students from all over the country as well as from the neighbouring countries like China. Under ChapterII. the methodology of conceptual analysis is explained. Accordingly concept denotes which generalises objects of a certain class according to their specific attributes. One of the logical functions of concept is to single out in thougt by definite attributes of objects which interest us from the point of view of practice and of condition. There are two interconnected sides of a concept viz. extent and the content. Extent

refers to a class of objects generalised in a concept whereas content is the some total of usual (Essential) properties, according to which objects are generalised and singled out in the given concept. By formulating the content of a concept we single out the identical (general) in objects of the given class. Accordingly the study of the Buddhist Monasteries of ancient India observed the features of these monasteries functioning as centres of higher education-as Universities of ancient Hindu India. Chapter IV gives a brief account of the salient features of University, as revealed by the fifteen centuries of life: (1) It is by its nature universal, (2) it must be a community of scholars with internal autonomy rested in the community. (3) It should offer both scholarship and profesional training to its students, (4) It should attack the frontiers of knowledge, (5) It should allow and be allowed academic freedom and lastly, (6) It should have certain privileges in order to carry out its mission.

The University of the Buddhist system of higher Education and learning centred around monasteries as Vedic Culture centred round the sacrifice. The Buddhist world did not offer any Educational Opportunities apart from or independently its monasteries. All education, sacred as well as secular was in the hands of the monks.They had the monopoly of learning and of the leisure to impart it. They were the only custodians and bearers of the Buddhist culture. Since the Monastry was a federation of individual educational groups or schools, the efficiency of its organisation depended upon the 'federal' principles of administration which aimed at three distinct objects viz. (a) the independence and efficiency of each constituent group of pupils bound to an individual teacher, (b) the adjustment of relations between the different constituent groups and (c) the framing of laws governing the establishment as a whole and binding upon all its members, the teachers and the taught alike. Two fundamental principles mark out of the monastic life from the ordinary layman's of the world. The structure of the worldly life has its basic in marriage and property, that of the monastic life rests on their very opposites, viz. celibacy and poverty.

The second feature speaks about the federation of scholars with internal autonomy rested in the federation of community. The Buddhist monasteries in general exhibit this feature very well. In the preceding paragraph it is shown the unit of the Buddhist educational system was the group of young Bhikkus or monks living under the guardianship of a common teacher, the Upajjhaya or Acharya, who was individually responsible for their health and studies, manners and morals, their spritual progress. But these groups or schools were not always existing as isolated and independent units or institutions in the Buddhist world, as they did so largly in the Brahmanical world of culture. They federated themselves into a large unit called the Vihara or monastery. Thus we have to view them as parts of that larger organisation and in their relations to its general, collective life which developed its own code of discipline and regulations binding upon all. While Brahmanical culture was the product of confederations of such schools in larger monastic institutions comprising numbers of teachers and students (e.g. 10000 students at Nalanda) promoting and partaking of a wider, collective , academic life with its own advantages as an educational and educative agency. That a university should offer scholarship and professional training to its students is aptly exhibited by the Buddhist Monasteries.

The main purpose of the Buddhist sytem of Education was to produce perfect monks for the monasteries in order to propagate the teachings of Lord Buddha. Besides the instruction the Buddhist Scriptures, the monks were educated in the study of Vedas and other humanities and sciences. The invariable mention of three Vedas shows that the study of Atharva Veda was not included in the curriculum for general education at the times of the Jatakas. The Vedas were of course to be learnt by heart. The Buddhist is frequently referred to as having learned the three vedas by heart. Instead of the three vedas, we sometimes find mention of "Sacred Texts", holy books or 'those which indicate explicitly the sacred literature of the Buddhists, arts and Crafts were taught.

The general education comprised the study of five subjects or Vidyaas viz. (1) Sabdvidya (grammar and lexicography) (2) Silpasthanavidya "art", (3) Chikitsavidya "medicine (4) Hetuvidya logic and (5) Adhyatmavidya "Science of the Universal soul" philosophy. In short, Liberal education was also prevalent in Buddhist monasteries besides the study of Buddhists scriptures. The study of these sciences and arts had a theoactical course. Knowledge of the literature of a subject had to be followed by its practical applications. In regard to some subjects like medicines, for instance, the practical course had to be gone through under the direction of the teacher. The practical course in medicine at Takkasila included a first - hand-study of the plants to find out the medicinal ones, as shown in the story of Jivaka's Education under chapter V. A practical turn indeed given to all instruction as a pedagogic principle.

There is a course of specialised and advanced studies in Vyakarana which was the name for the general secular literature. Students completing this advanced study were regarded as masters of grammatical science and earned the little of Bahusruta (much heard "or" knowing much of the Sruti). This course of specialization in Grammar was open to both priests and laymen. There were again courses of specialization in religious or priestly studies which were organised and offered by the monasteries. The most famous of such seats of higher learning in the time of I-tsing's visit to India were "the Nalanda monastery in Central India" and that "in the country of Valabhi in Western India."

The Vinaya texts refer to industrial education also. The Bhikkus were allowed facilities in their very monasteries for training and practice in the handicrafts such as spinning and weaving, tailoring etc. The Vinaya texts refer to a few other occupations pursued by the laity and the general public as sources of livelihood e.g. writing or the occupation of the clerk or scribe (Lekhan), Accountancy (Ganana) and Drawing (Rupan).

Hence it is argued that the Buddhist monasteries had functioned not only as centres of imparting religious education but also imparted secular education for the sake of scholarship and trained the monks as self-sufficient inmates of the monasteries.

As stated under the presumption that there was a gradual shifting from Faith to knowledge, it is argued that in fact the monasteries encouraged the scholar monks in their intellectual pursuit, thus displaying yet another feature of a university in real spirit. Provision for higher and specialized study stands to prove the presumption. Advanced studies in grammar were provided. It is argued that only students competing this advanced study were regarded as masters of grammatical sciences and earned the title of Bahusruta. There were again courses of specialization in religious or priestly studies which were organised and offered by the monasteries. The monks of the monasteries, like the students of colleges, were suitably graded according to their capacities and the level of advance they attained. With in the community of monks, the lowest grade is that of Sramanera who is promoted, after his Upasampada ordination, to the grade of the Dahara (small) Bhikshu. Higher than him is the Sthavira (elder), the Bhileshu, who has seen ten summers or passed then summer retreats in that capacity, and who, for his standing, can live by himself without having to live under a teacher's care. A Sthavira necessarily attains the position of an Upadhyaya and an Upadhyaya must be a Sthavira. The highest grade for a Bhikshu was that of the Bahusruta. This high title was conferred only on one who was learned both in the sacred and secular literature and famed as virtuous. But the gradations of the monks in a monastery were indicated not merely by title, but also by privileges. To venerable monks, if very learned, or those who had thoroughly studied at least one of the three Pitakas were assigned some of the best rooms of the monastery. These facts were observed by I-tsing at the Varaha monastery in Tamralipti.

Again it is argued that like modern universities the monasteries had the practice of conferring titles and honours for their intellectual achievements.

With reference to academic freedom, the very essence of a university, the monasteries allowed their students freedom of choices in studies, while all castes except the Chandalas were admitted to instruction. We thus see that youths of all sorts and conditions of life, of different classes and castes, had all the ridivisions and distinctions merged in the democracy of learning.

As we have seen, the academic debates and tournaments which formed so large a part of the intellectual life of the country under the Brahmanical system of education from the days of the Upanishads were also a marked characteristic of the Buddhist literary world. From Hiuen Tsang's collcetions about traditions and facts about India, we realize that these intellectual tournaments brought together scholars from distant and different parts of India, promoted active intercourse between different monsteries, representing different schools of thought, and created a broad brotherhood of letters in which were united the intellectuals of different provinces we find that even the distant South, overcoming the many physical factors of isolation, won for itself an honoured place in the Indian intellectual system as centred in the northern parts of India like Nalanda in the Magadha country. For instance, we read of the South Indian Buddhist scholar Deva, going with the permission of his master, the great Nagarjuna, to a monastery called Kukkutarama in distant Patalipputra where in a twelve days' discussion he defeated the Tirthikas of that place. The great Buddhist scholar of the South Dinnaya, a Brahaman of Kanchi by birth, made the buildings of the Nalanda monastery in Magadha resound with his victorious discussions with the exponents of various schools of thought of the times.

In the light of the aforesaid exposition, it is argued that these scholar monks enjoyed academic freedom to the greatest extent so that without any restrictions they partook in the intellectual tournaments and discussions.

Like the modern universities, the Buddhist monasteries enjoyed a uniques position in the then society by virtue of their missionary zeal to serve the humanity. Thus the Buddhist monasteries became the seats and centres of both sacred and secular learning, and being freely resorted to by the both, the Buddhist monks and laymen and even by non-Buddhists, materially aided in the diffusion of learning and culture in the country. The Buddhist monks also who came practically to have the monopoly in this learning and culture were catholic and generous enough to impart them to persons not belonging to their way of life. Not confusing their sympathies and valued services within the limited boundaries of their own church and faith, they thus became the Directors of Public Instruction in the country. They recognized in a noble spirit of toleration that the country was above creed culture and church? [6.6]

Chapter II deals with the methodology wherein the concept formation (Rickets') and conceptual analysis are discussed in detail. In the light of the interpretation it is argued that the content is the totality of the selectd ideas of immediate sensations: these ideas represent the common component elements of those concrete objects which are subsumed under the concept. The total number of these objects (e.g. all elephants as given in the Chapter II) constitutes the scope of the concept.

The selection in order to be valid requires the application of a standard of selection which is recognized as valid by everyday who wants to have scientific knowledge. This standard states what parts of reality are to be considered as "essential" for its valid representation. Elements which are common to many concrete phenomena are considered to be essential, whereas individual differences are neglected.

6.6 Mookerji R.K., (1951) Ancient Indian Education. (Brahmanical and Buddhist), (Page 546) Macmillan and Co. Ltd., St. Martins' Street, London.

Hence it is argued in light of the aforesaid explanation that the essential features of a university, as interpreted by the scholars especially by Newman and Jaspers are concretised as the content of the concept of a university, and accordingly the Buddhist Monasteries are exposed as exhibiting the salient 5 features of a university in general. Thus the content of a university as reflected by the Buddhist Monasteries is content- based and fabricated in the light of the explanations and interpretations given by the various scholars on the idea of a university. However, the Buddhist Monasteries, even before the emergence of the Medieval universities of Europe of 12th century blossomed on the Indian soil around 5th century thus representing the indigenous universities of ancient Hindu India.

In chapter II conceptual analysis of education by Prof. R.S. Peters has been taken for a sample study. But it is argued that Prof. R.S. Peters has attempted to fabricate a concept of education out of his own vision of what people ought to become (as commented by Prof.Dray) and Prof. Peters replied that his analysis is rather content free and his concept of education is taken as unspecific in terms of content, as something like'good' or 'worthwhile' with the notion of transmission of or of initiation into' prefixed to it. It is slightly more specific than good because of the cognitive criteria to do with depth and breadth of understanding and awareness also meant with it. But in the case of the Buddhist monasteries, concrete and specific criteria and building the concept and project the image on solid background of views and expressions, uttered by various scholars on the idea of a university. In Chapter II the scholar briefed about the interpretation and definition of 'Freedom' by Maurice Cranston (1967). Two types of definition viz persuasive and stipulative definitions are explained herein: what is the difference between persuasive definition and sound stipuplative definition? A man who stipulates soundly says 'This is how I see the word "X"' A man who gives a persuasive definition is trying to make you believe that the way he uses the word "X" is the correct way.

Accordingly it is further argued that R.S. Peters' concept of education and Saltis' concept of knowledge are governed by the persuasive definitions as they interpet the meaning in terms of what they feel "ought" to be incorporate. In the case of the study the concept of a university under the present title, the scholer has attempted to enumerate the essentialities of a university as expressed by the various scholars and thereafter stipulated salient features of a university and in the light of such features, the scholar attempted to discern the reflections in the Buddhist Monasteries.

II Following the line of thoughtt and mode of analysis, tthe scholar has given tentative areas for the future study.

A. The uniqueness of Platos' Academy as the First University of the world, Athtens as the International University, Sangham the Tamil Academy as the First University of South India- such studies highlighting their contribution to the respective countries and world may be undertaken.

B. Conceptual Analysis with reference to the University in Medieval India and Modern India and Philosophical analysis of the rationale for open University and Deemed University in Modern India may be taken for academic pursuit.

C. Contributory nature of the universities (Central Universities, open Universities, Deemed Universities, Universities with special mission such as Santinketan as propagator of Indian Culture) may be studied with their Philosophical implication.

After a perusal of views and opinions of scholars and Philosophers about the Univerities, it has been found that a university is a community of scholars, interested in the pursuit of knowledge. It is primarily a place of teaching universal knowledge. Thus it has become a seat of knowledge. The diffusion and extension of knowledge is its principal aim; but its real purpose is to produce more intelligent members of society, by fostering cultivation of mind and formation of character. In short liberal education is recommended to produce gentleman of the society, as expressed by the scholar like John Henry Newman. Teaching vitally needs the substance which only researh can give it, it is indeed the combination of the two that provide the spirit of University education.

The university is a social entity. The university exists only to the extent that it is insttitutionalized. The idea becomes conrete in the institution. The extent to which it does this determines the quality of the university. The university fulfils its tasks-research, instruction training, communication within an institution (as expressed by Karl Jaspers in his the idea of the University). It requires buildings, materials, books and institutes and then orderly administration. Privileges and duties must be distributed among its members. The university represents an independent corporate whole with its own constitution. The university, then, is an institution uniting people professionally dedicated to the quest and transmissioon of truth in scientific terms. Because truth is accessible to systematic search, research is the foremost concern of the university. Because the scope of truth is far greater than that of science, the scientist must dedicate himself to truth as a human being, not just a specialist. Hence, the pursuit of truth at the university demands the serious commitment of the wholeman. Oneness and wholeness are the very essence of man's will to know. The university is the corporate realization of man's basic determinaion to know. The university itself was planned on the principle that all things are part of a whole and must be done on an idea.

An image about a university is formed in terms of the aforesaid features. They become stipulatory in defining an institution as a university. The chosen model is constructed on a coognitive relation of somekind between the institution and its duties and functions towards the society.

The present study is an attempt to establish that the ancient Hindu India had developed a systematic higher education (University type education) which stands parallel to the European Medieval universities of 11th and 12th centuries A.D. The Buddhist Monasteries of the ancient Hindu India of 5th and 6th centuries B.C. exhibited similar features of the medieval European universities. Like the Christian Monasteries they too encouraged secular education, besides the religious study.

We are told that the Buddhist monasteries (Viharas) were built mainly for two purpses. First, that the Buddhist Sangha may mediate in peace with society. Secondly, that learned men may lodge in the Viharas. Gradually, however, the second object became the only object and in due course, became the main object too. As Viharas became repositories of learned men, they began to attract students from various parts of the land whose sole object was the acquisition of knowledge.

As seen in the ChapterIII Theoretical Build-up, both in Europe and in India monasteries had become Temples of Learning. But, whereas in Europe, educational activity passed out of the hands of the monks to those of secular clergy, with the spread of knowledge in the outside world,in India the monks were rather fortunate in retaining it. They saw what was emerging with foresight and they responded spontaneously to the demanding needs of the society. Therefore, instead of being swept away totally by the on-coming wave of reforms and social changes, they deemed it wiser to relax the rules of their order. The doors of the Buddhist Sangha which were open before only to those who had renounced the world, were now thrown open to the students as well, who, if they chose, were at liberty to leave the monastery and embrace once more the life of a householder, after their education was over. It is in this transformation of the monasteries that we find the seeds and semblance of the universities in general.

BIBLIOGRAPHY

Archambault, Reginald D (1965), Philosophical Analysis and Education, Routledge and Kegan Paul Ltd., London.

Bapat P.v. (1964), 2500 years of Buddhism, Publications Division, Ministry of Information and Broadcasting, Govt. of india.

Birch, William (1988), the challenge to Higher education, Reconcilng Responsibilities to Scholarship and to Society, The Society for Research into Higher Education and Open University Press, England.

Brog, Jalter R. and Meredith, D. Gall (1983) Educational Research; An introduction Fourth (Edition) Longman Inc. 1560, Broad way, New York.

Boyd, William & Edmand J.King. (1975). The History of Western Education, Adams and Charles Black Ltd., London.

Briggs, Kichal, H.,(1959) Hand book of Philosophy, Philosophical Library, New York.

Broun, S.C, (ed) (1975) Philosophers discuss education, Macmillan, London.

Brubacher J.S. (1977), Modern Philosophers of Education, Tata, Mac Graw HIll, New Delhi.

Chauhan E,P.S. (1990), Higher Education in India, Achievements, Failures and Strategies), Ashis Publishing Houuse, New Delhi.

Chopra P.N. (1983), Contribution of Buddhism to World civilization and Culture, S. Chand and Co. Ltd., Ram Nagar, New Delhi.

Connor, J.J.O. (1957), An introduction to the Philosophy of Education, Routledge & Kegan. Paul Ltd., London.

Cobban, A.B., (1975) The Medieval Universities: Their development and Organisation, Methuen & Co. Ltd., London.

Das Santosh Kumar (1986) The Educational system of Ancient Hindus, Glan Publishing House, Shakti Nagar, Delhi.

Deutsch, Karl (ed) (1965)- Karl Jaspers, The Idea of the University Peters Oun Ltd., Kendrich Place, London, S.W.

Dockrell W.B. & David Hamilton (1980)- Rethinking Educational Research, Holder and Steughton Ltd., Great Britian.

Durant, Will (1953)- The Story of Philosophy, the lines and opinions of the Great Philosophers, Washington, New York.

Dutt, Sukuman (1962)- Buddhist Monks and Monasteries of India (Their History and their contribution to Indian Culture), George Allen and Union Ltd., Ruskin House, London.

Enturstle, Noel (ed) (1990)- Handbook of Educational ideas and Practices, Routledge, London, New York.

Feinberg, Walter (1983)- Understanding Education, toward a reconstruction of Educational Inquiry,Cambridge University Press, New York.

Fletchar, Basil (1968)- Universities in the Modern World, Pargamon Press Ltd., London.

Gorovity and Rori G. William - Philosophical Analysis. An Introduction to its Language & Techniques (2nd edition). The university of Chicago, Illinois.

Goheen, Robert. F. (1969)- The Human Nature of a University Princeton, University Press, U.S.A.

Granston, Maurics (1967)- Freedom. A New Analysis, Longman, Green & Co. Ltd. (3rd Edition), London.

Gregorius, Panlcr Mam (1989)- Enlightenment: East and West , Pointers in the Quest for Indian's Secular Identity, Indian institute for Advanced Study, Shimla.

Gutck, Gerald.L. (1972)- A History of the Western Educational Experienc, Random House, New york.

Hommadi, A.N., (1984)- University Administration in Developing Countries, Indian Bibliographers Bureau, Delhi (India)

Kabir, Humayun (1961)- Education in New India, George Allen & Union Ltd., Ruskin House, London.

Ker, I.T. (ed) (1976)- The Idea of a University. Defined and Illustrated by J.H. Newman. The University Press, Oxford, London.

Keay, F.E. (Rev) (1980)- Ancient Indian Education, (An Inquiry into its origin, development and deals), cosmo Publications, New Delhi, INDIA.

Jaffar S.M. (1973)- Education in Muslim India, (Reprint) Idarah-I-Adabiyat-I-Delhi.

Justin, Wintle (ad) (1982)- Maker of Ninteenth Century Culture Routledge & Kegal Pvt. Ltd., storer Street, London, W.C.T.E.

Lawrence, G. Thomas (1972) Philosophical Redirection of Educat-ional Research. The 71st Year Book of the N.S.S.E., University of Chicago press, Illinois.

Levi Edward H., (1969)- Point of view a Talk on Education, The University of Chicago across, U.S.A.

Leavis F.R. (1979)- Edudcation and the University, Cambridge University Press, London.

Marrow H.I. (1982)- A History of Education in Antiquity (Translated by George Lamb). The University of Wisconsin Press (first Wisconsin Printing) U.S.A.

Minogue, Kenneth R. (1973)- The conept of University, Willmor Brothers Ltd., Briken head, London.

Mookherji R.K. (1951)- Ancient Indian Education (Brahmanical and Buddhist) Mac Millan and Co. Ltd., London.

Moraes Frank (ed) (1966)- Science, Philosophy and Culturs, Asia Publishing House, Bombay, India.

Mac Millan, James H.&Sally Sehumachar (1984)- Research in Education. A Conceptual Introduction,Little Broun and Co. Ltd.,Canada.

Nehru, Jawaharlal (1981) (reprint)- The Discovery of India, Jawaharlal Nehru Memorial Fund, Teen Murti House, New Delhi.

Oz Mon, Howard A & Samuel M Craver (1990)- Philosophical Foundations of Education (4th edition), Merrill Publishing Co. Columbia, Ohio, USA.

Pappu, S.S, Ra,a Raoj (ed.) & R. Puligandla (1982) Indian Philosophy Past and Future, Motilal Banarasi das, New Delhi.

Perkins, James A (1966) -The University in Transition, Princeston University Press, New Jersey.

Peterson A.D.C. (1971) - A Hundred Years of Education. (ELBS) and Gerald Duekworth & Co Ltd. Great Britain.

Peters R.S. (ed). (1973) - The philosophy of Education, Oxford University Press, London.

Peterfreund, P & Theodore C. Denise (1968) Contemporary philosophy and its origin (Text and Readings) Affiliated East-West Press Pvt, Ltd., New Delhi.

Phillips D.Z. (ed) (1980) - Education and Inquiry : John Anderson (values and philosophical inquiry) Basil Blackwell,publishers Ltd. Oxford (England).

Ray, Krishnalal (1984) - Education in Medieval India, B.R. publishing Corpn. (India), Delhi.

Ranganathananda, Swami (1988) - Science and Religion, Advaita Ashrama (3rd Reprint), - Calcutta (India).

Robson, John M. (ed.) (1984) - Essays on Equality, Law and Education, by John Stuart Mill (Collected Works of J.S. Mill) Vol. XXI. University of Toronto Press, Canada.

Robbins, Lord (1966) - The University in the Modern World and other Papers on higher education, Max Millan, St. Martins Press, New York.

Ross G. Murray (1976) - The University - The Anatomy of Academy Mc. Gram-Hill Book Co. - New York.

Robert, Peters: (1958) Adult Education : A Comparative study, London Routledge & kegal Paul, New York, Humanities Press

Sangharakshita (Bhikshu) (1967) - The Three 'Jewels' (An Introduction to Buddhism) Rider & Co. Great Port land Street, London W1.

Sankalia H.D. (1972) - The University of Nalanda, Oriental publishers, Pataudi House, Darya Ganj, Delhi (India).

Singh, Amrik & G.D. Sharma (ed.) (1989) - Higher Education in India (The Social Context), Konark Publishers Pvt. Ltd. Delhi.

Singh Bhansi Pratap (1990) - Aims of Education in India, Ajanta Publications (India), Delhi.

Swaminathan Gurumurthy - (1979) - Education in South India (Ancient and Medieval period) New Era Publications, Madras.

Svagha, Martin J. (ed.) (1960) - The Idea of a University (Defined and Illustrated) by John Henry Cardenal Newman, Holt, Rinehart and winston Ine, USA.

Smith, Aher kidd (ed.) (1970) - Handbook of Adult Education, A publication of the Adult Education Association, USA.

Soltis. F.Johar ed. (1981) - Philosophy and Education. 80th Year Book (NSSE), The University of Chicago, - Illinois.

Tewari, Udai Narain (1983) - Indian A Culture Voyage (A Culture Survey of the Land of Eternal Resurgence) Select book Service Syndicate, New Delhi (first Edn.) 1983.

Taylor, William, (1973) - Research Perspective in Education, Rout ledge and Kegan Paul Ltd. London.

Varma M. (1965) An Introduction to Education and Psychological Research, Asia publishing House, Bombay (India).

Wolff, Robert Paul (1969), The Idea of the University Beacon Press, Boston (USA).

Woodroffee, Sir John (1978) - India, Culture and Society, Light and Life publishers, Tilak Street, Paharganj, New Delhi.

Runes Dagobert (Ed) TREASURY OF PHILOSOPHY MCMLV Philosophical Library New York, USA.

JOURNALS

1. Higher Education policy Vol. 3 No.1. 1990 Special theme : Higher Education and Culture Editorial. Guy Neave.

2. Higher Education Policy No.3. No. 1 1990, Page no. 9- 12 Sheldon Rothamblatt, The carriers of Civilization.

3. Higher Education Policy Vol.3 No.1990 Page 13-14 Rudiger Stolz, Heritage and Tradition.

4. Higher Education Policy Vol.2.No.3 Sept. 1989 Page 7 Editorial Gay Neave.

5. Higher Education Policy Vol.2 No3. 1989 Page-44-45 Philip G. Altbach, Research and Higher Education in newly Industrialized Countries.

6. Interchange Vol.20 No.4 (Winter) 1989. (A quality review of Education) page 1-8, Elmer J. Thiessen, R.S. Peters on Liberal Education -A Reconstruction.

7. Jorunal of Philosophy of Education, Vol.23 No.2, 1989 Page 213, Hamlyn D.W., Education and Wittgenstein's Philosophy.

8. Journal of Philosophy of Education Vol.23 No.2 1989 Page 241-50, Charles Clerk, why Teachers Need Philosophy.

9. Educational Researcher, Vol.20, No.2 March 1991 Pages 3-10, Richard S. Prawat, The Value of Ideas : The Immersion Approach to the Development of thinking.

10. Higher Education Policy Vol. 3 No.1. 1990 pp. 38-40. Felik Gross, A University Academy : Coping with change in an urban Multiversity.

11. Higher Education Policy Vol.3 No.1. 1990 pp.41-45, Hans Joas, The Federal Republic of Germany: University and Career Opportunities for young Scientists,

12. Higher Education Policy.3, No.1, 1990 page-47 - 48: Chronicle -Reform proposals in Japanse Higher Edcuation.

13. Higher Education Review Vol. 22, No, 1Autumn 1989 pp. 7-19, L.Brownstein, University Education in a free society : a preliminary defence.

14. Higher Education review. Vol.22, No. 1Autumn 1989 pp. 35-46. Harry L. Gray and Charles H. Hoy University Development : The Balance between research and teaching.

15. Higher Education Policy Vol.4.No.1 March 1991, pp. 45-48, Lucien Michael, An Idea of the University.

16. Higher Education Policy Vol. 4.No. 1. March 1991.pp. 49-51, Chronicle, Magna Carta of Catholic Universities.

17. Higher Education Policy Vol. 1. No.2. July 1988 pp. 41 - 42, Claudine Langlis Chronicle, The International associations of Universities and the Promotion of Academic Mobility. The TRACE project.

18. Journal of Educational Planning and Administration Vol, iv. No.4 Oct. 1990 pp. 59-64, J.V.D. Cruz, Universities of Ancient Asia, Africa and Medieval Europe.

19. Education. Vol.39.1989. (Biannual Collection of recent Germanic contribution to the field of Educational Research) pp. 32-65, The Idea of the University in the contemporary world.

20. Educational Theory, Fall 1989, Vol, 39. No.4 The Board of Trustees of the Universities of Illineois) pp., 301-306 Nimrod Altoni-The three Pedagogical Dimensions of Nietzche's philosophy.

21. Educational Theory. Winter 1983 Vol.33 No.1. pp. -1-9., Ignacio L.Gotz, Heidegger and the art of teaching.

22. Higher Education Quarterly, Vol.43, No.3 Summer 1989 pp. 205 -215, Christopher Ball, B.P RSA Fellow in Higher Education, the Problem of Research.

23. Higher Education Quarterly, Vol.43 No-3, Summer 1989 pp. 216-227, Rowland Eustace, Society for research into Higher Education, Freedom for Academic (Abstract).

24. Journal of Higher Education Vol.12, No. 1-3, 1986-87 pp. 29-49, M.S.Yadav Lokesh Kaul, S.Roy and T.k.S. Lakshmi, Research Policy in the Perspective of National Development.

25. Higher Education review Vol.22, No.2. Spring 1990 pp 59-69, Ronald Barnett, Responsiveness and fulfil ment : the value of Higher Education in the Modern world.

26. European Journal of Education, Vol.24, No.4,1989 (Higher Education and Europe after 1992) I.pp.333- 343. Roger Dillemans, Autonomy responsibility and responsiveness of Higher Education Institutions after 1992.

27. Aryan Heritage Vol. vi, No.57,Feb. 1989 pp. 31-33, Dr. Satyavrata Siddhantalankar, the concept of Vedic Realism.

ENCYCLOPAEDIA

1. Encyclopaedia of Religion and Ethics James. Hastings (ed) Vol.2 Jan. 1958, pp. 128-131 ASRAMA.

2. Encyclopaedia of Religion and Ethics Vol.8. 1964 pp 781-805, Monasticism.

3. Encyclopaedia of religion and ethics Vol.9, 1961, pp. 126-127. Nalanda.

4. Encyclopaedia Britannica Vol.5 1959 pp. 33-35. Cathedral.

6. Encyclopaedia Britannica. Vol.18 1959 pp. 48-58. Plato.

7. Encyclopaedia Britannica. Vol. 22 1959 pp. 862-880 Universities.

DICTIONARIES

1. The Concise Dictionary of Education : Higher Education (page 107) by Gene R. Hawes, Lynne Salop Hawes A Hudson Group Book published by Van Nostrand reinhold co. Inc. New York,1982.

2. Dictionary of Education : Foundations in Education Higher Education - page (267), Editor Carter V good Winifred R Merkel. MC Graw Hill Book Co. INC, New York 1959.

3. Dictionary of Philosophy : Edited by I. FROLOV Translated from the Russian - English translation (c) Progressive publishers 1984 (second Revised edition), Moscow USSR.